ISSUES IN SOCIETY
Series Editor: Tim May

Current and forthcoming titles

Zygmunt Bauman: *Work, Consumerism and the New Poor*
David Byrne: *Social Exclusion*
Graham Crow: *Social Solidarities*
Mitchell Dean: *Governing Societies*
Gerard Delanty: *Citizenship in a Global Age*
Steve Fuller: *The Governance of Science*
Les Johnston: *Crime, Justice and Late Modernity*
David Knights and Darren McCabe: *Organizational Change*
Nick Lee: *Childhood and Society*
David Lyon: *Surveillance Society*
Graham Scambler: *Health and Social Change*
Piet Strydom: *Risk, Environment and Society*

Social solidarities

Theories, identities and social change

GRAHAM CROW

OPEN UNIVERSITY PRESS
Buckingham • Philadelphia

Open University Press
Celtic Court
22 Ballmoor
Buckingham
MK18 1XW

email: enquiries@openup.co.uk
world wide web: www.openup.co.uk

and
325 Chestnut Street
Philadelphia, PA 19106, USA

First Published 2002

A catalogue record of this book is available from the British Library

ISBN 0 335 20230 6 (pb)   0 335 20231 4 (hb)

Library of Congress Cataloging-in-Publication Data
Crow, Graham
    Social solidarities : theories, identities, and social change / Graham Crow.
      p. cm. – (Issues in society)
    Includes bibliographical references and index.
    ISBN 0-335-20231-4 – ISBN 0-335-20230-6 (pbk.)
    1. Solidarity. I. Title. II. Series.

HM717.C76 2001
301–dc21

                                                 2001021579

Typeset by Graphicraft Limited, Hong Kong
Printed in Great Britain by Biddles Limited, Guildford and Kings Lynn

Contents

Series editor's foreword

Collectively, the social sciences contribute to a greater understanding of the dynamics of social life, as well as explanations for the workings of societies in general. Yet they are often not given due credit for this role and much writing has been devoted to why this should be the case. At the same time, we are living in an age in which the role of science in society is being re-evaluated. This has led to both a defence of science as the disinterested pursuit of knowledge and an attack on science as nothing more than an institutionalized assertion of faith with no greater claim to validity than mythology and folklore. These debates tend to generate more heat than light.

In the meantime the social sciences, in order to remain vibrant and relevant, will reflect the changing nature of these public debates. In so doing they provide mirrors upon which we can gaze in order to understand not only what we have been and what we are now, but to inform possibilities about what we might become. This is not simply about understanding the reasons people give for their actions in terms of the contexts in which they act and analysing the relations of cause and effect in the social, political and economic spheres, but also concerns the hopes, wishes and aspirations that people, in their different cultural ways, hold.

In any society that claims to have democratic aspirations, these hopes and wishes are not for the social scientist to prescribe. For this to happen it would mean that the social sciences were able to predict human behaviour with certainty. One theory and one method, applicable to all times and places, would be required for this purpose. The physical sciences do not live up to such stringent criteria, whilst the conditions in societies which provided for this outcome, were it even possible, would be intolerable. Why? Because a necessary condition of human freedom is the ability to have acted otherwise and thus to imagine and practice different ways of organizing societies and living together.

It does not follow from the above that social scientists do not have a valued role to play, as is often assumed in ideological attacks upon their place and function within society. After all, in focusing upon what we have been and what we are now, what we might become is inevitably illuminated: the retrospective and prospective become fused. Therefore, whilst it may not be the province of the social scientist to predict our futures, they are, given not only their understandings and explanations, but equal positions as citizens, entitled to engage in public debates concerning future prospects.

This new international series was devised with this general ethos in mind. It seeks to offer students of the sciences, at all levels, a forum in which ideas and topics of interest are interrogated in terms of their importance for understanding key social issues. This is achieved through a connection between style, structure and content that aims to be both illuminating and challenging in terms of its evaluation of those issues, as well as representing an original contribution to the subject under discussion.

Given this underlying philosophy, the series contains books on topics that are driven by substantive interests. This is not simply a reactive endeavour in terms of reflecting dominant social and political preoccupations, it is also proactive in terms of an examination of issues which relate to and inform the dynamics of social life and the structures of society that are often not part of public discourse. Thus, what is distinctive about this series is an interrogation of the assumed characteristics of our current epoch in relation to its consequences for the organization of society and social life, as well as its appropriate mode of study.

Each contribution contains, for the purposes of general orientation, as opposed to rigid structure, three parts. First, an interrogation of the topic that is conducted in a manner that renders explicit core assumptions surrounding the issues and/or an examination of the consequences of historical trends for contemporary social practices. Second, a section which aims to 'bring alive' ideas and practices by considering the ways in which they directly inform the dynamics of social relations. A third section then moves on to make an original contribution to the topic. This encompasses possible future forms and content, likely directions for the study of the phenomena in question, or an original analysis of the topic itself. Of course, it might be a combination of all three.

Graham Crow's book is written with this ethos in mind. In charting what may be characterized as the causes, contexts and consequences of social solidarity, he provides us with an insightful account of how and under what circumstances, with what effects and utilizing what resources, groups exhibit particular characteristics in their relationships. In a world that appears fragmented into compartments formed by modes of consumption that are indifferent to their effects, the conditions for social solidarity appear to be diminishing. Yet it is those very conditions that provide for the possibilities of freedom and security.

In the face of these seemingly contradictory pressures – the demand for freedom based on a limited individualism and that of security based upon collective notions of solidarity – there are still systematic forms of social cohesion that exist within communities. Here we find practical/political issues mixing with key themes in classical social theory: for example, individualization, democratization and industrialization. Durkheim, in particular, was concerned with the evolution of society in terms of its propensity towards an individualism that was nothing more than egoism. What peace, he was to ask, could be derived from such a situation? Instead he was to argue that a form of individualism was not in tension with solidarity and brought the two together in terms of society being an active, moralizing force. A retrieval of the potential within this legacy, as Graham Crow notes, is a core theme informing this book.

For this reason he starts with an overview of contemporary issues in relation to social solidarity and then moves on to examine the productive legacy that emerges from classical social theory. A basis is then given for an interrogation of contemporary theoretical concerns via the works of those such as Bauman, Beck, Bellah, Castells, Etzioni, Giddens, Melucci and Sennett. For some, the answer to social solidarity lies in communities. Here we find the tension between a celebration of difference as manifest in individual freedom from constraint, mixing with a recognition of difference that is seen to necessitate the exercise of a group's power to limit freedom. From this latter point of view individual rights may be tempered in the name of collective survival. As Zygmunt Bauman has expressed it in his book *Postmodernity and its Discontents*, both liberalism and communitarianism represents dreams that have been born 'in the plight of autonomous individuals'. Bauman thus regards solidarity as episodic, contingent and short-lived. However, as William Beveridge understood during the period in which the British welfare state was born, one must act in the name of the liberty of all, not just those who can exercise freedom. Why? Because free choice and fear and anxiety coexist.

An illuminating discussion of such issues provides the author with a basis upon which to ground these arguments via a sociological interrogation of three case studies. They are families, solidarity in mining communities and the Polish *Solidarity* movement. We are then furnished with a detailed understanding of the basis of solidarity according to the different circumstances through which it arises, as well as the forms of its manifestation, dynamics and consequences. Here we see mixes of economic interest and symbolism, consent and coercion, inclusion and exclusion and the demands for intimacy and community, producing particular outcomes. As he notes, taken alongside lines of alliance around class, gender, sexuality and disability, we see changing forms of solidarity with self-help groups, for example, moving apart as quickly at they might come together. Solidarity should thus be seen as the result of conflict and change, as well as order and consensus.

Graham Crow shows a persistence in certain forms of solidarity despite a change in the original conditions in which it emerged. At the same time he also notes that new forms of solidarity should be examined in order to add to how thinking sociologically can contribute to greater understanding and tolerance. This requires a sensitivity to the conditions in which people find themselves and a recognition of the relations that exist between those conditions, forms of identity and actions and beliefs.

When governments seek conditions in which peace and security in a society may flourish, whilst also promoting policies that are in tension with such aspirations, a clear gap in understanding the dynamics of social relations is apparent. It is to an understanding of this gap that Graham Crow has turned his analytic gaze. Therefore, this book should be read not only by social scientists, but politicians, business people and all those concerned with the trajectories of the societies in which they live for that informs their dispositions, aspirations and actions.

Tim May

Acknowledgements

A number of people have contributed to the writing of this book in various ways. Thanks are due to Tim May, the editor of the series, for his insights and encouragement, and for suggesting the title. Other people have also read drafts of the book and discussed the ideas that it contains. These include Wendy Bottero, Fiona Devine, Sue Heath, Catherine Maclean, Kate Reed, Tony Rees and Rose Wiles, and I am grateful for all their help and advice. Colleagues in the Department of Sociology and Social Policy at the University of Southampton helped to provide a supportive working environment within which to write the book. Some of the themes developed in Chapter 3 had their origins in an ESRC-funded research project on step-families and their wider kin (award number R000237504), on which Graham Allan and Sheila Hawker also worked. Chapter 4 benefited from my role as co-supervisor (with Susan Halford) of Jane Parry's ESRC-funded PhD research into the former mining communities of South Wales. Other academics and students have also played their part in assisting the development of the book's argument through discussions in numerous different contexts. These individuals include those who responded in a constructively critical fashion to my proposal to write the book when invited to by the publishers. At the publishers, Gaynor Clements, Ros Fane, Justin Vaughan and their colleagues have provided the expertise without which the book would never have come to fruition, and I am grateful to them for keeping faith with the project. Finally, I must thank my parents, who many years ago (unwittingly) sowed the seeds of my interest in solidarity. I dedicate this book to them, with thanks.

Introduction

This book is concerned with how people strive to come together and act as a coherent, united force. Social solidarity is important in many areas of our lives, or at least in how we wish our lives to be. Family and kinship relationships, community life, trade union activity and the identity politics of new social movements are just a few of the many ways in which solidarity can feature in contemporary social arrangements. There is, of course, no inevitability that these or other collective activities will be characterized more by unity than by division. Indeed, it is a central theme of the book that social solidarities are often precariously based and difficult to sustain over time; there is nothing 'natural' or automatic about people's ability to achieve and maintain solidarity in their social relationships. As the historical sociologist Moore (1978: 507) observed, 'fissiparous tendencies exist in all societies and cultures of any size . . . Where cooperation exists, it has to be created and continually re-created'. The forms through which social solidarity comes to be expressed are diverse and range from the spectacular to the mundane. This remarkable diversity and the consistency of the underlying patterns that produce it help to explain why the causes, contexts and consequences of its presence, and also its absence, have been the subject of extensive and sustained investigation over the years.

There is certainly no shortage of current interest in social solidarity. Governments concerned to tackle 'social exclusion' are immediately confronted by the difficulties of promoting solidarity among citizens (Jordan 1996; Lister 1997; Levitas 1998; Byrne 1999), and similar sentiments underpinned the United Nations 'Year of the Elderly and Solidarity between the Generations' (Laslett 1996: viii). Such developments can be considered to be the latest phase of what Baldwin (1990), in his study of welfare state histories, refers to as *The Politics of Social Solidarity*. Welfare states continue to be confronted by the age-old problem of reconciling 'conflicting claims of self, family and community' (Lees 1998: 1) and by the related issue of whether (and, if so, under what circumstances) solidarity extends to strangers. Solidarity is equally important for communitarians, who share with the architects of the welfare state the same broad objective of social inclusion but who regard the State as being unable to deliver it. Their task is to provide an alternative account of how a supportive social environment can be attained and sustained. The term 'community' undoubtedly conveys a sense of solidarity built around some common purpose, but many critics have identified as problematic the way in which such language may be used to smuggle in romanticized notions of informal social relationships (Frazer and Lacey 1993; Hoggett 1997).

Nor is concern with the issue of solidarity confined to discussions of welfare states and communities. At the more intimate level of personal life, much attention has been paid to the question of what it is that holds members of families together in an age frequently characterized as one of 'individualization' (Beck and Beck-Gernsheim 1995; Silva and Smart 1999). On a more global level, the rise of new social movements in the South has generated growing interest not only in the nature but also the limitations of their solidarity (Wignaraja 1993; Scott 1994). Appeals to 'transnational collective solidarity' have, for example, been criticized by Hoogvelt (1997: 243) for their reliance 'on some magic wand that waves away the fragmentation of class, gender, ethnic and nationalist loyalties'. Equally instructive are developments in post-communist societies, about which Castells (1998: 64) argues that an important part of the transitions taking place involves coming to terms with 'the mockery that the Communist state made of the values of human solidarity'. Such histories make all the more difficult the project of strengthening the 'feelings of solidarity and mutual obligation' (Offe 1996a: 49) that many commentators have identified as having been eroded by disenchantment with communist regimes.

This revival of interest in the place of social solidarity in contemporary social relations has been accompanied by renewed engagement in recent years with solidarity as a theoretical problem. Beck's (1992: 49) analysis of *Risk Society* suggests that it is possible to discern in contemporary societies a fundamental shift 'from the solidarity of need to solidarity motivated by anxiety', while his later work pursues the theme of 'the withering away of solidarity' (Beck 1998: ch.3). Parallels can be drawn between this perspective on 'individualization' and Melucci's interpretation of 'individuation', since this too emphasizes the link between the growth of choice and anxiety. According to Melucci (1996a: 130), '[w]hen human relations are almost entirely governed by choice, the foundation of solidarity is undermined and the social bond is dangerously weakened'. Likewise, Offe (1996b: 96) refers to individualization as 'drying out . . . the seedbed of solidarity'. These ideas run counter to the pioneering thesis developed by Durkheim (1984) over a century ago that individualism and solidarity are intimately connected rather than being in tension with one another, and the retrieval of this legacy constitutes an important part of this book.

A rather different concern with solidarity underlies Maffesoli's (1996) writings, in which he directs attention to the way in which contemporary solidarities are in important respects coming to be tribal in their defining characteristics. For Maffesoli, what stands out about current developments is that the tension between individualism and tribalism is being resolved in favour of the latter, and with it the emotional dimension of social life is displacing more rational arrangements. Maffesoli's work illustrates the more general point, that what Elias (1991) refers to as 'changes in the we–I balance' are at the heart of many contemporary debates. A key matter of contention between the different positions is the question of whether contemporary solidarities are better understood as innovative or traditional – that is, as forward-looking or backward-looking – an issue that lies at the heart of what Giddens (1994a) identifies as 'the problem of solidarity'. Giddens is critical of the notion that what he calls 'damaged solidarities' can be repaired by the revival of 'civil society', but others attempting to analyse contemporary solidarities have given this idea a more positive endorsement (Keane 1998).

Informed by these and related debates, Misztal (1996, 2000) has sought to specify why it should be that solidarity has so much importance attached to it. She suggests that particular attention deserves to be paid to the association of solidarity with trust, and an absence of solidarity with lack of trust. The desirability of enhancing trust between individuals is a familiar theme in a range of literatures, including both those that have direct policy-relevance and others that are more abstract and theoretical. Much of the impetus behind the current engagement with the issue of solidarity can, therefore, be attributed to the understandable concern to grasp how social relationships come to be solidary in character and how this process can be reinforced for the common good. The current focus of attention on the causes of solidarity derives to an extent from concern to enhance their capacity to bring people together in ways that are mutually beneficial. In turn, this has led to the recognition that certain contexts are more favourable than others to the development of solidarity. An illustration of this point is provided by the transformation of the ethos of community work in recent decades, as top-down, state-centred initiatives have given way to 'looser and more flexible networks' (Taylor 1995: 109) and new forms of political alliance that more readily embody the spirit of solidarity.

There is, however, another dimension to the problem of solidarity, as both Misztal and Taylor recognize when noting that solidarity is not universally regarded as an ideal. Although the absence of solidarity is more often regarded as problematic than is its presence, nevertheless there are standpoints from which solidarity appears to pose a threat to individuals' autonomy, creativity and scope for being different. Misztal (1996) refers to communities in which this outcome occurs as inward-looking and marked by 'sectarian solidarity', resting as they do on hostility to outsiders. In like fashion, Bauman (1999) has warned of the dangers of solidarity that is rooted in 'parochial sentiments', while Albrow (1999: 25) has noted that '[t]he ideal of solidarity is utopian, but also in an important sense anti-social'. How people come to distinguish between those with whom they have solidarity and others to whom they have no such obligations is a complex process of classification that has serious consequences, and it is in this light that Sennett's (1998) description of 'we' as 'the dangerous pronoun' makes sense.

Questioning the desirability of solidarity may arise out of recognition that a tension exists between the solidarity of a group and the individualism of its members, or it may be prompted by the existence of tensions between the solidarities of competing groups. Wrong (1994: 185) describes as a sociological commonplace the observation that '[s]olidarity based on shared norms, commitment to collective goals, and the maintenance of a system of differentiated roles, are defining criteria of *all* stable organized groups, including groups whose *raison d'être* may be conflict with other groups' (emphasis in original). It is, indeed, widely acknowledged that solidarity among members of a group can be heightened by emphasizing the group's distinctiveness, and it is only superficially paradoxical that 'solidarity . . . may be strengthened by antagonistic relations with other groups' (Wrong 1994: 201). For example, urban sociologists have long recognized that 'conflict from without creates solidarity within' (Pahl 1970: 102). Put another way, solidarity with some people may commit an individual to rivalry with others if competition exists between the two groups. Where solidarity extends only as far as the boundaries of the group to which an individual regards herself or himself as belonging, the nature of that solidarity will be influenced by whether others beyond these boundaries are considered to pose a threat (Johnsen 1998). The trust on which solidarity between group members is founded may be regarded as forced if it arises against a background of uncertainty and mistrust in other relations. If Douglas (1987: 1) is correct in her characterization of solidarity as something which 'involves individuals being ready to suffer on behalf of the larger group and their expecting other individual members to do as much for them', the forced nature of some solidarities may help to explain why individuals behave in this way rather than in a more narrowly individualistic fashion. Of course, Douglas (1996: 33) is aware of the existence of alternative perspectives that emphasize 'good will, kindness and self-denial', but altruism is as much of a puzzle as self-interested behaviour and it remains the case that '[s]olidarity always needs explaining'.

It is apparent, therefore, that social solidarity is open to many different expressions, and this is the reason for entitling the book *Social Solidarities* in the plural. In addition to the distinction between inward-looking and outward-looking solidarities and the distinction between backward-looking and forward-looking solidarities, it is also possible to distinguish between solidarities that have rational foundations and those that are founded on affect or emotional attachments (Doreian and Fararo 1998). Of course, analytical distinctions such as these rarely translate neatly into concrete examples, but they do provide a framework through which the 'messiness' of empirical reality can be investigated. The importance of considering social solidarity analytically was recognized by many of the founding figures of sociology. Durkheim's (1984) celebrated distinction between 'mechanical' and 'organic' solidarity has unquestionably been the most influential of early attempts to theorize social solidarity, but valuable contributions were also made by other classical figures and these are considered along with Durkheim in the opening chapter of the book. This lays the foundation for consideration in Chapter 2 of contemporary theorists of social solidarity, many of whom take the ideas of the classics as their starting point, even if they seek (with varying success) to go well beyond this legacy.

By the end of the first part of the book, it will be evident that it is possible to approach social solidarity in various ways. Some of these approaches are particularly concerned with solidarity at the micro-level of interpersonal relations, while others focus on the broader canvas of solidarity at the macro-level of national and international social forces. For this reason, Part two is devoted to three case studies in which social solidarity is explored at different levels, ranging from the micro-level of step-family households to the macro-level of the Polish *Solidarnosc* movement. The case study of mining communities is at an intermediate level between these two ends of the spectrum. The choice of these three case studies has been guided by other considerations in addition to the contrasts between solidarity at different levels that they allow. One of these is that they are all cases in which it is useful to consider the issue of contention in contemporary debates noted above, the relative importance of the rational and emotional foundations of solidarity. Family relationships have often been treated as part of the private sphere in which rational calculation is subordinate to the expression of emotions, but closer inspection of the evidence considered in Chapter 3 reveals that this is a questionable assumption. The related assumption that rationality rules in the public sphere is equally open to question in the light of studies of work organization and political processes, as Chapters 4 and 5 show. Political actions are governed by emotional loyalties as well as by calculations of advantage, despite the fact that these two influences may be in conflict with each other.

Another consideration regarding Part two of the book is that the case studies are all ones in which it is possible to explore the complex connections that exist between solidarity and hierarchy. Solidarity does not necessarily require members of a group to be equal, as Torrance's (1977) distinction between 'horizontal' and 'vertical' solidarity and Runciman's (1989: 97) comment that 'collective action frequently arises out of vertical rather than horizontal cooperation' are designed to demonstrate. Indeed, the difficulties encountered in attempts to create 'communal solidarity' suggest that there may be an inherent tension between solidarity and equality (Abrams and McCulloch 1976). Certainly, the pursuit of solidarity involves individuals in 'an attempt to reconcile difference and similarity' (Touraine 2000: 153), and this is particularly challenging where differences are expressed hierarchically. The hierarchical nature of families is readily apparent, although there is extensive debate about whether inequalities between generations and between genders are being eroded by a process of 'democratization'. Step-families provide a particularly interesting reference point for the exploration of these ideas. Communities are in many ways the converse of families in this respect, since closer inspection of community relationships reveals several dimensions of inequality that are masked by the superficial appearance of community members being equal. Mining communities illustrate in particularly stark form the presence of hierarchies relating to gender, class, length of residence and a number of other variables, and they provide further insights in relation to the process of industrial decline and the transition to post-coal futures. The combination of solidarity and hierarchy in the third case study, the Polish *Solidarity* movement, reinforces these points and in addition serves to highlight the rapidity with which 'leadership' and the solidarity of supporters can change in volatile political environments.

The presence of hierarchies among members of solidary groups brings into sharp focus the importance of considering what it is that forms the basis of social solidarity. The specification of what it is that people have in common that leads to their social relationships being characterized by solidarity presents a notoriously difficult definitional problem. The range of phenomena to which the term 'solidarity' may be applied means that definitions are necessarily somewhat general. Reflecting this, Llewelyn-Davies (1978: 206) defined solidarity as 'a commitment to some kind of mutual aid or support, based upon the perception, by those who are solidary, that they share certain characteristics, or that they are equal with respect to some social principle'. On the basis of this definition, she goes on to note that solidarity constructed around some shared characteristics may have the effect of reproducing existing inequalities in contrast to solidarity constructed around more abstract principles like 'equality', which has greater potential to be subversive of things as they are. This is a significant observation because it highlights the point that the effects of solidarity are open, sometimes contributing to continuity in social relationships, while at other times promoting change. Part three of the book will consider such issues in the light of the material covered in the preceding parts, with a view to clarifying what might be concluded about the key matters of contention with the benefit of the case study analyses. The discussion there pays particular attention to how solidarity connects with both social inclusion and social exclusion, and to how solidarities are routinely hierarchical. It also revisits the central sociological dichotomy of social order and social change, mindful of what is argued in the preceding chapters about the importance of the time dimensions of social solidarities.

Writing this book has been sustained by the belief that social solidarity continues to matter, and that therefore the study of social solidarity continues to occupy an important place on the agenda of social scientific research. A number of prominent thinkers have suggested that solidarity is an increasingly elusive goal, among them Beck and Beck-Gernsheim (1995: 46), whose interpretation of the individualization process is that 'each of us is both expected and forced to *lead our own life* outside the bounds of any specific community or group' (emphasis in original). One of the objectives of the book is to arrive at a judgement about how far evidence relating to contemporary social relationships supports such contentions, and how far it is consistent with alternative perspectives such as that offered by Scott (2000), in which greater potential for the development of new forms of community solidarity is identified. There is no shortage of empirical evidence available to be drawn upon to arrive at a judgement about the place of social solidarity in contemporary societies, and it will be the argument of this book that pronouncements on the demise of social solidarity are not only premature but are likely to continue to be confounded by events. There are good social scientific reasons for believing that social solidarity will persist as a necessary feature of social relationships at all levels, even if the forms in which solidarity is embodied are subject to profound change in an age of individualization. Chapter 6 explores further the idea that 'traditional' solidarities are under pressure from various unsettling forces besides individualization, but it develops the argument that these forces are countered (more or less effectively) by other processes that have the potential to bring people together in new ways.

The task of charting the changing nature and force of social solidarity is approached mindful of the long history that the 'loss of community' perspective has, at least in Western cultures. Many versions of this influential idea have rested on dubious foundations, among which is the pervasive belief that the historical record supports a pessimistic interpretation of social change in which social relations in the past are treated as having been somehow better than they are now (Lee and Newby 1983; Crow and Allan 1994). Awareness of the dangers presented by myths of a golden age of solidarity now disappeared is due in no small part to the fact that the problem of solidarity has engaged the attention of some of the most powerful minds in the history of sociology, who have been concerned to challenge such thinking. The early sociologists were not the first people to identify the problematic nature of solidarity, but they were responsible for reformulating conceptions of the problem in ways that, well over a century later, continue to provide a productive starting point for contemporary investigations into this fundamentally important question.

PART ONE

Classical theories of
social solidarity

○───

Introduction

Concern with social solidarity has been present in sociology from the outset,
and it features as prominently in the work of the discipline's founding figures
as it does in contemporary sociological writings. It has even been suggested
that 'it is primarily as the study of the causes of solidarity and schism that
sociology . . . has its *raison d'être* as an autonomous discipline' (Lockwood
1992: 3). There are echoes here of Durkheim's (1984: 27) claim that 'the study
of solidarity lies within the domain of sociology'. Although the issue of social
solidarity has the potential to pose difficulties for many other subjects in the
social sciences and beyond, it is in sociological works that the problem is
confronted most frequently and directly. The fundamental sociological question about what makes 'society' possible necessarily raises the issue of solidarity, as does the equally basic sociological concern with explaining patterns
of social change. One of Durkheim's main messages was that social arrangements that are not underpinned by solidarity between the individuals involved
are vulnerable to fragmentation. In similar vein, Marx emphasized that the
likelihood of success of efforts to steer social relations in particular directions
is affected by the extent of solidarity among both those pushing for change
and others involved in resisting such efforts. These ideas have proved to be
important points of reference for many subsequent contributions to debates
about social solidarity.

Sociology's founding figures showed that social solidarity can be approached from several different angles. One approach is particularly concerned
to investigate the foundations of social solidarity by asking questions about
what it is that people have in common that makes it possible and desirable for
them to act in unison. Within this tradition, Durkheim was concerned to
emphasize that, in modern societies, common interests alone are not enough

to secure social cohesion and collective endeavour. His observation that 'if mutual interest draws men closer, it is never more than for a few moments' (Durkheim 1984: 152) leads directly to the conclusion that social solidarity between people (women and children as well as men!) requires shared understandings and beliefs if it is to be sustainable. For Durkheim, people need to be integrated into orderly social classifications with definite boundaries, and his work can be read as a warning against the dangers of 'declassification' that the absence of such a framework threatens to generate (Lockwood 1992). A distinct but related approach sets out to identify different types of social solidarity on the basis of the argument that the forms in which solidarity is expressed can vary significantly. Durkheim's distinction between 'mechanical solidarity' and 'organic solidarity' is the best known example of such thinking, but he was by no means the only author to have followed this pattern of thought. Rival typologies to that of Durkheim are to be found in the writings of several classical sociological figures, for example Spencer and Tönnies, and it is important to acknowledge that Durkheim's ideas developed in part as a response to these. A third approach involves consideration of the dynamics of social solidarity. This line of inquiry is exemplified in Marx's analysis of what Torrance (1977) calls 'negative solidarity' – that is, the collective actions and reactions of social classes seeking to consolidate their strength relative to other social classes with which they have antagonistic relationships. Marx was especially interested in the extent of solidarity among workers and employers, since he saw this as having a crucial bearing on what he referred to as 'the respective powers of the combatants' (Marx and Engels 1969b: 73). These approaches are not mutually exclusive, but they do illustrate an important theme of the book, that a different angle of vision is gained according to whether the principal concern is with social solidarity's causes, contexts or consequences.

The unfolding agenda around the problem of order

The concept of social solidarity has come to be associated first and foremost with Durkheim's writings, but it is important that these writings are placed in their appropriate intellectual setting and that they are recognized to have left important issues unresolved. Durkheim was not the first person to engage with the problem of social solidarity and many of his most significant ideas were developed as part of a critique of earlier writers' theories that he regarded as deficient in their explanations of what holds people together. In addition, there are numerous parallels between Durkheim's ideas and those of other writers that make it appropriate to consider them together rather than separately. According to Barbalet (1983), for example, Durkheim's famous point about the potential of the whole to be greater than the sum of its individual parts was already present in Marx's view of class as more than 'a conglomeration of individuals'. The argument that there is considerable overlap between what Marx and Durkheim have to say about social solidarity has been made several times (Torrance 1977; Alexander 1982; Lockwood 1992). Similarly, it is possible to find interesting parallels and instructive differences between Durkheim and other writers, for example Simmel (Frisby and Sayer 1986; Craib 1997). In the light of these points, Durkheim's ideas will be examined alongside those of others who shared his concern to illuminate the nature of social solidarity and grappled with the difficulties involved in its analysis.

The first thing to note about Durkheim's analysis of social solidarity is that he did not provide a ready definition of this key term. Poggi (1972) regards it as 'somewhat surprising' that, despite its centrality to Durkheim's argument, 'nowhere does he define solidarity itself'. Torrance's (1977: 106) explanation of this omission is that 'Durkheim was reluctant to venture a general definition of solidarity, which he feared would only be taken as an invitation to substitute philosophical or psychological speculation for sociological inquiry'. Certainly, it would be difficult to exaggerate the sense that Durkheim sought to convey of the distinctiveness (and superiority) of sociological standpoints; one of the ways in which he did this was by contrasting sociology with other disciplines. In Durkheim's view, a sociological approach needed to leave behind the speculative and a-historical generalities to which philosophy was prone, and it also needed to avoid the danger of reducing social phenomena to the mental states of the individuals involved, which he regarded psychology as doing. Solidarity for Durkheim involved much more than simply sentiment (Watts Miller 1996), although in making his case Durkheim was guilty of exaggerating the extent to which sociology and psychology are distinctive, as Ray (1999: 98) notes by observing that 'he actually grounds his account in a theory of human psychology'. It was also necessary, in Durkheim's opinion, for sociologists to go beyond the approaches of political scientists and economists that tended to privilege explanations framed in terms of people's interests. As Worsley has noted, Durkheim embodied the confidence shared with many of his late nineteenth-century contemporaries that sociology promised to add 'another dimension to the explanations of social solidarity – or lack of it. A whole range of *cultural* institutions and forms of association – non-economic and, as we would say to-day, "non-governmental" – were also crucial: not just the state, the party and the market, but institutions which expressed a conception of society as a cultural community too' (Worsley 1997: 269, emphasis in original). Durkheim's objective of improving on previous accounts of social solidarity was thus a highly ambitious one, involving as it did a direct challenge to the conventional wisdom of his day.

The relationship of the individual to society had long been recognized as an intellectual problem, but Durkheim argued that a properly sociological approach to the bases of social solidarity was distinctive from all previous attempts to resolve 'the problem of order', as Parsons (1968) later named it. What stands out in particular about Durkheim's approach is his identification of two complementary ways in which individuals come to be socialized, one involving regulation of behaviour through institutional controls and the other involving integration of individuals through their shared experience of interaction (Hornsby 1998). Previous attempts to account for social solidarity generally lacked the depth and subtlety of Durkheim's approach. One of the intellectual traditions which Durkheim sought to challenge was exemplified in the writings of the seventeenth-century political philosopher Hobbes, who famously described the state of nature as a war of all against all in which an individual's life would be 'solitary, poore, nasty, brutish and short' (Hobbes 1968: 186). In the light of this argument that no natural basis for a harmonious social order existed, Hobbes's explanation of solidarity was framed in terms of social order being imposed from above by a powerful state. The *Leviathan*, as Hobbes called it, stood above competing individual interests and passions. Without such a restraining force, society would be predominantly an arena of mistrust and fear. Human nature dictated that, 'except they be restrained through fear of some coercive power, every man will dread and distrust each other' (Hobbes 1949: 11), and it was therefore necessary for order to be imposed by the state before trust could be established between individuals. Hobbes's great innovation was to question the assumption that people were 'born fit for society' and to demonstrate that individuals acting rationally in pursuit of their ends do not necessarily generate outcomes that are orderly or beneficial to others.

By the nineteenth century, Hobbes's location of the basis of social order and solidarity in a sovereign who could secure the interests not of particular individuals but of 'Man-kind' as a whole had been questioned on several grounds. Among the various representatives of the emerging discipline of sociology, Comte accepted Hobbes's belief that force exercised by the state underpinned social unity, but differed in expressing the view that people's actions were not necessarily selfish. Comte's introduction of the concept of altruism has significance in the history of analyses of social solidarity not only because it challenged the assumption of egoism, but also because it played an important role in making the study of solidarity more dynamic and comparative. Comte's idea that societies progress from one stage to the next in a law-like fashion contained the suggestion that, as industrial societies replaced earlier stages of social development, so people's moral attachments broadened out from the family to 'the whole of the human species' (in Thompson 1976: 119). In his view, social evolution (and the growth of cooperation between specialized elements of society that it brought) opened up new opportunities for altruistic behaviour in widening arenas. As he expressed it, the general point was that 'civilization leads us on to a further and further development of our noblest dispositions and our most generous feelings, which are the only possible basis of human association' (in Thompson 1976: 154). Comte did not regard this as a matter of personal choice, since the development was the result of changes over which individuals had little control. The basis of the shift towards a more altruistic society lay beyond the individual in broad social forces that, as they unfolded, progressively restrained egoism and sponsored cooperation. Material forces were prominent among these. One such force was the development of the division of labour, about which the thrust of Comte's thinking was that 'separation of functions' was necessarily connected to 'combination of efforts' (Aron 1968: 97). Put another way, what Comte suggested was that '[s]ocial solidarity is enhanced in a system in which individuals are dependent upon others' (Ritzer 1992: 90), and this interpretation of the division of labour had a significant effect on subsequent writers.

The work of Spencer shows that it is possible to set off from many of Comte's starting points and arrive at quite different conclusions. Like Comte, Spencer emphasized the importance of 'human variability' in his criticism of any approach which 'assumes the character of mankind to be constant' (1868: 49, 44). He also shared the belief that social change had the potential to be beneficial in its effects, but his argument placed much greater emphasis on the growth of individuality and what he referred to as 'the law of individuation' (1868: 479). In Spencer's account, 'human progress is toward greater mutual dependence, as well as toward greater individuation' (1868: 483), a belief which he argued for by use of an analogy with other species in the natural world. The development of society from the militant type to the industrial type was linked by Spencer to the foundation of each type of society on different principles. In drawing this distinction, he made much of the contrast between 'the compulsory co-operation which military activity necessitates' and 'the voluntary co-operation which a developed industrial activity necessitates' (1971: 172–3). Spencer suggested that there was a diminishing role for the state as societies evolved towards the industrial type, and it has been commented that his 'ideal is a society in which the government is reduced to a minimum and individuals are allowed maximum freedom' (Ritzer 1992: 109). In such a society, people would be brought together by common interests, and these shared interests lie at the heart of Spencer's explanation of the increasing integration and coherence of social groups which he believed he had identified. Voluntarily entering into contracts to their mutual benefit, individuals in industrial society had little need of coercive state activity beyond the provision of a legal and political framework that ensured individual freedom to take appropriate advantage of the opportunities that the developing division of labour generated. And while Comte concluded that people would continue to need some form of religion to provide them with moral guidance, Spencer's (1868: 29) view was that 'the moral forces upon which social equilibrium depends, are resident in the social atom – man'.

The broad optimism that characterized the account of social development for which Spencer is best remembered gave way to a more pessimistic tone in his later writings. Peel (1971) interprets the changing fortunes of Spencer's ideas as part of the more general shift away from liberal thinking which marked the final quarter of the nineteenth century. It is certainly the case that the equation of the rise of individualism with social progress became increasingly difficult to sustain. Spencer's Social Darwinism, encapsulated in his phrase 'survival of the fittest', carried with it a harsh message about the limits of solidarity, particularly when it was applied to those sections of the population referred to by Spencer (1969) as 'the incapables' and 'good-for-nothings'. Other observers of the social problems that accompanied industrialization were less sanguine about the potential of individualism to provide a feasible basis on which social solidarity could flourish, and conveyed more of a sense of loss when comparing the present with the past. Among these writers, the position of Tönnies is particularly instructive, since he states explicitly that his sociology grew out of an engagement with the ideas of Hobbes, Comte and Spencer. Tönnies (1971: 122) felt that modern society could be 'conceived of as a mere aggregate of individual households, each pursuing its own interest, maybe at the cost of all the others'. The biological analogy that Spencer had used to analyse the basis of contemporary social relationships was one which Tönnies felt did not stand up to scrutiny, not least because its key notion of a 'social body' suffered from being 'indefinite'. Referring in 1905 to the idea that a social body evolves, he asked '[i]s it England that has taken a development of this kind? Or is it England and Wales? Or are Scotland and even poor conquered Ireland to be included?' (Tönnies 1971: 123). By approaching the question in this way, Tönnies highlighted the need to be clear about two things on which previous writers like Spencer had been unhelpfully vague, namely specifying what it is that the members of a social group have in common and identifying the boundaries of the group.

Tönnies sought to bring greater clarity to the issue of social solidarity by insisting that social entities are held together not only by individual members having rights in common, but also by what he referred to as social 'bonds' or 'ties'. Whereas Spencer had emphasized the voluntary and free nature of cooperation in industrial society, Tönnies (1955: 8) stressed that interdependence involved 'being bound to others', which 'is the exact opposite of freedom, the former implying a moral obligation, a moral imperative, or a prohibition'. Like Comte and Spencer had before him, Tönnies employed a simplified distinction between different types of social order, which he designated *gemeinschaft* and *gesellschaft*. These terms translate imperfectly as 'community' and 'association', given that the latter term can also be read as 'society' or 'organization' (Lee and Newby 1983: 44). For Tönnies, *gemeinschaft* involved people being held together by 'real and organic life', while *gesellschaft* links people through an 'imaginary and mechanical structure' (1955: 37). In the former, a dense web of relationships connects people in on-going ties of interdependence, at the heart of which is the family, 'the general basis of life in the Gemeinschaft' (1955: 267). These relationships have an enduring emotional dimension in which attachment to place is important. In *gesellschaft*, the bases of social solidarity have become weakened by greater geographical mobility and by the rise of urban, industrial capitalism, processes which, if taken to the extreme, reduce social relationships to an 'act of exchange . . . performed by individuals who are alien to each other, have nothing in common with each other, and confront each other in an essentially antagonistic and even hostile manner' (1971: 76–7). Tönnies employed a deliberate echo of Hobbes in his suggestion that 'the modern, urbanized, *Gesellschaft*-like civilization . . . represents a concealed war of all against all' (1971: 60). Tönnies regarded 'unconditional self-affirmation' and 'unfettered economic competition' (1971: 61) as more likely to lead to conflict than to cooperative collective endeavour, since the latter requires an enduring sense of common purpose and common identity with which individualism and the inequalities it generates are ultimately incompatible.

Tönnies's writings represent an advance on previous accounts in several important respects. First, he was more concerned to ground his sociological analysis in relation to observable evidence, being rightly sceptical of approaches that used ill-defined concepts in support of speculative pronouncements. He was particularly mindful of the 'enigmatic contradiction' whereby in *gesellschaft* it is presumed that 'all individuals are equal insofar as they are capable of engaging in exchange and entering into contracts' (Tönnies 1971: 78), while it is all too apparent that in practice social relationships are distorted by employer–employee inequalities. Tönnies's awareness of how the societies of his day were divided by social classes allowed him to link various social problems with 'the monopoly of wealth of the few'. His reference to widening inequalities as the 'social question' flagged up his concern with the practical outcomes of the shift from *gemeinschaft* to *gesellschaft*. Confronting this issue made it imperative to ask whether it was more appropriate to consider people as belonging to 'society' or some other social entity. Whereas the organic analogy took as given the integration of societies and the functional equality of their members, Tönnies drew on Marx's thinking to distinguish between the positions of the working and capitalist classes, referring to the latter as 'completely free' but the former as only 'semi-free'. Tönnies (1955: 270) suggested that such inequality promotes among the masses a movement 'from class consciousness to class struggle' which threatens to 'destroy society', and he looked to the revival of a more *gemeinschaft*-like culture to counter this threat and restore concord to social relationships. Tönnies was thus by no means optimistic about the course that social development was taking, and his concerns provided an important corrective to those approaches which simply assumed the progressive nature of social change. Furthermore, by highlighting that, in principle, *gesellschaft* is 'boundaryless', Tönnies drew attention to the way in which market forces worked to undermine the ties which formerly bound people together as members of discrete social entities such as families and local communities. The unity of *gesellschaft* is precarious because it is founded on what Tönnies called 'convention', where individuals are guided in their actions by their calculation of what is useful to them. By contrast, the *gemeinschaft*-like principle of 'tradition', where individuals follow the 'sacred inheritance of the ancestors' (Tönnies 1955: 87), offers a more stable basis for social order.

Durkheim's thesis concerning social solidarity can be seen as a reaction against the various ideas of Comte, Spencer and Tönnies, even though he sought to answer the same intellectual problem as they did. Lukes (1975: 141) sums up this problem as two related questions: 'if pre-industrial societies were held together by common ideas and sentiments, by shared norms and values, what holds an industrial society together? Or is it perhaps not being held together at all, but rather in the process of disintegration?'. Lukes goes on to show that Durkheim objected to the role Comte allocated to the state as a regulator of social life, which he regarded as impractical because solidarity could not be imposed from above in the context of a modern division of labour. Durkheim's objections to Spencer were that common interests provided only a tenuous basis for social solidarity, and that he overlooked the importance of the wider social framework that made economic exchange possible. In turn, Tönnies's ideas were rejected because Durkheim questioned the portrayal of *gesellschaft*-like relations. Durkheim (1972) regarded these as no less 'organic' than those of *gemeinschaft*, and thought therefore that their portrayal as 'mechanical' was inadequate. As if to emphasize this point, Durkheim's depiction of pre-industrial societies as founded on mechanical solidarity and industrial societies as founded on organic solidarity turned Tönnies 'on his head' (Kivisto 1998: 95). In making his distinction between mechanical and organic solidarities, Durkheim advanced the deceptively simple argument that the former was based on similarity among individuals and the latter on difference. When stated this bluntly, Durkheim's central thesis appears to be just as speculative as many of his contemporaries' ideas that he sought to criticize. It is, however, an argument that he elaborated on extensively and, in doing so, went well beyond speculation about the bases of social solidarities to consider how these different types of society actually functioned.

Durkheim's developing account of social solidarity

Social solidarity was the subject of Durkheim's first lecture course and of his first book, *The Division of Labour in Society*, and it remained a central issue throughout his career. It has been said of Durkheim that he regarded solidarity as 'the highest social and moral good, the *raison d'être* of society' (Lehmann 1994: 48–9). The approach that he adopted was characteristically broad in scope. He took as his subject matter nothing less than 'the totality of bonds that bind us to one another and to society, which shape the mass of individuals into a cohesive aggregate' (Durkheim 1984: 331). The contrast between the two broad types of solidarity that he identified, mechanical and organic, underpinned a bold theory of the evolution of societies in which interdependence grew as the latter replaced the former. Equally characteristic was the style in which he delivered his argument about social solidarity, establishing it by use of propositions that appear in common-sense terms paradoxical. The relationship between individuals and society was introduced by Durkheim as a puzzle: '[h]ow does it come about that the individual, whilst becoming more autonomous, depends ever more closely on society? How can he become at the same time more of an individual and yet more linked to society?' (p. xxx). When posed in this way, the shortcomings of alternative explanations of solidarity framed in terms of either compulsion by the state or the pursuit of self-interest were highlighted, since neither could account satisfactorily for the connection between the growth of individualism and increasing interdependence. Furthermore, Durkheim sought to go beyond these approaches by being more rigorous in methodological terms. He argued that 'generalities' had the capacity to produce only 'a very incomplete explanation' of solidarity, and that what was necessary for analysis to be scientific was greater attention to detail. As an empirical sociologist, Durkheim was sensitive to the fact that '[w]hat exists and what is really alive are the special forms of solidarity – domestic, professional, national, that of the past and that of today, etc. Each has its own special nature' (p. 27). It followed that comparisons between them needed to be undertaken systematically and methodically.

Much has been written about Durkheim's distinction between mechanical and organic solidarities, and several commentaries have questioned how far he practised what he preached concerning methodological rigour when developing his argument in *The Division of Labour in Society*. Abrams (1982) describes Durkheim's account as 'an extremely general framework' that is 'notably unhistorical', while Thompson (1982) suggests that 'Durkheim's own moral and political preferences creep back in' as the book proceeds. There are indisputably major difficulties with Durkheim's designation of certain forms of the division of labour as 'abnormal' or 'pathological', since this entails specification of a 'normal' pattern which is not as objective as it is presented as being (Bryant 1976). His choice of the law as an indicator of how patterns of social solidarity have changed is equally problematic. To argue that mechanical solidarity is associated with laws that have 'repressive' sanctions designed principally to punish transgressors, whereas organic solidarity is reflected in legal codes that are less punitive and more 'restitutory' (described by Durkheim as, 'restoring the previous state of affairs'), is, as Aron (1970) puts it, 'rather over-simplified'. It is also, as Parkin (1992: 26) has noted, 'quite out of character for Durkheim to have posited a close connection between something so eminently social as solidarity and the administrative process of the central political power, a body whose impact upon society he is usually at pains to minimise'. The additional observation that Durkheim did not employ the terminology of mechanical and organic solidarity in his writing subsequent to *The Division of Labour in Society* might lead us to suppose that these various difficulties led him to abandon it as an analytical framework. It is, however, more appropriate to see Durkheim's work that followed as engaging with these difficulties and developing this framework rather than abandoning it.

Several elements of Durkheim's discussion of the division of labour remained central to his later analyses of social solidarity, even though the language that he used to discuss them and the phenomena on which he focused left behind 'the massive and cumbrous concepts of organic and mechanical solidarity' (LaCapra 1985: 79). The first of these common threads is that Durkheim continued to proceed from the proposition that social collectivities are composed of more than simply the aggregate of the parts that make them up. In *The Rules of Sociological Method*, Durkheim (1982: 129) insisted that 'society is not the mere sum of individuals'. He used the example of crowd phenomena to illustrate the point: 'an outburst of collective emotion in a gathering does not merely express the sum total of what individual feelings share in common, but is something of a very different order . . . It is the product of shared existence, of actions and reactions called into play between the consciousness of individuals' (Durkheim 1982: 56). It follows from this that the study of solidarity requires that attention be paid to what Durkheim called the 'conscience collective', a term which neatly captures the group and moral dimensions of the phenomenon by meaning both collective consciousness and collective conscience (Craib 1997). When he wrote *The Division of Labour in Society*, Durkheim was already aware of the existence of powerful objections to using the law as an indicator of the 'conscience collective'. His argument that laws are normally in harmony with custom and tradition merely compounded the problem by raising the difficulty of identifying what is 'normal'. Durkheim subsequently found his attention shifting towards the way in which religion integrated people into society, and he described his discovery of 'the capital role played by religion in social life' as 'a revelation' and 'a watershed in my thinking' (Durkheim 1982: 259). This line of reasoning led ultimately to Durkheim's last great work, *The Elementary Forms of the Religious Life* (1976), in which he elaborated on the unifying force that shared beliefs about what is sacred exert on members of a collectivity. This work develops a point of view already present in embryo form at the outset of Durkheim's career, that the explanation of social life needs to take into account not only its 'material foundation' but also the 'whole world of sentiments, ideas and images' which shape individual behaviour.

Related to this is a second continuity in Durkheim's work revolving around his rejection of explanations of solidarity as something that is purely rational. Durkheim continued to argue that common interests are not enough to sustain cohesion among group members, who need to be committed to a moral code for more than instrumental reasons. His later work suggested that people's commitment to shared values requires periodic revitalization through gatherings which constitute an 'effervescent social environment'. Ritual gatherings have the capacity to renew solidarity by transporting people beyond everyday routines and, Durkheim (1976: 210) argued, '[t]his is why all parties, political, economic or confessional, are careful to have reunions where their members may revivify their common faith by manifesting it in common'. Durkheim thus recognized that modern societies continue to have a need for such 'collective effervescence' because, as Torrance (1977), Pickering (1984), Hornsby (1998) and Pope (1998) have all noted, he was acutely aware of the place of emotion in reinforcing people's commitment to solidary modes of behaviour. Sentiments of solidarity with others were in Durkheim's view strengthened where social relationships were more intense, and the element of renewal that gatherings involve helps to explain why it is that traditions have the force that they do. Networks of social relationships link individuals to the broader collectivity and, where these relationships are only weakly maintained, the individual is less regulated by tradition and more at risk of becoming detached from the wider society. In the extreme, weak ties to the collectivity make the individual vulnerable to suicide, as Durkheim's (1970) celebrated study argued. Campbell (1981: 157) interprets such ideas as an indication that what Durkheim offered was not a stark opposition between organic and mechanical solidarity as alternatives, since 'the latter can exist without the former but the former cannot exist without a measure of the latter'.

The recognition in his later works that the distinction between mechanical and organic types was insufficiently subtle to capture the complexity of social solidarities did not lead Durkheim to abandon comparison altogether. A third continuity in Durkheim's work was his firmly held belief that the form which social solidarity takes has to be seen in its appropriate social structural context and classified in this light. Social solidarity was in his view open to being expressed in several forms, depending on whether the social structure functioned by promoting people's similarities or their differences. He regarded historical sociological comparisons as demonstrating that different societies operated with different moral orders, and he was aware that the 'conscience collective' had tended over the course of social evolution to give way to a moral order in which individualism was more prominent. He held to the belief that the specialization inherent in the division of labour meant that 'solidarity by similarities' became increasingly difficult to sustain, and that as homogeneity gave way to heterogeneity, so 'the cult of the person and individual dignity' (Durkheim 1984: 333; frequently translated more simply as 'the cult of the individual') grew in importance.

The idea that individualism could be the basis of solidarity in modern societies was not contradictory to Durkheim, since he attached great importance to the distinction between individualism and egoism, as a number of commentators have noted (Bryant 1976; Cladis 1992; Ritzer 1992). Durkheim's view was that the development of the division of labour promoted the process of individuation, whereby 'the individual no longer shares the same characteristics as all other individuals in his society' (Giddens 1972: 9). Individualization in the sense of growing awareness of individual differences was regarded by Durkheim as a development to be welcomed where it embodied 'glorification not of the self but of the individual in general', but it was an entirely different matter when it took the form of 'infatuation with oneself' (Durkheim 1973). According to Dawe (1979: 391), Durkheim was centrally concerned 'with the creation of a truly moral individualism, as the necessary basis for moral solidarity, out of the egoistic individualism in terms of which he saw the society around him'. The former reinforced solidarity through the growth of awareness among people of their interdependence and mutual obligations in complex societies. The latter, by contrast, was the antithesis of altruism and other-regarding behaviour, and by taking the process of individuation too far was destructive of solidarity. Durkheim's view was underpinned by his belief that every person confronts 'a permanent tension between the demands of social life and those of his individual, organic nature' (Lukes 1985: 286) and that the latter needed to be kept in check.

In *The Division of Labour in Society*, the case for believing that '[v]ery often we happen to feel drawn to people who do not resemble us, precisely because they do *not* do so' (Durkheim 1984: 16, emphasis in original) is unconvincing. One of the reasons for this is that it is at odds with the extensive evidence of the weakness of solidarity in the 'abnormal forms' of the division of labour that are considered at the end of the book. Durkheim's discussion of the abnormal forms of the division of labour is an acknowledgement that it is by no means inevitable that the emergence of new forms of social solidarity based on difference will replace the old ones based on similarity. Having recognized that the development of the division of labour could in practice be accompanied by social division, disorganization and conflict, Durkheim went on to devote much of the rest of his career to the analysis of how social solidarity might be promoted in the modern context. In the Preface to the second edition of *The Division of Labour in Society*, Durkheim (1984: liv) flagged up the importance of civil society in this respect: '[a] nation cannot be maintained unless, between the state and individuals, a whole range of secondary groups are interposed. These must be close enough to the individual to attract him to their activities and, in so doing, to absorb him into the mainstream of social life'. He suggested, for example, that occupational associations that linked employers and employees in groups of related industries had the potential to act as a bridge between the individual and society as a whole. This role could be enhanced if they went beyond narrowly economic matters and adopted further responsibilities relating to such things as 'pensions, welfare, culture and recreation' (Bryant 1976: 86). He was careful to note, however, that on their own such associations would not reverse social disintegration if unfair inequalities between rich and poor people persist, since these produce a forced division of labour which runs counter to the ethos of individualism.

Durkheim saw occupational associations as in important respects similar to the family as an institution through which social solidarity could be effected. Family ties are an illuminating element of his account of social solidarity, since he represented them as relationships that need to be enduring if they are to be effective in directing and controlling individual members. Treating the family as a prime example of 'a group of individuals who have drawn close to one another in the body politic through a very specially close community of ideas, feelings and interests', Durkheim (1984) could describe it as 'a kind of complete society' in miniature. Among these family ties, the 'marital solidarity' present between spouses was attributed by Durkheim to the way in which their sexual division of labour embodied their 'mutual dependence'. He treated the sexual division of labour between spouses as mutually beneficial and also functional for the wider society, even though it was not an egalitarian arrangement but part of an 'order of domination' (Gane 1992: 85) in which men's position within the domestic hierarchy was superior to that of women. The most important characteristic of the division of labour for Durkheim (1984: 17) was that it serves 'to create between two or more people a feeling of solidarity', and he took the evolution of the sexual division of labour as a telling demonstration of this point. He was aware of the fact that family relations could in practice come to be 'maintained at the expense of women' (Sydie 1987: 24), but his account nevertheless treated a wife's subordination to her husband as 'a necessary condition of family unity' (Durkheim 1980: 20). The argument that there existed a 'natural' basis for such inequality was considered but it proved difficult to sustain, not least because it was at odds with what Durkheim wrote elsewhere about individualism. He was, however, reluctant to pursue the alternative explanation framed in terms of unequal power which more radical writers of the time (including early feminists) promulgated. Organic solidarity for Durkheim involved a positive attraction between individuals conscious of their interdependence, and was quite distinct from the forced division of labour and forced solidarity to which powerless individuals would acquiesce only because of the absence of alternatives.

These debates over the family serve to highlight more general issues regarding social solidarity. Durkheim's approach aligned him with the tradition of thought that treated family solidarity as enduring to the extent that family members placed commitment to the group ahead of rational calculation of individual interests. Durkheim's work has some similarities to Tönnies's treatment of the family as the epitome of *gemeinschaft*, and neither writer was confident about the prospects of family solidarity surviving into the future. Durkheim (1970) was conscious of various social and economic forces that were working to undermine 'the indivisibility which was once the family's strength', and Tönnies (1955) was particularly mindful of the corrosive effects of women's employment that made them 'enlightened, cold-hearted, conscious'. Tönnies likened this development to the growth of class consciousness among the working class, and in this respect his position was closer to that of Marx than that of Durkheim. What is at issue here is the way in which Durkheim's approach prioritized the unity of the whole and played down the issue of subordination within the entity under consideration (be it family, society or any other collectivity). Lehmann (1993: 9) may be overstating the case to say that 'Durkheim does not discuss the differences of race, class and sex (or sexuality)', but she is correct in pointing to his approach having serious problems in its treatment of hierarchies within collectivities. Other writers of the time attached considerably more importance to internal divisions within families and societies, and their greater awareness of the potential for difference to generate conflict rather than consensus produced a contrasting perspective on social solidarity.

Social solidarity and social divisions

When considering the intellectual legacy bequeathed by Hobbes in the form of his problem of order, it is possible to trace several other lines of response besides that leading to Durkheim. McDonald (1994: 21), for example, has detailed the on-going engagement with Hobbes in the writings of 'the women founders of the social sciences', among whom there was a notable 'stress on positive social bonds', which she argues continues to inform contemporary feminism's support for collective welfare provision. In addition, by criticizing what Sydie (1987) has called 'the assumptions about the nature of human nature' as 'sex-blind', feminists posed in stark relief the question of whose solidarity was under discussion. The way in which the debate about the relationship between the individual and society was set up often overlooked important differences between the positions of men and women. This matters because taking men as a norm can transform women into 'minor subjects'

(Gane 1992: 106) in the analysis of social relationships, or it can even make them effectively invisible by treating them as an unacknowledged 'other'.

A similar point was made by Marx and Engels about social class differences, since it was evident to them that class position had a strong influence on how an individual fitted into relationships of solidarity. Solidarity entails different things depending on whether an individual occupies a superior or subordinate position within a mode of production, and they regarded it as misleading to refer to individuals as abstract entities, separate from their class situations that might endow them with distinctive interests. Such analyses led directly to questions about the desirability of solidarity where it reproduces systematic inequalities by stifling change, and much of Marx and Engels's work was devoted to the analysis of how solidarity comes to be channelled in particular directions. In turn, the focus on class solidarity rather than the solidarity of whole societies was subjected to critical scrutiny by Weber, whose research led him to regard 'status groups as agencies of collective action that serve as alternatives to class-oriented action' (Parkin 1982: 99). Simmel, too, questioned the merit of focusing on solidarity at the abstract levels of 'society' or 'class', and a major thrust of his analysis was that solidarities are often forged most intensely among smaller groups, especially where other individuals or groups constitute a recognizable enemy. In different ways, what all of these approaches emphasize is that social solidarity is frequently constructed around the domination or exclusion of others. What Weber (1978: 342) called 'the closure of social and economic opportunities to *outsiders*' (emphasis in original) is something which the method of looking beyond the generality of the individual–society relationship revealed to be an important aspect of social solidarity.

The recognition that the issue of solidarity concerns the individual's relationship not only to 'society' but also to other levels of social collectivity that may be in competition with each other broadens out the discussion of the Hobbesian 'problem of order'. Other classical sociologists attached greater importance than did Durkheim to what have been called 'the functions of social conflict' (Coser 1956), emphasizing in the process the unifying effect which having an opponent can have on a group. Marx and Engels (1969a: 63–5), for example, noted in *The German Ideology* that '[c]ompetition separates individuals one from another' and is corrosive of 'community', before going on to argue that '[t]he separate individuals form a class only insofar as they have to carry on a common battle against another class; otherwise they are on hostile terms with each other as competitors'. Marx recognized that the extent to which individuals are united as members of social classes influences their capacity to control what happens in their lives, but he was well aware of how material circumstances can limit the scope for such unity. The analysis of the peasantry in mid-nineteenth century France that he offered highlighted that a common economic situation does not necessarily lead to effective class solidarity. As he described their situation in *The Eighteenth Brumaire of Louis Bonaparte*, '[t]he small-holding peasants form a vast mass, the members of which live in similar conditions but without entering into manifold relations with one another. Their mode of production isolates them from one another instead of bringing them into mutual intercourse'. As a result, they form a collective entity only in the limited fashion that 'potatoes in a sack form a sack of potatoes'. All the while that 'the identity of their interests begets no community, no national bond and no political organization among them, they do not form a class' (Marx and Engels 1969a: 478–9). The acknowledgement by Marx and Engels that class solidarity was not an inevitable outcome of people having class interests in common highlighted the need to explore what precisely solidarity is founded upon and what processes operate to sustain it.

Marx and Engels's identification of the potential for solidarity to emerge among the workers of the world is framed in terms of shared interests, but the specification of interests is by no means straightforward (Barnes 1995). Marx indicated as much by distinguishing between different types of interests (Barbalet 1983). Class consciousness tends to promote solidarity through the recognition that '[b]y acting together the members of a class can obtain more than they could by acting in isolation' (Elster 1985: 347), but there is no guarantee that individuals will put class interests first. Where people take a purely selfish stance, there is a constant danger that '[t]he common interest is appreciated by each only so long as he gains more by it than without it' (Marx 1959: 194). There are clear parallels here with Durkheim's point about the unstable basis for solidarity that interests provide and the need for some element of altruism or of the coercion inherent in forced solidarity if solidary relationships are to be sustainable (Pearce 1989). In addition, as Mills (1963: 113) has noted, 'the fact is that men are often concerned with temporary rather than long-run interests, and with particular interests, of occupational trades, for example, rather than the more general interests of their class'. Even when class interests are readily identifiable, it is not a foregone conclusion that people will put these ahead of other interests that they may have.

Awareness of points like this led Weber to reject the idea that class interests had the overriding significance as a basis for solidaristic action that Marx attributed to them. According to Barnes (1995: 173), 'Weber was content to take class as just one potential basis for collective action, and one that might or might not become actual'. Indeed, it might be regarded as less rather than more likely to occur given Weber's conception of economic action as 'the antithesis of solidarity, of collective action for a common cause or of altruistic self-sacrifice' (Albrow 1990: 265). Weber worked from the premise that people's conduct was directly governed by 'material and ideal interests' (in Gerth and Mills 1970: 280) and thus operated with a much wider sense of the potential bases of solidarity. His sociology of religion is replete with instances of how 'shared religious ideas' can 'serve as a bulwark of group cohesion' (Bendix 1966: 87), for example. Weber's analysis of 'communal and associative relationships' drew on Tönnies's distinction between *gemeinschaft* and *gesellschaft*, since the contrast between solidarity based on tradition and emotion and solidarity based on rationality was one that Weber sought to develop. Of the two, communal relationships derive their strength from the fact that they are 'based on a subjective feeling of the parties, whether affectual or traditional, that they belong together'. In addition to noting that the family typified communal relationships, he cited an extremely diverse set of examples: 'a religious brotherhood, an erotic relationship, a relation of personal loyalty, a national community, the *espirit de corps* of a military unit' (Weber 1978: 40–41). Such relationships may be open or closed to outsiders, but it was the process of social closure that had greater significance in Weber's analysis of solidarity because of its greater relevance to his concern with the distribution of power and the reproduction of inequalities and domination (Parkin 1979; Murphy 1988).

Weber suggested that what Marx and Engels observed about solidarity among class members being strengthened by the identification of a recognizable opponent may be a feature of interest groups more generally. In any circumstances where competition exists for a scarce resource, it can be expected that one group will take an 'externally identifiable characteristic of another group of (actual or potential) competitors – race, language, religion, local or social origin, descent, residence, etc. – as a pretext for attempting their exclusion. It does not matter which characteristic is chosen in the individual case: whatever suggests itself most easily is seized upon'. In turn, such closure 'may provoke a corresponding reaction on the part of those against whom it is directed' (Weber 1978: 342), with the implication that collective identities may quite possibly be modified or reinforced over time. Social closure is thus a feature of 'categorical inequality' (Tilly 1998: 7) and class is but one of many potential categories around which solidarity may be mobilized. One of the things which led Weber to question how far social closure would take place around class differences was his awareness that people do not always perceive the world in terms of abstract notions like class, as Giddens (1971) has noted. Thus, Weber (1978: 931) observed, 'It is not the rentier, the share-holder and the banker who suffer the ill will of the worker, but almost exclusively the manufacturer and the business executives who are the direct opponents of workers in wage conflicts'. He therefore felt it more likely that collective identities would develop against opponents who are visible and confronted directly than they would against more abstract macro-level entities such as classes.

The move away from the problem of order couched in terms of the relationship between the individual and society was taken further still in the work of Simmel. In his analysis, Simmel stressed the diversity of social processes that unite people and of the social forms that this unity can take. He drew various instances from everyday life to illustrate the general point that a 'whole gamut of relations' exists 'that may be momentary or permanent, conscious or unconscious, ephemeral or of grave consequence', but which all 'incessantly tie men together' (in Wolff 1964: 10). The interests which bring people together were described in similarly broad terms by Simmel, yet despite being based on different foundations and expressed in different forms, it was quite possible to identify common patterns in the way that particular types of social relationships operated. Thus 'inner solidarity coupled with exclusiveness toward the outside' could be found 'in the state, in a religious community, in a band of conspirators, in an economic association, in an art school, in the family' (in Wolff 1964: 22). By this reasoning, Simmel suggested that much could be learned about group dynamics from studying how any one of these operated. According to Simmel, group identity is particularly strong in secret societies because there one finds unusual clarity about the boundary between insiders and outsiders and about the mutual obligations of members. Although they constitute an extreme example of group solidarity, secret societies shed light on the more general processes by which people come to be socialized into behaving appropriately in relation to others within a group hierarchy. Reciprocity among members of a secret society is reinforced through rituals which heighten their consciousness of what they have in common and of the mutual trust which ensues from their shared secret (Misztal 1996; Watier 1998).

Collins's (1994: 117) assessment of Simmel's contribution to the study of solidarity is that it can be reduced to the propositions that '[c]onflict sharpens the sense of group boundaries' and that 'groups often search for external enemies in order to maintain internal order'. There is considerably more to it than that, however, since Simmel was at pains to explain why so much signi-ficance should be attached to group boundaries in this way. Like many of his contemporaries, Simmel was very much aware of how the growth of a more individualistic culture signalled the end of the old order and heralded a more uncertain future. His view of the development of a money economy was that it sponsored 'the feeling of individual self-sufficiency', but at the same time the benefits of this liberation from personal dependence had to be set against the alienating effects of 'the complete heartlessness of money' (Simmel 1978: 298, 346). As a result, social relationships come to be at risk of losing much of their meaning, and it is against this background of ambiguity and uncer-tainty that the attraction of exclusive social groups that offer a more positive identity must be seen. The impersonality and fragmentation of life which are inherent in modernity and which have been taken furthest in the modern metropolis represented a paradoxical development for Simmel because, as Coser (1965: 11) expressed it, '[s]ociety allows the emergence of individual-ity and autonomy, but it also impedes it'. The approach that Simmel adopted was distinctive in important respects, but the underlying problem that he addressed was a familiar one to the classical sociologists of his generation (Nisbet 1970).

The commonalities and differences to be found in what the classical soci-ologists wrote about social solidarity are worth drawing together at this point. All were aware that they were living through a period of transformation in which traditional social arrangements were being re-cast, and that this neces-sitated paying attention to the implications of these changes for social order. In their analyses of change, they frequently made use of stark comparisons such as those between militant and industrial societies, *gemeinschaft* and *gesellschaft*, and mechanical and organic solidarities. The process of individualization is a common theme in these accounts, although important differences exist between explanations of how and why this has come about. The linkage between individualization and the development of the division of labour is given prominence in several accounts, while others point to the influence of processes like secularization, urbanization, democratization, the development of the modern state and the development of capitalism. Assessments of the implications for social solidarity of these changes are correspondingly diverse, although they all in some way confront the tension between nature and rationality which Everingham (1994), in her discussion of Tönnies's work, identifies as 'the paradox of modernity'.

Opinions varied among the classical sociologists about whether individualization was better understood as liberation from oppressive constraints or herald of alienation, anomie and social fragmentation, although in general the mood of optimism was replaced by one of pessimism as the nineteenth century wore on (Hughes 1974). Opinions varied, too, on what might be done in response to these developments. Rose (1999: 79) has traced how sociological ideas fed into interventionist politics which 'tried to re-invent community governmentally' on the assumption that 'the bonds of solidarity could be rendered *technical*, that is to say, made amenable to a technique' (emphasis in original). He refers to Durkheim as 'intimately involved in the French politics of solidarism' (Rose 1999: 118), and while others have played down this association (Lukes 1975; Bryant 1976), Durkheim's work undoubtedly offers a rationale for the active promotion of civil society. Other positions were more backward-looking in seeking to restore elements of the old order, or more radical in their assessment of what needed to change, or sceptical of the role of political interventions. Underpinning these arguments lay more fundamental disagreements about the nature and purpose of social solidarity. Debates about whether solidarity is better regarded as a rational or non-rational phenomenon, the level at which it operates, and whether it is always desirable were by no means resolved by sociology's founding figures. Nonetheless, the power of their analyses is indicated by the influence that they continue to have on current thinking.

2

Contemporary theories of social solidarity

Introduction

Many contemporary theorists of social solidarity acknowledge their debt to the classical theorists before going on to identify the ways in which they regard this legacy as problematic. In most of these accounts, the need to go beyond the work of the founding figures is associated with the ways in which the social world has changed in the period since they were writing. The development of welfare states and the emergence of new expressions of individualization are among a number of processes which can be regarded as having brought with them fundamental changes in the way in which the issue of social solidarity is confronted. Giddens (1994b: 186), for example, has argued that '[w]e need . . . to question today the old dichotomy between "community" and "association" – between mechanical and organic solidarity. The study of mechanisms of social solidarity remains as essential to sociology as it ever was, but the new forms of solidarity are not captured by these distinctions'. Similar sentiments underlie Beck's (1994: 13) identification of the decline of traditional institutional arrangements as the expression of the 'disembedding and re-embedding' ushered in under the auspices of welfare states 'as they have developed since the 1960s in many Western industrial countries'. Such developments necessarily take us beyond the 'parallel interpretations' offered by Simmel, Durkheim and Weber. The same implications about the need to reconsider inherited analytical frameworks can be drawn from Bauman's (1999: 54) rather pessimistic suggestion that patterns of social change have produced a situation in which '[o]ur sufferings divide and isolate: our miseries set us apart, tearing up the delicate tissue of human solidarities'. The 'short-lived explosions of human solidarity' that Bauman describes as being more characteristic of the contemporary world are quite distinctive because of their fleeting nature and consequent unpredictability. It is his view that 'more often than not common actions do not live long enough to precipitate solidary institutions and command stable loyalty of their participants' (Bauman 1995: 274). From another angle, Meštrović's (1997: xii) account of 'postemotional society' makes explicit contrast with Durkheim's ideas by claiming that 'contemporary "collective effervescence" is staged and rationally induced. The "collective consciousness" no longer exists: It has succumbed to a process of fission, a Balkanization of social identity into fragmented group identities that are hostile to one another'.

Arguments that start from the premise that nineteenth-century approaches to social solidarities need to be updated in the light of subsequent developments are the subject of intense debate. The extent of change is an important issue to consider when gauging the validity of claims about the emergence of new solidarities and the decline of old ones, not least because there are legitimate questions to ask about how far such claims are based on evidence. Within the literature that highlights the novelty of contemporary patterns of solidarity, it is not difficult to find examples of what Marshall (1997) refers to as 'data-free sociology', and the arguments contained in such works need to be treated with a good deal of caution. Claims about the past should be scrutinized with similar rigour, since historical evidence does not always tally with the image of a 'golden age of community' that is frequently deployed in support of the thesis that social solidarities have undergone a radical transformation. Referring specifically to social class solidarities, Marshall and his colleagues (1988: 206) have questioned the 'dualistic historical thinking whereby a communitarian and solidaristic proletariat of some bygone heyday of class antagonism is set against the atomized and consumer-oriented working class of today'. The point they make has applicability to other solidarities besides those of class that are equally susceptible to being romanticized. There are clear echoes here of earlier debates about the supposed transition from *gemeinschaft* to *gesellschaft*, even if the terms in which contemporary debates are conducted have evolved somewhat.

A further aspect of contemporary theories of solidarity that requires attention is the preparedness of some writers to ask awkward questions about the purpose and desirability of solidarity. The positive associations of the idea of 'solidarity' (and related concepts like 'community', 'civil society', 'social capital' and 'social support') make it easy to assume that the phenomena under discussion are more or less generally welcomed and that, conversely, it is appropriate to treat their absence as problematic. Williams's (1976) observation that the word 'community' 'seems never to be used unfavourably' has often been cited in this context, but it no longer holds true. Sennett's (1977a) characterization of contemporary *gemeinschaft* as 'destructive' is just one expression of a perspective whose proponents are critical of the taken-for-granted desirability of solidarity where this entails social arrangements that are regarded as oppressive. Young's (1995) critique of the ideal of 'community' because of its denial of opportunities for people to be different is another powerful statement of this position, as is Oakley's (1992) questioning of the assumption that social support is always beneficial. It also underlies Baron and co-workers' (1998: 105) comment that 'societies characterized by high social capital, such as Nazi Germany, might be deeply unpleasant places in which to live'. Points such as these help to explain why it is that the apparently innocuous agenda of promoting social solidarity (embodied, for example, in the writings of communitarians) has turned out to be so contentious.

Contemporary social solidarities perceived as breaks with the past

The changing nature of citizenship is a key point of reference in contemporary theories of social solidarity. As has been noted many times, the founding figures of sociology were writing in advance of twentieth-century developments in the scope and rationale of State activity, most obviously (but by no means exclusively) those associated with the growth and consolidation of welfare states. Their ideas are of limited contemporary relevance for writers such as Bendix, according to whom the centralization of government has revealed the inherent nostalgia of the intellectual legacy of Durkheim and others. For Bendix (1996: 168), it is a hard truth that '[t]he "great transformation" leading to the modern political community makes the decline of social solidarity inevitable'. The framework of the modern nation-state necessarily produces citizens whose interconnections do not have 'the intense reciprocity of rights and duties' characteristic of local communities that in the past operated with the norm of mutual aid. The modern context does witness people coming together in organizations to promote their common interests, but such organizations are less and less able to draw on the intensity of 'group feeling or fraternity' that characterized the social life of earlier times. In sum, Bendix's (1996) view is that 'national allegiance grows at the expense of group solidarity' and it is unsurprising to find a number of cases in which 'citizenship as such does not mean much integration' (Bendix 1984). Twentieth-century conceptions of citizenship emphasized everyone's common membership of 'society' understood as 'nation' or 'the people', and the construction of national welfare states around the idea of enhanced citizenship promoting a new unity formed an integral part of this project of redefining 'solidarity' (Baldwin 1990; Esping-Andersen 1996; Lewis 1998). Solidarity, or 'fraternity', was allocated a key role in reconciling the potentially conflicting objectives of freedom and equality, making it 'the concrete expression of citizenship' (Touraine 2000: 236), albeit that it was understood as being 'amenable to a technique' (Rose 1995: 221) and open to manipulation in a rather mechanistic fashion.

The way in which welfare states provide a distinctive context for the reshaping of social solidarities is central to Beck's influential account of 'risk society'. According to Beck, the modern welfare state has given great impetus to the process of 'individualization' that is corrosive of traditional solidarities. The emergence of modern welfare states has made redundant Marx's ideas about class solidarities founded on people coming together on the basis of shared economic adversity. Beck (1992: 95) accepts the Marxist thesis that capitalism leads to people being 'uprooted in successive waves and wrested loose from tradition, family, neighbourhood, occupation and culture', but he sees the process working out in quite different ways in contemporary circumstances where material constraints have become less pressing. Beck also distinguishes his position from that of Weber, who he claims failed to anticipate how the solidarities of status-based community organizations would disintegrate in the context of trends such as rising standards of living, widening opportunities for personal educational advancement, and intensified mobility. What has changed is that '[w]ithin the welfare state the individual has acquired, in historical terms, a new economic status. He is not primarily an employee in a specific business but a participant in the labour market, organized and buffered by collective bargaining and social safeguards as a reward for his qualifications and mobility' (Beck and Beck-Gernsheim 1995: 39). People now have both the opportunity and the responsibility to exercise choice as individuals, since individualization tends to undermine arrangements which in the past 'obligated and forced . . . individuals into togetherness' (Beck 1997: 97). It is thus possible to describe the welfare state as 'an *experimental arrangement for conditioning ego-centred ways of life*' (Beck 1997: 97, emphasis in original) because it has had the effect of emancipating people from traditional patterns of dependency (for example, that of unpaid housewives on 'breadwinner' husbands).

Beck's view is that the process of opening up opportunities for individual advancement and self-realization that welfare states bring with them is not realistically reversible. Things have come a long way from when 'the social mesh of the family and village community was tight, and possibilities of control were omnipresent' (Beck and Beck-Gernsheim 1996: 33). Even cursory consideration of the possibility of restoring traditional solidarities highlights the extent of the changes which individualization has brought, for example in the area of gender relations. Traditional solidarities were founded on fixed gender roles, and it follows that '[a]nyone who wishes to restore the good old solidarity must turn back the wheel of modernization, that is to say, push women out of the labour market . . . [and] out of education as well' (Beck 1998: 34). Put another way, individualization's stress on the rights of individuals to welfare has the effect of destabilizing the nuclear family (where this is structured around the male 'breadwinner' norm) at the same time that it works to destabilize traditional class relations. Beck can thus posit that 'the labour market society protected by the welfare state dissolves the social foundations of class society as well as of the nuclear family' (1992: 153). A further dimension of individualization is that 'traditional forms of community beyond the family are beginning to disappear' (1992: 97) as people's greater mobility leads them to discriminate more actively between the different social relationships and social networks open to them. Furthermore, a culture that lays emphasis on individual choice and responsibility inevitably promotes a degree of competitiveness and, as Beck rather graphically expresses it, 'community is dissolved in the acid bath of competition' (1992: 94).

It is important to note that Beck (1994: 16) distances himself from what he refers to as the 'litany of lost community'; such ideas are backward-looking and fail to give an adequate account of the present. The 'withering away' of traditional forms of solidarity does not necessarily usher in a void; Beck's argument is rather that '[a] new relationship between individual and society is announcing itself here' (1998: 35). The other side of people's withdrawal from the institutions through which traditional solidarities found expression is their 'emigration to new niches of activity and identity' that allow 'a new mode of conducting and arranging life' (1997: 102, 95). These shifts reveal that '[c]ommunal spirit can no longer be ordained from the top down' (1998: 35), but comes rather from the active engagement of individuals struggling through a process of reflexivity to make sense of their biographies. New social movements embody these principles in the sphere of political activity, and provide one example of how the decline of traditional class solidarities requires us to pay attention to '[n]ew sources for the formation of social bonds' (1992: 99). The emergent and often contradictory nature of these new forms of solidarity reflects the fact that 'nothing "goes without saying" any longer'. The dilution of traditional forms of solidarity thus presents contemporary individuals with 'the tribulations of finding (or inventing) commonality and communal spirit' (1997: 102, 43). A good illustration of the need to look for new bases of solidarity is provided by Beck's argument that community is less and less tied to place. By speeding up the movement towards 'places without community', globalization means that 'the relationship between community and locality has been transformed' (1998: 33, 36). There are gains as well as losses involved in this process, since the shattering of neighbourhoods also shatters 'their limitations and their opportunities for social control' (1992: 97). Beck's further comment that 'there is not just the danger of too little community, but that of too much as well' (1998: 13–14), also serves to distinguish his position from that of the communitarians who seek to restore and revitalize lost community traditions.

Parallels can be drawn between Beck's analysis and that developed by Durkheim, discussed in the previous chapter. Just as Durkheim criticized backward-looking responses to the social problems of his day as unrealistic in their expectation that traditional solidarities could be revived, so Beck is critical of communitarians' responses to individualization on the same grounds. His assessment of their ideas is that they involve 'the flight to an ideal world' and are guilty of 'preaching instead of analysing' (Beck 1998: 148). The communitarian agenda is unsatisfactory from Beck's point of view because it represents an attempt 'to exorcise the evil of egoism with a sanctimonious rhetoric of community spirit, a home remedy from grandma's medicine cabinet which, as we know, costs nothing and is worth every penny' (1998: 13). Communitarians' complaints about individualization are criticized for being nostalgic, involving as they do 'the invocation of "we-feelings", the disassociation from foreigners, the tendency to pamper family and feelings of solidarity' (1997: 96). Beck characterizes communitarians as offering a variant of the 'loss of community' thesis, which is treated as problematic because its backward-looking perspective fails to recognize the signs of new forms of solidarity that are emerging. Beck further echoes Durkheim's analysis by arguing that individualization rules out the possibility of solving today's social problems by reinforcing traditional institutions. The new circumstances of 'risk society' require that a different approach be adopted to the relationship between individuals and collectivities.

Beck's theses about individualization are presented with a fair degree of generality, but he does not claim that they have universal applicability. The extensive welfare state arrangements of countries such as Sweden, Switzerland and western Germany have allowed a pattern of *comprehensively insured individualization*' (Beck 1997: 101, emphasis in original) that is inconceivable in most former communist countries and those of the third world, most of whose people have considerably less prosperity and social security. He would readily acknowledge, too, that such countries have quite different traditions of collective activity independent of the state, as is revealed by discussions of 'civil society' in former communist countries (Offe 1996a; Elster *et al.* 1998; Keane 1998) and of the role of 'community' organizations in development processes (Scott 1994; Craig and Mayo 1995). Questions about the extent to which Beck's ideas are applicable are not restricted to the world beyond Western welfare states, however, since doubts can be raised concerning the ability of these welfare states to maintain the framework within which 'comprehensively insured individualization' was nurtured. Beck's (1997: 97) comment that '[p]articipation in the material protections and benefits of the welfare state presupposes labour participation in the greatest majority of cases' suggests that difficulties will be encountered regarding the social integration of those groups whose members are located outside the labour market. Beck refers to housewives in this context, but mention could equally well be made of pensioners, unpaid carers and people whose disabilities prevent them from working.

Beck's account of how social solidarities came to be re-shaped in the second half of the twentieth century treats welfare state arrangements as broadly empowering of individuals. Other writers are significantly less upbeat about these matters, notably where welfare states are understood to have gone through a transformation, replacing the aim of promoting the welfare of all citizens individually and collectively with more limited goals. Writing about the situation in the USA, Gordon (1994: 1) has argued that '[i]n two generations the meaning of "welfare" has reversed itself . . . Today "welfare" means grudging aid to the poor, when once it referred to a vision of a good life'. A similar assessment has been offered by Bauman, who suggests that it is possible to identify various consequences of the shift whereby welfare states have moved away from universal benefits and towards means-testing. As he describes it, the situation of the 'new poor' is distinct from that of poor people in earlier and more generous periods of welfare state provision. In contrast to the overriding concern with the common good which underpins universal benefits, means-testing produces a situation in which 'the community is immediately split into those who give without getting anything in exchange, and those who get without giving . . . Rationality of interest is thereby set against the ethics of solidarity

. . . The overall effect of means testing is division instead of integration; exclusion instead of inclusion' (Bauman 1998a: 50). Developments in this direction undermine the commitment of individuals to the active promotion of citizenship.

Bauman argues that the project of securing social inclusion around the norm of employment has become increasingly problematic in an age that no longer attains full employment. Approaching social inclusion as a goal to be achieved through employment has the effect of marginalizing and excluding those citizens who, for whatever reason, are unable to work. This has presented an acute political challenge in recent decades. Bauman's analysis emphasizes the changing nature of welfare state commitments against the broader background of the fragmentation of contemporary life. He refers to the welfare state as 'a product of a unique historical conjuncture' (Bauman 1999: 184) and suggests that it has entered a period of 'downsizing' (1998a: 50), which contrasts with the expansionary decades of the mid-twentieth century. In that earlier period, '[t]he welfare state used to institutionalize *commonality* of fate' (1996: 55, emphasis in original), but the sense of all citizens engaged in a collective endeavour and enjoying common entitlements has broken down as individuals have come increasingly to calculate whether they are winners or losers in such arrangements. Welfare states no longer have the capacity to unite citizens in the way they once did, and in such circumstances other, more exclusive bases of collective identity gain in prominence. They produce a situation in which people pursue '[n]ot togetherness, but avoidance and separation' (1998b: 48) in their relationships with others, a development expressed for example in the rise of so-called 'gated communities'.

One way of approaching the analysis of these alternative solidarities to those engendered by welfare states is Bauman's discussion of 'forms of togetherness' in which he sets out their distinguishing characteristics. Togetherness may be 'mobile', as is the case of the togetherness of people in a busy street, or 'stationary', as occurs among the occupants of a waiting room. Alternatively, togetherness may be 'tempered', where people are brought into contact with each other by their common purpose, as happens when people assemble together in their workplace. He also refers to 'manifest' togetherness, where the pretext for gathering may be instrumental but the more fundamental purpose is 'the unloading of the burden of individuality' (Bauman 1995: 47). Bauman's examples of such togetherness include a football crowd and a disco. In contrast, 'postulated' togetherness refers to the imagined community of nations, races, classes and similar constructions, part of the appeal of which is the promise of '[r]esiding in the future perfect tense' (1995: 48). The sixth type of togetherness is the 'meta-togetherness' or 'matrix-like' togetherness that characterizes pubs and holiday beaches, the attraction of which is their openness and the sociability that stems from this, even though participants know that the togetherness of such situations is impermanent. Bauman acknowledges that this is not necessarily an exhaustive list, but argues that nevertheless it serves the purpose of demonstrating that time has a crucial bearing on how 'togetherness' is experienced.

Bauman's discussion contains echoes of the long-standing debate in which writers have attempted to identify the various bases of 'community'. It is possible to distinguish between communities in which people have place in common, communities founded on common interests and communities that are the expression of common identity (Willmott 1986). Time matters to the quality of community relationships in all of these cases, given that geographical and social mobility can have the effect over time of destabilizing place and interest communities respectively, while the expression of common identity is a notoriously mercurial phenomenon (Crow and Allan 1995). Bauman (1990: 72) recognizes that community is strongest where it 'is thought of as a *natural* unity' (emphasis in original). At the same time he is aware that the circumstances most conducive to such thinking have disappeared as the ability of even the most isolated groups to maintain separate and distinctive ways of life has been eroded. The paradox of the contemporary world is that post-modernism has spawned an 'infatuation with community' (Bauman 1996: 50) while simultaneously people are increasingly conscious of the fragile and impermanent nature of community relationships. Commenting on the Hobbesian problem of order, Bauman observes that 'it is not so much the way we live together that has changed, as our understanding of how we go on achieving this remarkable feat . . . What has changed is that we now know just how difficult the task is and suspect that no easy escape from the difficulty can be found' (1995: 20). Togetherness has come to be 'fragmentary' and 'episodic' (1995: 49), and is expressed in 'cloakroom communities' or 'carnival communities' (2000: 200) that are distinguished by their short lifespan. As a result, contemporary solidarities become more 'contingent' (1991: 236), and the associated uncertainty has generally negative and potentially far-reaching implications for trust in social relationships and the toleration of social differences.

Beck and Bauman are by no means the only analysts of contemporary solidarities to direct attention to purportedly new ways in which individual and collective identities are forged. A similar theme can be found in the writings of Melucci, who claims that the coming of 'post-material society' heralds the displacement of 'the right to *equality*' by 'the right to *difference*'. This change 'opens the way for a new definition of solidarity and coexistence' (Melucci 1989: 177–8, emphasis in original) that has the potential to transcend inherited patterns of social inclusion and exclusion built around conventional notions of citizenship. Present trends undermine traditional solidarities, but they do not automatically generate new solidarities to take their place. Societies in which people 'are pushed to become individuals' (1996a: 147) continue to generate collective action, but not all of it is solidaristic, since in some cases 'collective action arises as an aggregation of atomized behaviours'. Such action is treated by Melucci as distinct from that which involves solidarity, defined as 'the ability of actors to recognize others, and to be recognized, as belonging to the same social unit' (1996b: 23). This analytical distinction between solidarity and aggregation is an important one, especially when it is combined with the recognition that solidarity cannot be reduced to individuals pursuing what is in their rational self-interest. As Melucci expresses it, '[w]e feel a bond with others not chiefly because we share the same interests, but because we need this bond in order to make sense of what we are doing' (1996a: 32). Solidaristic identities have an emotional dimension 'which cannot be reduced to cost–benefit calculation' (1996b: 71). There is for Melucci a link between solidarity and 'passion' (1996a: 130), and it is this that helps to account for people's preparedness to engage in altruistic action.

Melucci is aware that the arguments that he advances relating to contemporary solidarities do not readily translate into empirically testable hypotheses. It is, for example, difficult in practice to disentangle what an individual does in response to their personal need for 'self-centred, defensive solidarity' (Melucci 1989: 49) from actions that are undertaken more purely for the benefit of others. These difficulties are not insurmountable, however, and it is possible to identify several strands of contemporary debates about the changing nature of social solidarities in which empirical research provides a key point of reference. One such strand is that relating to the purported weakening of place-based social solidarities. Giddens (1994a: 96), working from the premise that globalization creates a situation in which 'absence predominates over presence', has expressed the opinion that '[n]ew forms of social solidarity might often be less based upon fixed localities of place than before' (1994b: 186). Running counter to such thinking are alternative assessments of the evidence like that offered by Castells (1997) that report the current vitality of territorially based community identities. A second strand of debate revolves around the issue of whether contemporary solidarities make more sense when treated as predominantly emotional phenomena than they do when approached as the embodiment of rational calculation. Durkheim's emphasis on the emotional character of collective expressions is echoed in Maffesoli's (1996: 93) view that 'solidarity is not an abstraction or the fruit of rational calculation; it is an imperious necessity which causes us to act with passion'. Conversely, it is challenged in Meštrović's (1997: xii) account of how, in today's 'postemotional society', '"collective effervescence" is staged and rationally induced'. There is much to be learned in relation to such issues from the detailed historical research that has been undertaken into the nature of the connection between collective action which is community-based and that which is class-based, as Barnes (1995) has noted. Historical evidence of this sort is also crucial to the resolution of a third area of debate, namely that concerning the question of whether solidarity is a declining phenomenon in an age characterized by individualization and the growing significance of individual differences. Processes of fragmentation operate alongside other processes that generate more solidaristic entities, and the relationship between the two is open to empirical investigation, as has been shown in different ways by Bradley (1996) and Warde (1997). The evidence available for examination in all of these cases may be considered less than ideal, but it does nevertheless allow a measure of how well the speculative ideas which abound in the field stand up to scrutiny.

The balance of change and continuity in contemporary solidarities

There are good theoretical grounds for anticipating that place will be of declining significance as a basis for social solidarity. Globalization is associated with the erosion of local communities' capacity for self-sufficiency, and also with new possibilities emerging for spatial barriers to be transcended, most obviously through the development of communications. Beck identifies various examples of 'living and working together in separate places' as 'a new form of social bonding', and as the reverse side of 'the destruction of local communities' that globalization ushers in. It is thus possible to regard emergent 'transnational or transcontinental "communities"' as expressions of 'new kinds of "communality"', although he goes on to note that his work provides 'an *empirical working hypothesis*' (Beck 2000: 49–52, emphasis in original) which requires further investigation. The tentative nature of such speculation about the transcendence of place-based solidarities reflects in part an awareness that globalization may be associated with a process of 'localization', as is suggested by the concept of 'glocalization'. Robertson is right to say that '[m]uch of the talk about globalization has tended to assume that it is a process that overrides locality', and right also to be sceptical of this assumption. His counter-argument that 'globalization has involved the reconstruction, in a sense the production, of "home", "community" and "locality"' (Robertson 1995: 26, 30) suggests that glocalization by no means heralds the demise of local social solidarities. Similar points are made by Hall (1992), who notes that local identities are being transformed rather than eliminated by globalization, and by Sennett (1998: 138), who observes that '[o]ne of the unintended consequences of modern capitalism is that it has strengthened the value of place, aroused a longing for community'.

Castells's research in this area acknowledges that the new forms of solidarity embodied in identity politics can be understood as defensive reactions to globalization and the culture of individualism with which it is associated. His conclusions are nevertheless at odds with those of writers like Beck and Bauman when they speculate about what Albrow (1996: 158) has termed 'the delinkage of community from place' brought by 'deterritorialization'. What Castells (1997) refers to as 'networks of solidarity and reciprocity' may be constructed around many different identities, including religious, ethnic and territorial ones. Such networks illustrate the point that 'new' solidarities do not necessarily entail a radical break with the past, and may instead involve a re-working of previous arrangements. Such 'communal havens' emerge from 'defensive identities that function as refuge and solidarity, to protect against a hostile, outside world'. Social movements made up of people seeking to defend 'my neighbourhood, my community, my city' (Castells 1997: 65, 61) are paradoxically the product of global forces working to loosen people's ties to their localities, and in such circumstances locality can offer a fixed point around which collective identity can coalesce. The use of the internet to mobilize place-based community action provides an interesting illustration of this point. The potential of the internet to foster the development of global networks is unquestionable, but its power to reinforce local attachments should not be overlooked, as Castells (1996: 362) indicates by observing that 'local democracy is being enhanced through experiments in electronic citizen participation'. Such initiatives are undoubtedly confronted by a number of difficulties, but they also have great potential, as Mele's (1999) case study shows. Electronic communication's capacity to transcend spatial constraints on the patterns of solidaristic social relationships in which people can engage does not mean that cyber communities have to be divorced from place. Doheny-Farina's (1996: 123) assessment of developments to date may be that 'the net, in connecting everyone, furthers our isolation by abstracting us from place and virtualizing human relations', but he goes on to note that there is nothing inevitable about this trend. Indeed, he detects numerous signs of emergent community networking being pioneered by 'wired communitarians' whose agenda is to use the new technology to reinvigorate place-based solid-arities through promotion of 'the wired neighbourhood'. Hornsby's (1998) observations about the propensity of Internet group members to 'meet socially in real life' also illustrate the capacity of the technology to reinforce place-based solidarities.

The extent to which contemporary social relationships have come to be spatially 'disembedded' from 'traditional' expressions of solidarity is thus a matter of continuing dispute. Current disagreements are in many ways a con-tinuation of earlier debates about the impact of technological change in the field of communications (Wellman and Gulia 1999). Research conducted by Wellman and his colleagues in Toronto suggests that innovations such as telephones and cars liberated individuals from exclusive dependence on close-knit and all-encompassing neighbourhood networks. The 'personal com-munities' that people went on to create were characterized by greater diversity in terms of the people involved and of the content of their relationships than were suggested in prevailing models of community (Wellman *et al.* 1988), although it is possible to interpret such findings as signalling the enhance-ment rather than the displacement of previous patterns of social relationships. In any event, it would be dangerous to generalize on the basis of particular case studies. Fischer's study of the early users of the telephone who sought 'to enhance their existing social networks of communication, and to rein-force their deep-rooted social habits' (Castells 1996: 363) shows that techno-logical developments do not dictate that people change their behaviour in fundamental ways, although they may make such change possible.

Doubts about the extent to which traditional solidarities are being eroded by a process of spatial disembedding are part of broader concerns in relation to the 'detraditionalization' thesis. Whether or not contemporary solidarities have been liberated from spatial constraints, the very idea of a qualitative shift away from 'traditional' solidarities invites reassessment of the images of the 'traditional' past that are entailed. The notion of 'detraditionalization' invokes a picture of traditional arrangements that historical researchers have come to regard as at best elusive, and more commonly to involve a misinterpretation of the evidence. Wellman and Berkowitz (1988: 125) noted how '[t]he supposed communalism of the preindustrial past now appears to be in large part an artifact of the focus of earlier scholars on localism and solidarity rather than on internal cleavages and external ties'. Constructions of 'traditional' solidarities as expressions of unreflexive identification with existing arrangements on the part of group members overlook the extent to which social solidarity in previous eras was calculated and conditional. 'Traditional' working-class communities, for example, were characterized by social divisions that set very definite limits to the expression of solidarity, notwithstanding the conventional wisdom that relations between members were governed by an ethic of loyalty to the group and mutual aid (Crow and Allan 1994). The same point can be made more generally about working-class solidarity, given that 'sectionalism, privatism and instrumentalism have always been close to the surface of working-class life' alongside the 'sociability and altruism' (Marshall *et al.* 1988: 206) to which more romantic accounts pay disproportionate attention.

One of the most important findings of historical sociologists with regard to working-class solidarity has been that there was often a strong element of local attachment underpinning collective endeavours. Calhoun's (1982: 149) point that 'the popular protest movements of the early nineteenth century . . . were largely based on the social foundations of local communities' is part of his wider case that collective action needs to be placed in the context of the community ties of those involved. Marx's thinking about class is open to criticism on the grounds that he 'did not have a sociological account of what turned an aggregate of individuals into a grouping capable of concerted collective action' (1982: 218). Appeals to class solidarity did not carry the same force as 'immediate social relations' and, as a result, '[t]he mutuality of experience in a closely knit community is a much more likely and solid foundation for collective action than is the similarity of experiences among the members of a class defined in external terms' (1982: 226). Calhoun's account combines elements of explanations of solidarity framed in terms of the calculation of interests with an acknowledgement of the importance of identity as a springboard for action. People's obligations to express solidarity with others will be greater where their relationships are more 'established' – that is, where 'the cognitive, affective, and material costs of violating their premises or disengaging from them increase, along with the rewards of maintaining them' (1982: 233).

Calhoun's approach highlights the dangers of generalizing about 'traditional' solidarities by emphasizing the variability of social ties in different historical contexts. The general point that 'community may be stronger or weaker, and a pattern of sociation may be more or less communal' can be illustrated by the situation of a hypothetical individual: '[i]f . . . a worker, unsure of whether or not to join his fellows in a strike, feels that he must necessarily live out the rest of his life among them (like it or not) then his decision will be far more constrained than if he regards these relationships as mere consequences of a coincidence of residence or employment which he might alter at any time' (Calhoun 1983: 91–2, 90). Calhoun (1987: 57) is prepared nevertheless to advance the general observations that '[c]ommunities offer pre-existing relationships as a potential foundation for collective struggle', and that '[w]here classes have less prior social solidarity on which to draw, they are weaker', not least because they are likely to be less durable. It follows that it is important to make the analytical distinction between collective action that is class-based and that which is community-based, and that references to 'traditional' solidarities that gloss over this distinction are a poor basis on which to gauge the direction and extent of social change.

Debates about the extent to which the community and class bases of 'traditional' solidarities have been eroded have a direct bearing on discussions of modern industrial organization, most obviously in relation to trade unions and collective action such as strikes. Studies by Fantasia (1988) and by Wellman (1995) illustrate the continued relevance of the language of community solidarity to industrial action, a theme that will be explored further in Chapters 4 and 5. These debates have an equal significance for discussions of changes to welfare state arrangements. Welfare states have been described as bodies that, as they expanded in the decades following the Second World War, compelled citizens into 'mass solidarities' (Jordan 1996: 6) that were constructed around the idea of the nation as a collectivity whose members were to be linked to each other by 'civic obligations and the principle of reciprocity' (Jordan 1998: 53). The compulsory character of welfare state arrangements contrasted with the voluntary ethos of many of the organizations that these developments were designed either to complement or to supersede. In Britain, the Friendly Societies that insured against a variety of contingencies such as sickness and that dated back to the early nineteenth century took diverse forms, but they were engaged in the common pursuit of 'providing for mutual help among the working class in a situation in which individual self-help was impossible for so many of them'. Thane's (1982: 29) account of these societies also notes that they 'were unlike commercial insurance companies in holding popular, convivial meetings . . . and in their sense of comradeship and obligation among members'. The drawbacks of these voluntary organizations were that they tended to be run without the benefit of professional expertise, and that they excluded people considered to be socially inferior, as De Swann has chronicled. He presents mutual-aid societies as characterized by 'authentic solidarity' among members alongside 'exclusion of the less privileged', and advances the more general proposition that '[a] system of small, autonomous collective provisions always excludes a substratum' (De Swann 1988: 148, 147).

The exclusion of poorer people by voluntary welfare organizations illustrates the point that solidarity can be the expression both of rational calculation and of members' sense of identity that rests on more emotive foundations. De Swann observes that it made sense for workers who were regularly employed to exclude people who had no such security, because 'to these paupers, wretches, *lumpen*, the pressures of daily survival were often too great for them to afford a penny a week for the burial society, let alone for the sick fund'. At the same time, identity issues were also involved, since those who regarded themselves as '"decent working men" . . . did not identify at all with casual or itinerant workers or with all those others whom they too saw as "the dregs of society"' (De Swann 1988: 147). According to Baldwin (1990: 33), the presence of shared identification is crucial to the development of solidarity in relation to welfare arrangements, for 'Without some sense of collective identity, of community or "sameness", even a shared predicament is unlikely to prompt mutual aid'. Baldwin's account of the development of welfare states emphasizes the way in which the case for universal benefits was most effective when made in terms of such arrangements bringing advantage to everybody, in principle if not necessarily in practice. In particular, he argues, the extension of welfare state provision would have been more limited had members of the middle classes not been convinced that their interdependence with other members of society gave them an interest in participating. The ethical case for solidarity with others, constructed in terms of altruism, is for Baldwin much less significant than the case framed in terms of 'a generalized and reciprocal self-interest' that involves all members of society.

Current debates about the welfare state have thrown up contrasting perspectives on the extent to which arrangements are characterized by a weakening sense of generalized reciprocity and what might be the cause of any such change. The argument that people have become more ready to calculate the costs and benefits to themselves of collective provision ties in with the idea of individualization, or at least the notion that people are increasingly looking to 'put the family first'. In their explanation of such developments, Jordan and his colleagues (1994: 2) attach particular importance to policy decisions taken by British governments informed by New Right thinking that were 'designed to realign the links and loyalties of large groups of citizens, replacing an order based on public services and communal solidarities by one founded on property ownership, commercial systems and family responsibilities'. Vail's account of the situation has a somewhat different emphasis, identifying governments as only one of the powerful groups that have eroded the collective security promised (if not always delivered) by welfare states. Arguing that attention should be focused on economic as well as political power, Vail writes that '[i]t is a hallmark of insecure times that those who have the greatest resources and power will attempt to shift the burden of insecurity onto the weakest members of society'. This in turn undermines solidarity, since 'the more individuals are able to insulate themselves from insecurity and off-load their collective responsibilities to others, the harder it is to achieve a spirit of community and mutuality' (Vail 1999: 12). Renewed commitment to market principles in economic and social life has provided a sharp reminder that '[t]he market may indeed be an efficient mechanism of allocation, but not of building solidarities' (Esping-Andersen 1996: 27).

Several reasons can be advanced in support of the view that state agencies are poorly placed to engender solidarity between citizens, even where the political will to attempt this is present and there is a favourable position regarding the availability of resources. The relationship between the formal institutions of citizenship and the more informal institutions of community or civil society is characterized by '[a] series of reciprocities and antagonisms', and '[b]lame for many of the problems experienced by community institutions is often lain at the door of citizenship' (Crouch 1999: 367). Welfare states are open to criticism on account of the essentially passive role that citizens are allocated rather than being encouraged to engage more actively in the wider society. A related line of criticism of welfare state organization concerns its impersonality, suggesting that organization at the level of the nation state may be too remote from the individual to instil a sense of collective endeavour, even if bureaucratic procedures can be made to run in ways that are regarded as efficient and fair. Wolfe (1989: 146) concluded that '[t]he trends associated with the welfare state do not abolish community, but . . . they do alter its character', suggesting in particular that elements of sociability with known others are more enduring than are bonds of moral obligation to strangers. The theme of the growth of welfare states coinciding with the loss of the moral grounding of social solidarities has been an especially prominent feature of communitarian thinking in which a central concern has been to re-establish the importance of the idea of obligation. By doing this, communitarians have prompted fundamental debates not just about the feasibility of the revival of social solidarities as vehicles of social renewal, but also about the desirability of such developments.

Communitarian conceptions of solidarity and their critics

Communitarian thought has numerous variants, but what is common to all of them is a concern to safeguard and promote people's sense of belonging to groups whose members are committed to supporting each other. Inherent in this agenda is an opposition to self-interested behaviour that disregards obligation to others, since other-regarding moral obligations are treated as essential to the successful functioning of community relationships. In turn, community is regarded as vital to people's quality of life because of the impersonality of formal government structures and their association with coercion. According to Etzioni (1997: 140), 'the more a society relies on a government per se, the more *both* the moral order and autonomy are diminished, the less communitarian the society becomes' (emphasis in original). The solution to contemporary social ills proffered by communitarians is the reinvigoration of community, defined by Etzioni in terms of 'a web of affect-laden relationships among a group of individuals . . . and second, a measure of commitment to a set of shared values, norms, and meanings, and a shared history and identity' (1997: 127). The communities that communitarians seek to promote are identified at several different levels; in Etzioni's words, 'communities are best viewed as if they were Chinese nesting boxes, in which less encompassing communities (families, neighbourhoods) are nestled within more encompassing ones (local villages and towns), which in turn are situated within still more encompassing communities, the national and cross-national ones' (1994: 32). Attachment to such communities is encouraged by communitarians on the grounds that the solidarities that they engender are more deep-rooted than those grounded in market-based interests or in state-sanctioned rights.

The Durkheimian roots of contemporary communitarian thinking are evident, first of all in terms of the emphasis placed on the need for normative agreement among community members if social solidarities are to be realized without at the same time unduly subordinating the individual to the group. Cladis (1992) refers to this shared set of beliefs as a 'common faith', although this does not have to be expressed in the form of a conventional religion. A second parallel relates to the concern of communitarians to engage with the issue of how to understand and counter the anti-social effects of contemporary economic change. Bellah and his co-authors have suggested that globalization has spawned 'a deracinated elite' made up of people who are 'located less securely in communities than in networks linking them, flexibly and transiently, to others like themselves who are scattered all over the world', while at the same time members of the middle class suffer from 'a sense of uncertainty about the economic future so pervasive that concern for individual survival threatens to replace social solidarity' (Bellah *et al.* 1996: xii, xv). Third, the case made by communitarians for the integrative role of the informal institutions of community carries strong echoes of Durkheim's analysis of the need to develop intermediate institutions that would tie the individual into the wider society by forming a connection between personal and public life. Neglect of this dimension of social cohesion is regarded as a source of social problems, and this point informs Gray's (1997: 77) judgement that '[c]ommunitarian thought works as a corrective to the central errors of the New Right'. Just as Durkheim's work offered a critique of those Victorian thinkers whose approaches focused on self-interested individuals, so communitarian ideas can be understood as a reaction to the revival of their ideas a century later.

One response to communitarianism has been to regard it as essentially backward-looking in its appeal to 'community'. Beck (1998: 132) suggests as much through his reference to the way in which individualization promotes the appeal of '[t]he idyllic – grandma's apple cake, forget-me-nots, communitarianism', implying that current uncertainties promote a longing for the imagined security of an idealized past. Calhoun makes a related point in his assessment of Bellah and colleagues' *Habits of the Heart*. According to Calhoun (1995: 228), this approach 'calls for a renewal of communitarian commitments and a reigning [*sic*] in of American individualism, without seriously considering the political, economic, or social structural features of American society which fundamentally differentiate today's community life from that which supported New England town meetings'. The extent to which communitarians are committed to an essentially backward-looking agenda that involves a return to 'dense networks of solidaristic and (to some extent) self-regulating locales' (J. Clarke 1996: 80) varies considerably between authors, some of whom are at pains to establish the differences between their views and those of conservative thinkers. Etzioni (1997: 6), for example, distances himself from the idea of communities as villages and small towns by arguing that '[c]ommunity is a set of attributes, not a concrete place'. He goes on to claim that communitarians differ from 'social conservatives' by the weight they attach to 'the moral voice of the community, education, persuasion and exhortation' (1997: 16) rather than compulsion through the law. The community may be place-based, but it need not be, since people 'are members of many communities – families; neighbourhoods; innumerable social, religious, ethnic, work place, and professional associations; and the body politic itself' (1998: xxv). On this basis, Etzioni claims that new communities are less oppressive than 'old communities [that] had monopolistic power over their members. New communities are often limited in scope and reach', and because individuals are likely to be part of several communities they can enjoy 'a fair measure of autonomy' (1997: 128).

Communitarians may not necessarily be committed to treating 'community' as synonymous with place, or to the wholesale restoration of past patterns of community life, but they do stress the importance of shared norms. For Etzioni, the social order to which communitarians are committed involves more than 'civil society', because 'the civic order . . . is far too thin a concept'. The social fabric of the communities envisaged by Etzioni entails a stronger commitment to group values than is embodied in the notion of 'civil society', desirable though it is that 'people are civil to one another' (Etzioni 1997: 14). The shared values that bind together community members are identified as being more strongly held when they have historical depth, and it is for this reason that Bellah and his colleagues emphasize the importance of 'communities of memory'. The meanings that these contain 'can allow us to connect our aspirations for ourselves and those closest to us with the aspirations of a larger whole and see our efforts as being, in part, contributions to a common good' (Bellah *et al.* 1996: 153). Families, neighbourhoods, ethnic groups, religious organizations, and nations are all considered to be the stronger for being 'communities of memory'. Concern for the common good is embodied in traditions that take members beyond the narrow utilitarian calculation on which 'communities of interest' are based and in which 'self-interested individuals join together to maximise individual good' (Bellah *et al.* 1996: 134).

Bellah and his colleagues (1996) find parallels between their understanding of the threats posed by unchecked individualism to these communities of memory and the notion that the stock of 'social capital' is declining. Both approaches are concerned with trends like the 'withdrawal into gated, guarded communities' of affluent groups, for example, and both recognize the importance of economic and social relationships being underpinned by trust. The 'social capital' approach focuses attention on 'features of social organization, such as trust, norms, and networks, that can improve the efficiency of society by facilitating co-ordinated actions' (Putnam 1993: 167). Social situations are more likely to be characterized by social capital where judgements about the trustworthiness of individuals can be made with confidence, and Putnam illustrates this point by noting that the organizers of mutual aid groups will 'select members with some care', paying particular attention to the reputations of people wishing to join. Members are also constrained in their actions 'by strong norms and by dense networks of reciprocal engagement' (Putnam 1993: 168). Fukuyama offers a similar message about the economic benefits of a social environment in which trust is a prominent feature. Social capital requires the presence of trust, 'the expectation that arises within a community of regular, honest, and cooperative behaviour, based on commonly shared norms' (Fukuyama 1995: 26). Fukuyama goes on to argue that there are no easy short-cuts to the acquisition of social capital by communities that lack such traditions, a point that has direct relevance to the project of re-casting post-communist societies that will be explored further in Chapter 5.

The identification of the cultivation of greater community-mindedness as a solution to situations marked by a solidarity deficit has prompted critical responses at several levels. A number of writers have noted that communitarians tend to avoid awkward questions about the broad structure of social inequalities within which solidarity is seen to be lacking. Byrne (1999: 27) regards communitarians as leaving 'intact the very tightly possessed property rights of those who have them . . . They readily impose obligations of behaviour on the poor but there is no equivalent discussion of the obligations of the rich'. Another way of putting this is that, by locating 'the causes of social problems in the value systems of individuals', communitarians 'fail to recognise the importance of social, economic and political environments in which people must function' (Freie 1998: 160). Communitarianism's failure to offer a systematic challenge to structures of political and economic power leads Freie to associate it with 'counterfeit community' rather than with the 'genuine community' in which there would be greater scope for the expression of social diversity. A further reason for questioning the case for the communitarian programme is the 'disturbing tendency for civil society and the community to be reduced to an arena of unpaid work, a means of mopping up problems created by the market' (Levitas 1998: 169). Levitas also advances the criticism that communitarianism contributes to the reproduction of social exclusion among people whose beliefs or practices place them outside of the community's value consensus and who come to be treated as 'lesser citizens'. It is in addition difficult for Etzioni and his fellow communitarians to present inclusion and participation as voluntary, as a matter of personal choice, when there is marked pressure from peers to conform.

Communitarianism's identification of the need to revitalize community relationships thus encounters the difficulties of communities being exclusive as well as inclusive, and controlling as well as empowering. Communitarians' concern with group boundaries does have sound sociological foundations, since it is not only communitarians who argue that 'groups by their very nature are exclusive rather than inclusive' (Wolfe 1992: 309). Harris (1990a: 93), for example, treats as axiomatic the proposition that '[s]ocial processes do not merely unite, create solidarity and include; they divide, create opposition and exclude . . . A category with no non-member has little practical value'. What is more contentious is Wolfe's (1992: 311) claim that '[w]ithout particular groups with sharply defined boundaries, life in modern society would be unbearable . . . We could never belong to anything with texture and character'. Sharply defined and carefully policed boundaries can lead to parochialism and promote disempowering social exclusion through the emphasis that is placed on the difference between insiders and outsiders, particularly when the values of the latter are characterized as inferior. Where this happens, the communitarian agenda can be seen to produce 'an obsessive particularism' (Weeks 2000: 182), and awareness of this danger has prompted consideration of alternative conceptions of community that are more compatible with the idea of 'solidarity in difference' (Lister 1997: 80). Sibley's (1995: 90) argument that social differences are 'less likely to be noticed, less likely to be a source of threat, in a weakly classified environment' contests the proposition that sharp group boundaries promote the common good. In similar vein, Weeks, drawing on Foucault's distinction between 'given' communities and 'critical' communities, proposes moving beyond traditional identification with family and neighbourhood and into the realm of 'new subjectivities' that seek to establish communities embodying 'a solidarity which empowers and enables' (Weeks 2000: 182, 185).

Other writers have gone further in expressing doubts about both the possibility and the desirability of recasting community along communitarian lines. Young has made fundamental criticisms of what she regards as utopian conceptions of community in which unity and similarity are treated as more authentic bases for social relationships than is difference. Not least among the problems with such idealization of community is its tendency to reinforce traditional gender roles by identifying as feminine 'the values associated with community – affective relations of care, mutual aid and cooperation' (Young 1995: 238). The idealization of community predisposes us to thinking in terms of static arrangements rather than recognizing that community relationships have change inherent in them. From the standpoint of his 'process view of community', Sennett (1998: 143) has criticized communitarianism on the grounds that it 'falsely emphasizes unity as the source of strength in a community and mistakenly fears that when conflicts arise in a community, social bonds are threatened'. He goes on to contrast 'the often superficial sharing of common values' with 'strong bonding', arguing that the latter involves people 'engaging over time their differences'. These ideas build on Sennett's (1971) earlier critique of the unrealistic desire for the order and coherence of the 'purified community' and his account of how such imposed rigidity hampers rather than promotes the development of constructive and meaningful relationships. Unless there is acknowledgement that diversity can serve a useful purpose, individuals who promote it will be regarded as 'betraying' the community because of the challenge they pose to the idealized sense of order on which it is based. In circumstances where people's 'fantasy' of community life is brought into question, Sennett (1977b: 311) suggests, '[d]istrust and solidarity, seemingly so opposed, are united', with fragmentation being the likely outcome.

The communitarian response to social change has been to reassert the importance of traditional values while at the same time positing that these can be adapted to contemporary circumstances. The sustainability of this position is open to debate. The argument advanced by Etzioni that new communities are less oppressive than those of former times because each individual can be a member of several different communities is open to criticism on the grounds that it fails to appreciate how this may intensify rather than resolve problems of belonging. As Ignatieff (1996: 94) has noted, '[w]e belong to families, work-groups, networks of friends, private and public associations of all kinds. These forms and sites of belonging present us with constant conflicts of loyalty: how much time, how much effort, how much money can we afford to devote to each of these spheres [?]'. Membership of numerous communities offers an individual an escape route from all-encompassing control by any one of them, only to present her or him with the dilemma of how to demonstrate sufficient commitment to them all when the demands they make are in competition with one another.

Communitarians would not be surprised to find people responding to such pressures by 'putting the family first', although their preference for 'traditional' family arrangements is confounded by 'the rising numbers of people . . . whose family arrangements do not conform to the nuclear norm' (Ignatieff 1996: 95). Like 'community', 'family' has become a key focus of commentators seeking to identify how social solidarity is expressed in contemporary social relationships. The theoretical debates considered in this chapter all have a potential contribution to make to this analysis. The purpose of the next chapter is to examine this potential in the light of research findings as they relate to families in general and to step-families in particular.

PART TWO

Family solidarities

───────── ○ ───────────────────────────────────

Introduction

The material considered in Part One indicates that solidarity has long been
central to the analysis of a range of social phenomena. Debates about solidarity, and in particular debates about its causes, contexts and consequences,
continue to be at the heart of contemporary analyses of relationships ranging
from the micro-level of families to the macro-level of whole societies. These
debates may have moved on in terms of the details of the phenomena under
investigation, but many of the fundamental problems relating to solidarity
that the founding figures of sociology confronted persist. Consideration of
empirical evidence is crucial to the attempt to tackle these problems, although
there remains a good deal of scope for disagreement about precisely how
such evidence is best interpreted. Careful selection of case studies can play a
key role in the process of evaluating the merits of the competing theoretical
perspectives available, as the three chapters that make up Part Two are
intended to demonstrate. The analysis of controversial topics is often especially illuminating, and the extent to which family relationships continue to
be characterized by solidarity is unquestionably an area of fierce debate. The
topic of family relationships is therefore an appropriate one with which to
commence Part Two of the book.

   The connection between the ideas of family and of solidarity is well established. It was noted in Chapter 1 that Tönnies regarded family solidarity as
constituting the core of *gemeinschaft*, and the association of solidarity with
family obligations is equally prominent in communitarianism, as noted in
Chapter 2. It is instructive that writers from a range of other theoretical perspectives besides communitarianism have also made use of what Frazer (1999:
150) refers to as 'the rhetorical and political power of the link between "family"
and "community"'. Equally instructive is Dempsey's (1990: ch. 4) account of

how readily residents of Smalltown refer to their community as being like 'one big happy family' in their efforts to convey the mutually supportive character of their relationships. Wider kinship ties are another important element in people's networks of obligation and support, as Dempsey's and many other community studies have shown. Roberts's research into working-class communities of the mid-twentieth century found extensive evidence of kinship solidarity which she accounted for by reference to 'individuals acting from a mixture of love, duty, affection and obligation', the essence of people's sentiments being captured in the axiom '[b]lood is thicker than water' (Roberts 1995: 180). It is a matter of on-going dispute how far such an orientation has survived down to the present time, as was noted in Chapter 2. Whatever current practices are, in their ideal form family and kinship connections promise to provide an enduring basis for reciprocal aid founded on a shared sense of identity and mutual trust (Harris 1990a). In addition, the apparently 'natural' qualities of family and kinship relationships give them an appeal that it is difficult for people to contest, at least in their 'public' accounts (Cornwell 1984).

Closer scrutiny of how family relationships actually operate reveals that, to the extent that solidarity is present, it is by no means a spontaneous 'natural' phenomenon. There are numerous decisions that people have to make about how to arrange their family relationships, for example whether to allocate resources equally between members or to follow more hierarchical principles, and whether to make greater or lesser allowance for individual differences. The recognition that family life must of necessity have some underlying principle of organization but that in practice people's domestic arrangements are characterized by great diversity has led Douglas and Ney (1998: 109) to observe that 'The family is probably the best site for understanding the tremendous tensions triggered by the effort to organize'. Evidence of this can be seen in the attention paid to the function of periodic family gatherings for ritual occasions such as weddings, funerals and Christmas festivities, emphasizing that they are powerful symbols of family solidarity and belonging (Firth *et al.* 1969). The significance of more commonplace activities such as everyday meals shared by family members also warrants acknowledgement. Charles and Kerr (1988: 21) comment that family togetherness is a key ingredient of a 'proper' meal, since this is defined (in British culture at least) as a meal that 'requires all members of the family to be present'. Similar attention deserves to be paid to gift-giving as part of what Cheal calls 'the struggle to institutionalise feelings of solidarity'. Cheal argues that people's management of their personal relationships is problematic because '[i]nterest and contact cannot be sustained at high levels with everyone, and so each person specializes in cultivating a limited number of intimate ties' (Cheal 1988: 39, 108). Gift-giving is a central part of the everyday reproduction of intimate family relationships, but decisions about gifts (for example, when, what, how much and to whom to give them) are by no means straightforward ones because of what they symbolize about reciprocity, dependence, inclusion and exclusion.

It is not coincidental that the examples of mealtime organization and gift-giving are aspects of family life associated more with women than they are

with men, since the maintenance of family and kinship ties is typically assigned
to women. Cheal (1988) notes that women's preparedness to take primary
responsibility for 'kin-keeping' and for the achievement of family unity
presents 'something of a sociological puzzle', given that the rationale for their
doing so is by no means self-evident. Part of the explanation can be found in
the power of tradition. Women's connections with family solidarity have
deep historical roots. Roberts's (1985: 169) account on working-class life in
the 50 years from 1890 contains the comment that '[w]orking-class solidarity
has usually been discussed in terms of organisations like trade unions, the
Cooperative Movement, and the Labour Party. It is rather more meaningful
to discuss female solidarity in terms of the extended family and the neighbourhood'. Campbell's (1993: 319) argument about the 1990s is that it is the
latter which has been more enduring, at least in the deprived neighbourhoods
she studied where men's priorities are focused on other things and, as a result,
'[s]olidarity and self-help are sustained by women'. According to Campbell,
the tradition of solidarity is preserved by women through their commitment
to the values of inclusion and equality that contrast with men's more individualistic and calculating responses to their situations. There are echoes
here of Weber's (1978: 41–2) observation that there exists 'a wide variation
in the extent to which the members of a family group feel a genuine community of interests or, on the other hand, exploit the relationship for their own
ends'. Women's primary responsibility for family and kinship solidarity may
thus also be explained in terms of their different perception of what family
and kinship relationships involve and their different emotional engagement
with these relationships. Family solidarities are not the exclusive preserve
of women, but it is important to keep in mind the highly gendered nature
of the contributions to the maintenance of solidarity that take place within
families.

Family solidarity and family diversity

The impact of social change on family solidarity is an issue of central importance in much contemporary debate. The emphasis placed by communitarians
on the family as an institution where people are socialized according to established norms of responsibility tends in practice (if not always explicitly) to
give moral approval to 'traditional' family forms (Frazer 1999). From this
perspective, alternatives to the 'traditional' pattern of family relationships
(such as families headed by lone parents and step-families) are associated with
social problems, even though the continued growth in their numbers means
that households comprising married parents and their dependent children are
less and less 'normal', at least in statistical terms. In turn, the growth in alternative family arrangements is championed by Ignatieff (1996: 95) as an expression of people's 'desire to live a life expressive of one's own needs and choices',
and it is in this context that reference can be made to lesbian and gay partnerships as 'families of choice' (Weeks et al. 1999a). Bauman (2000: 182) describes

this debate as the latest instalment of 'the long and inconclusive search for the right balance between freedom and security', with communitarians positioned 'fast on the side of the latter'. By invoking the value of family traditions and positing the need for predictability and consensus in family relationships, the communitarian perspective leads to a conservatism about family forms and gender roles that critics like Gray regard as increasingly unworkable. For Gray (1997: 81), 'communitarian thought will be fruitless or harmful if it engages in propping up traditional forms of social life or recovering any past cultural consensus'. Much attention is focused, therefore, on the extent to which competing perspectives embrace, question or reject family and other diversity, including arrangements that embody non-traditional expressions of solidarity.

In a similar fashion to Gray, Stacey's (1998) critique of communitarianism and other programmes engaged in the promotion of traditional family values is essentially that these perspectives have failed to come to terms with 'the irreversibility of family diversity'. As a result, communitarians are mired in 'the politics of nostalgia'. Stacey is, of course, aware that ideas about the 'naturalness' of 'traditional' families continue to be influential across a wide spectrum of opinion, not least because of people's propensity to think one thing and act quite differently. In the 1990s, Stacey (1999: 189) suggests, '[m]any who contributed actively to such postmodern family statistics as divorce, remarriage, blended families, single parenthood, joint custody, abortion, domestic partnership, two-career households, and the like still yearned nostalgically for the "Father Knows Best" world they had lost'. A parallel explanation can be advanced to account for the fact that, in Aitken's study of contemporary American families, many of his respondents reported that '[l]iving up to traditional family values was a significant source of stress'. The aspiration to do so is nevertheless widespread because, in the context of such values being perceived as natural, 'there is little societal support for the multiple realities of family life' (Aitken 1998: 34). Aitken goes on to suggest that part of the reason for the growth of 'gated communities' is that they appeal to 'fantasies' of traditional family normality. In support of this contention, he refers to an instance where in order to preserve this fiction the community more or less effectively 'excludes minorities and single mothers' on the grounds of their perceived deviation from the ideal of the full-time housewife and mother.

The assumption that all communities have the capacity to control their destinies embodies what Stacey (1996: 77) refers to as 'the PMC (professional middle-class) bias of communitarian ideology', and goes against the evidence collected by her and others that the growth of family diversity reflects the markedly different economic circumstances within which people live. Stacey's (1998: 252) argument is that '[r]ising divorce and cohabitation rates, working mothers, two-earner households, single and unwed parenthood, and matrilineal, extended, and fictive kin support networks appeared earlier and more extensively among poor and working-class people. Economic pressures more than political principles governed these departures from domesticity'. Put another way, it is easier to conform to the norms of white, middle-class family life where people have available to them the income levels on which these patterns are founded. Linked to this debate is the long-standing dispute about where power lies and how much control individuals can exercise over their family relationships. Communitarians have been taken to task on the grounds that their approach 'lacks a critical theory of power, and is ill equipped to identify, let alone analyse, the social conflict that is a systematic feature of life inside families' (Frazer 1999: 159). Etzioni's (1997: 181) exhortation to couples to 'manage their conflicts in a more constructive manner' is consistent with the communitarian premise that power lies with people as members of communities, but fails to acknowledge the variation that exists between families in terms of their exposure to pressures that are liable to generate difficulties. Gibson's (1994: 138) reference to '[t]he association between low income and a high rate of divorce' and Kiernan and Mueller's (1999: 388) mention of '[t]he higher probabilities of partnership breakdown among the socio-economically disadvantaged' are relevant in the context of this discussion.

It is a prominent theme running through much of the recent literature on family diversity that family solidarity can be expressed in many ways, not all of which necessarily involve marriage. Silva and Smart (1999: 7) emphasize the point that 'while there are new family forms emerging, alongside new normative guidelines about family relationships, this does not mean that values of caring and obligation are abandoned. On the contrary, these are central issues which continue to bind people together'. People can be bound together and understand their relationship as a 'family' one without necessarily having 'formal, objective blood or marriage ties'. This would be true, for instance, of the lesbian and gay 'families of choice' referred to by Weeks and his colleagues. Members of these 'families of choice' regarded their situation as having 'some at least of the qualities attributed (in ideology at least) to the traditional family: continuity over time, mutual support, a focus for identity and for loving and caring relationships' (Weeks *et al.* 1999b: 44). It is also well documented that traditional family relationships can in practice fall some way short of the ideological ideal. Domestic violence is the extreme expression of the potential divergence between ideal and reality, but it is nevertheless instructive that Dobash and Dobash describe women's refuges as places within which it is possible to find the sorts of relationship qualities more typically associated with families. They report how '[s]afety, an end to isolation, companionship, solidarity, independence and mutual assistance are themes running through the comments of thousands of women from all over the world' (Dobash and Dobash 1992: 90). In the light of this, Etzioni's (1997) stated aim 'to strengthen families' and to 'strengthen marriage' in preference to other household forms deserves to be scrutinized in terms of its assumptions about the superiority of traditional family solidarities and in terms of the evidence that is available about how families operate.

The concept of family solidarity thus confronts researchers in this area with a number of difficulties in an age characterized by growing diversity in family forms. One difficulty is that the language that it is necessary to use is ideologically charged and contested. There is no consensus about what is meant by 'family' or about precisely what to look for when researching families, and the range of perspectives from which it is possible to approach the subject has expanded enormously as theorists have mounted challenges to what Cheal (1991) calls the 'standard theory of the family'. A second difficulty relates to people's propensity to say things about family life that are at odds with their actions. Cornwell discusses this in terms of the discrepancy between people's 'public accounts' and their 'private accounts'. Her research among residents of East London found that '[t]he images of family life in public accounts were images of unity' but that '[t]he private accounts told a different story' (Cornwell 1984: 84). Family unity was buttressed in particular by popular beliefs about the family being 'a "natural" social unit' and by 'pursuit of the common objective of "doing the best for the children" ', but in their less mediated private accounts of their personal relationships Cornwell's respondents furnished her with 'stories of internal rifts within families, and of the stresses and strains individuals suffer because of their families' (Cornwell 1984: 94, 102). She goes on to note that apparently well-defined family ties in practice vary significantly in terms of their content, citing mother–daughter relationships as an example: '[s]ome relationships are based on shared skills and practical activities and that is all; others involve a degree of emotional intimacy and the mother and daughter are each other's confidante; still others are based on family loyalty and a sense of duty . . . It is possible for there to be regular and frequent contact between mothers and daughters without either of them particularly liking the other' (p. 112). This side of relationships is glossed over in romanticized representations of family life such as that contained in Young and Willmott's (1957) classic study *Family and Kinship in East London*, conducted in the same fieldwork site to which Cornwell returned. She argues that there is limited value in concentrating on the formal arrangements between family members unless one can also discover 'the reasons people have for seeing each other and how they feel about their relationships'. It is illegitimate to assume 'that the formal properties of relationships are a valid indicator of their content and quality' (Cornwell 1984: 115), and it follows that quantitative data (such as those relating to divorce rates) will need to be interpreted carefully and with an eye to what they mean to the people involved.

Cornwell's point about the time people spend together being an unreliable indicator of their feelings about each other is given particular importance by the significance attached to 'togetherness' in contemporary family relationships. Charles argues that togetherness at mealtimes is important because of what it symbolizes about community and sharing among family members, including shared conversation. She suggests that people regard talking 'as an important part of the "proper" family meal. This is often linked to the fact that the main meal is the only time during the day when the family are all together'. Against the background of high expectations of mealtimes reinforcing family unity, it is perhaps unsurprising that '[t]he reality of family meals . . . is often not one of peace and harmony'. Mealtimes have the potential to uncover family tensions and divisions that may be less evident at other times during the day when family members are apart, but when family togetherness does generate conflict 'it is women who feel responsible for this disjuncture' (Charles 1990: 65–7). Similar findings have been reported elsewhere. Richards (1990: 146) refers to aspirations of family togetherness as 'a dream of a self-contained family capsule fuelled by love and communication', but while her respondents were aware of the potential of family life to fall short of this ideal, the majority did not consider togetherness to be an 'unreachable star'. Again it was the case that the achievement of family togetherness was made possible by the preparedness of mothers to take on primary responsibility for ensuring the smooth running of activities undertaken together. Being a 'good' mother was perceived to mean putting other family members first, particularly in terms of the allocation of time, and Richards (1990: 149) remarks that among her respondents '[n]obody suggested that a good mother has her own life'. This point about family togetherness entailing self-sacrifice on the part of mothers is echoed in Ribbens's discussion of how board games with children require active coordination by mothers. Her respondents understood the role of mother to commit them 'to spend time creating and sustaining "the family"', even though such activities were not necessarily ones that they enjoyed and despite the fact that they associated 'considerable strains and tensions' (Ribbens 1994: 63, 64) with family togetherness.

One of the things that such studies of contemporary family life reveal consistently is that togetherness does not automatically generate solidarity. Indeed, it is worthwhile considering why it might be expected to do so, given the frequency with which researchers have reported finding people experiencing conflict and stress alongside cooperation and supportiveness in their family relationships. It is a common assumption that family unity arises on the basis of members having shared interests, but it is by no means axiomatic that this assumption is correct. Oakley and Rigby have drawn attention to this point by posing the question '[a]re men good for the welfare of women and children?' and by going on to refer to the growing body of evidence of the 'disbenefits of traditional father-present households'. They argue that these disbenefits fall principally on wives and mothers who perform the majority of caring tasks within families, have more limited access than their partners do to material resources, and suffer poorer health and well-being as a consequence. They also suggest that, to the extent that children are better off materially when their fathers are present, 'this benefit in part depends on the ability of their mothers to protect them from some of the disbenefits associated with living in a nuclear family' (Oakley and Rigby 1998: 123). These are controversial arguments that have been hotly contested (Daniels 1998), but they are only an extension of what has been demonstrated beyond doubt, that families are unequal in terms of the contributions made by different members and in terms of their outcomes (Bittman and Pixley 1997; Dempsey 1997).

Attempting to establish the veracity of the argument that the nuclear family brings advantages to men at the cost of women's disadvantage necessarily involves consideration of how alternative arrangements generate different outcomes, and this is a complex and contested methodological procedure, as

Oakley and Rigby acknowledge. One way of doing this is to compare the position of women who are alike except for their marital status. On this basis (and using statistics for Australia), Bittman and Pixley (1997: 106) have calculated that '[c]ompared to a single woman of equivalent age living alone, a married woman spends 40 per cent more time in cooking, time spent cleaning increases by 17 per cent, and the time taken for laundry by 37 per cent'. Other research, such as Sullivan's (1997) analysis of UK data, also indicates that married women experience intensified time pressures as a result of similar inequalities. It follows that any explanation of what holds families together that emphasizes the material benefits that accrue to all members is unlikely to be convincing, at least for women members. Oakley and Rigby suggest that an alternative explanation would give more emphasis to the point that the individualistic calculation of who gains what from family relationships runs against the grain of the prevailing ideology of marriage as 'an intrinsically supportive relationship'. Thus while their research did find that 'being married to or living with a man is not coterminous with being helped or supported by him', they were also made aware of how much women's perceptions are influenced by the powerful ideological formulation that partners can be expected to bring 'affection, support and a shared life' (Oakley and Rigby 1998: 116, 117, 124). In other words, people participate in family relationships for a range of reasons besides narrowly instrumental ones. Finch's (1989: 77) discussion of how relations between family members are structured by 'the delicate balance between feelings of affection, moral imperatives of duty, and calculations about personal advantage and disadvantage' is pertinent here, not least because of her emphasis on the tendency of men and women to operate with different understandings of how best to go about striking a balance between these various principles.

Finch's work is also instructive because of the challenge it contains to the idea that there has been a general trend in family relationships away from what Meyer Fortes called 'sharing without reckoning' (quoted in Finch 1989: 231). Finch's overview of the historical evidence concerning family obligations casts doubt on the claim that people today are more calculating than their ancestors were about the support they are prepared to provide. There are strong grounds for believing that the principle of reciprocity figured prominently in family relationships in the past, even if this principle was open to being expressed in different ways. This is not to say that the bases of family solidarity have remained unchanged over time. The mid-twentieth century witnessed the growth in popularity of the ideology of 'companionate marriage', which incorporated a set of ideas ranging 'from the notion that there should be greater companionship between partners . . . through the idea of marriage as "teamwork", to the concept of marriages based on "sharing"' (Finch and Summerfield 1991: 7). This ideology has evolved over time and in the process the economic rationale of family life has had reduced emphasis placed upon it because 'marriage has come to be defined as a personal relationship' (Mansfield and Collard 1988: 161). Mansfield and Collard's (1988: 179) study of newly married couples echoes the points made earlier about the importance attached to the idea of togetherness, with brides in particular seeking '*a common life* with an empathetic partner, who was to provide both material and emotional security. Women wanted a close exchange of intimacy which would make them feel valued as a person not just a wife' (emphasis in original). What is aspired to is 'a partnership of sharing and mutual caring' (Bittman and Pixley 1997: 105) – that is, one that delivers a satisfying personal life, including an appropriate depth to intimate relationships.

What Bittman and Pixley (1997) refer to as 'the rise of intimacy' can be considered to have had contradictory effects on family solidarities. On the one hand, the growing emphasis on emotional fulfilment may have contributed to the strengthening of independent nuclear families by prioritizing intimate relationships with close family members over links with wider kin. According to Harris (1990b: 200), 'to be a family it is necessary to assert the primacy of practices and obligations arising out of familial activities over kinship obligations'. Jordan and his colleagues (1994: 38) found a strong commitment to 'putting the family first', and that 'the definition of "the family" was usually one in which partnership and parenthood were given much greater priority than other kinship relationships'. This ties in with the trend whereby families are much more likely to have a separate dwelling from the outset than was the case in the years around the middle of the twentieth century when, for example, no fewer than 50 per cent of newly married couples in Swansea lived with one or other set of parents and a further 8 per cent lived with other relatives (Rosser and Harris 1965). Links with kin beyond the nuclear family can also be expected to have become less prominent as a result of higher levels of geographical mobility and the growth of child-centredness. Rosser and Harris (1965: 14) allude to the former in their reference to 'the importance of physical proximity in the effective maintenance of a relationship', and elsewhere Harris (1980: 400) has traced the connection between isolation from wider kin and the rise of 'the child-centred family in which the parents' lives are given meaning and purpose primarily through their children'. The search for greater emotional fulfilment through family-centredness and in particular child-centredness may be understood to reflect changing priorities as wider kin become less central figures in people's lives.

At the same time as the search for greater intimacy within the narrow compass of the immediate family promises to deliver a more fulfilling life, it also carries with it new threats to solidarity between members. Harris refers to the danger of the family's 'implosion' – that is, bursting inwards under the excessive pressures placed upon it – and he cites approvingly Lomas's observation that isolation from wider kin 'may lead to excessive interdependence and to an idealization of their mutuality' (Harris 1980: 399). Heightened expectations of what family relationships have the capacity to deliver are quite consistent with trends towards family disintegration, expressed for example through rising levels of divorce, and they may even be seen to have contributed to them. This theme has been developed by Giddens in relation to the idea that contemporary societies are witnessing 'the transformation of intimacy'. Family relationships are not exempt from broad trends towards the democratization of modern life, and it is against this background that people are said by Giddens (1992) to be increasingly propelled into engaging in 'everyday social experiments'. The pursuit by individuals of what he calls 'the pure relationship' is potentially destabilizing for family ties, not least because of the implication identified by Giddens (1991: 89) that 'marriage becomes more and more a relationship initiated for, and kept going for as long as, it delivers emotional satisfaction'. This assertion is echoed in Beck and Beck-Gernsheim's (1995: 11) claim that '[p]eople marry for the sake of love and get divorced for the sake of love'. The freedom brought by individualization includes the freedom to leave relationships with which individual members are no longer satisfied.

These arguments are acknowledged by their authors to be ideal-typical and speculative, and it is appropriate to recall from the previous chapter Marshall's (1997) reservations about 'data-free sociology' when assessing ideas advanced as 'provisional, hypothetical and risky' (Beck and Beck-Gernsheim 1995: 10). The change underway in family relationships that they detect promises to usher in 'the negotiated family, the alternating family, the multiple family, new arrangements after divorce, remarriage, divorce again, new assortments from your, my, our children, our past and present families. It will be the expansion of the nuclear family and its extension in time' (Beck and Beck-Gernsheim 1995: 2). Assessments of these ideas against the available evidence on various aspects of contemporary family relationships such as couple relationships and the impact of divorce have already been undertaken (Jamieson 1998; Smart and Neale 1999), and their treatment of gender inequalities and their neglect of children have quickly been identified as key problems requiring further analysis. Step-family relationships occupy a pivotal position in the debates generated by theorists of individualization, and as such deserve exploration in some detail. Step-families are 'intrinsically highly complex social organizations' (Gorell Barnes *et al.* 1998: 5) and it is no easy matter to determine the likely outcome of the re-working of intimate relationships within them. The organization and management of gender and generational relationships within step-families sits uneasily alongside traditional notions of family bonds having a 'natural' basis, but it does not necessarily follow that step-family members will regard themselves as being in the vanguard of Stacey's (1998) 'postmodern family pioneers' or Giddens's everyday experimenters actively engaged in developing new modes of post-traditional family life.

Step-family solidarities

Step-families are not a new phenomenon, but in the contemporary world they are far more likely to come into existence through re-marriage following parental separation and divorce rather than the death of a parent (Humphrey and Humphrey 1988; Robinson 1991). Estimates of these proportions and of the total number of step-families are necessarily approximate, given that there is no agreed definition of what a step-family is, but Morrow's (1998) figure for the UK of one in twelve children living in step-families gives some sense of scale. Narrow definitions focus on married couples with dependent children brought to the family by one or both partners from previous relationships, but other definitions would include partners who cohabit (as well as those who are married) and sets of relationships including non-dependent children. Joint parenting arrangements between a divorced couple may also be regarded as creating two step-families, with children moving between the households of their mother and step-father and their father and step-mother at different stages of the week. It is possible to distinguish between many different types of step-family according to whether children are brought with them by one or both partners, whether further children are added, whether the adults entering step-families are widows or widowers, divorcees or were not previously married, and related permutations. This approach has been used by De'Ath (1992) to identify no fewer than 72 different step-family types. For these reasons, Gorell Barnes (1998: 271) and her colleagues criticize as misleading 'any attempt to describe stepfamilies as if they were one discrete and definable family form'. What they do have in common is that they can be distinguished from the norm of the nuclear family in which married parents live with children who are linked biologically to both of them. Put another way, step-families have to deal with the fact that 'blood relationships continue to be a powerful determinant in conceptualizing identity' (Davidoff *et al.* 1999: 263), and that as a result the relationships between step-family members have to be grounded in something other than the conventional ideology that emphasizes the 'naturalness' of blood ties.

In their pioneering research in this field, Burgoyne and Clark (1984) found that the ideology of nuclear family normality and naturalness was sufficiently strong for the majority of the forty couples of Sheffield step-parents whom they interviewed to aspire to living as an 'ordinary' family. One of the striking things about their findings is '[t]he pervasiveness of the nuclear family norm', even though a quarter of their respondents reported that their pursuit of an 'ordinary' family life was frustrated by the disruptive legacy of past marriages. This latter situation saw 'continued contact, intervention by, and, on occasion, conflict with the children's non-custodial parent undermine the stepparent's attempts to be a full "social" parent and disrupt the autonomy of the family's daily domestic routine' (Burgoyne and Clark 1984: 193). At the time when this research was undertaken, the pattern of step-parents taking on the role of 'natural' parents was an obvious course to follow given that Burgoyne and Clark (1984: 21) report finding that '*negative* images of stepfamilies' (emphasis in original) were the most pervasive in the literature of the day and in the wider society. The intervening period may be regarded as having witnessed a decline in the stigma attached to step-families as an alternative family form as their numbers have increased. In addition, the increased emphasis on the interests of children being served by continued contact with both of their natural parents has become enshrined in various pieces of legislation (Edwards *et al.* 1999). This is indicated in Simpson's (1998: 85)

observation that 'a powerful consensus has emerged concerning the importance of maintaining links between fathers and children after divorce'. There
is correspondingly less support for the idea that step-families offer their members the chance of a fresh start following a clean break between divorcing
parents (Clark and Haldane 1990; Smart and Neale 1999).

Only a minority of Burgoyne and Clark's respondents conformed to the
step-family type that they identified as 'progressive', and its increased popularity more recently may be attributed to the way in which this alternative
model of step-family organization offers scope for non-resident parents to be
included rather than excluded. Burgoyne and Clark (1984: 193) described
their respondents who fell into this 'progressive' category as people whose
'imagery of family life is pluralistic; they are aware of a diversity of patterns
in family and domestic life and depict themselves as making choices and
responding to constraints in a way which would exploit the advantages of
their circumstances for their children'. More recently Stacey (1998) has referred
to such arrangements in which children have active relationships with both
of their biological parents and their new partners as 'a divorce-extending family'. Benefits are seen to flow from creatively re-drawing the boundaries around
the step-family household in this more positive celebration of the legacies of
the past. Simpson's account of what he calls 'the extending family' echoes
this view by noting that 'choice and the possibilities for continuity in social
relations would appear to be maximised', but he makes an important qualification by noting that 'cultural expectations and economic constraints shape
relational possibilities in practice' (Simpson 1998: 44, 39–40). It is significant
that his case study of the extending family is middle-class, while the example
of step-relationships built more exclusively around the nuclear mould features
a working-class family living in rented accommodation. There is an instructive parallel here with Burgoyne and Clark's (1984: 193) comment that their
'progressive' step-families typically had 'few outstanding sources of conflict
with ex-partners and financial worries were rare'. The drive to develop workable arrangements along the lines of such 'progressive' step-families can be
understood as a reaction to the problems of trying to reproduce 'ordinary'
family life that are associated with the 'fresh start' approach to step-family
life. According to Robinson (1991: 128), the idea that step-families can be the
same as nuclear families is a 'phantasy that encourages unrealisable expectations, as well as adding to the conflicts between biological parents whose
children may be members of stepfamilies'. At the same time, it needs to be
acknowledged that step-family arrangements of the 'progressive' type are
easier to sustain where resource constraints are less pressing, and are not without problems of their own.

Simpson's (1998) identification of 'the nuclear mould' and 'the extending
family' as two 'opposite ends of a spectrum' ties in with his wider argument
that recent decades have witnessed the steady displacement of the nuclear
family by 'the unclear family'. For Simpson (1999: 121–2), 'the emergence
of families which are reconstituted, blended, recombinant, step- or otherwise
"unclear" when measured against the former certainties of the nuclear family'

represents a 'fundamental transformation'. Within step-families, changing legal, economic and cultural influences have tended to undermine the simplicity of the arrangement whereby the step-parent 'replaces' the biological parent who is no longer present, and encouraged what Le Gall and Martin (1997: 190) refer to as 'the search for a new behavioural model'. Previously it was estimated that over one-third and perhaps as many as a half of all children whose parents divorced completely lost contact with their non-residential fathers (Gibson 1994; Gorell Barnes *et al.* 1998), it being the case that children are far more likely to live with their mothers than their fathers following divorce. American data suggest that, where they and/or their former partner had remarried, up to three-quarters of non-custodial parents had lost contact with their children 5 years on from divorce (Pasley and Ihinger-Tallman 1988). In such circumstances, the arrival of step-fathers meant that step-families could more or less readily 'pass' as 'an ordinary family' (Burgoyne and Clark 1984). More recent figures indicate that a much higher proportion of non-residential fathers are maintaining contact with their children. Bradshaw and his colleagues (1999) found that almost half of the non-resident fathers to whom they spoke saw their child at least once a week, and over two-thirds had at least monthly contact. These figures are higher than those produced in other recent studies, but even on this basis it does appear reasonably safe to conclude that a major change is underway. The involvement with their children of non-residential parents means that exclusive models of step-family life need to be modified, and the negative portrayal of absent fathers as 'deadbeat dads' has to be reconsidered in the light of findings that '[t]he majority want to fulfil all their parental obligations, social, emotional and financial' (Bradshaw *et al.* 1999: 232). The pursuit by step-families of 'ordinary' family life conceived in terms of the nuclear family has become less viable as a result of this change, although no blueprint exists of precisely how step-family arrangements might be re-worked in a more inclusive way.

Comparison between step-families made in 'the nuclear mould' and those pursuing 'the extending family' directs attention to both the number of people involved and the range of viewpoints that they hold. Step-families provide a good illustration of how 'the unclear family is characterised by a polyphony of voices' (Simpson 1998: 50), and it is readily apparent that a good deal of flexibility is required if a sense of common purpose is to be achieved among the various people involved. Gorell Barnes and her colleagues emphasize the gender differences that exist in terms of contributions to the development and maintenance of 'a sense of cohesion' in step-families, noting in the process 'the overwhelmingly important role played by women in helping children to cope with loss and transition' (Gorell Barnes *et al.* 1998: 31, 147). Within step-families, women are more likely than men to have to deal with the practical and emotional consequences of the fact that '[d]ivided loyalty is a common problem for the children' (Humphrey and Humphrey 1988: 127). Women's efforts to secure integration and harmony within step-families led Chandler (1991) to describe them as 'family diplomats'. This links in with Smart and Neale's (1999: 52) more general observation about the difference between biological fathers' and mothers' involvement with their children following divorce, that 'fathers have more freedom to opt in or out of such interactions and to choose how and when to balance fatherhood with their other commitments or interests'. It follows from this that negotiations between former partners concerning their children are not conducted between equals, however much they may aspire to be fair and act in the best interests of the children. Another reason for doubting the appropriateness of Beck and Beck-Gernsheim's (1995) model of 'the negotiated family' when examining step-families relates to the way in which giving greater voice to non-residential biological parents may marginalize step-parents. In Smart and Neale's (1999: 58–9) research, the pursuit of co-parenting resulted in a situation whereby 'new partners were not regarded, and did not regard themselves, as step-parents and so limited their involvement with the children'. Such an outcome is perhaps unsurprising given that step-parents are often 'invisible' (Edwards *et al.* 1999) in official thinking.

Edwards and her colleagues have argued that step-families are confronted by 'a clash of moralities concerning whether children need (biological) parents or whether they need (social) families'. Each involves a very different understanding of family solidarities, the former treating blood ties as generating 'more intense and enduring emotional relationships . . . characterised by absolute commitment and loyalty' and the latter founded on the belief that children 'need to feel they "belong" to a clear-cut social unit, which can be provided by a "family"' (Edwards *et al.* 1999: 88–9). The finding that middle-class respondents tended to identify with the former way of thinking, whereas working-class respondents were more likely to express the latter view, is consistent with the class differences of Simpson's (1998) case studies noted above (although there is a need for caution about generalizing on the basis of such qualitative data derived from small samples). The gulf between these two perspectives is substantial enough for there to be doubts about whether parents holding to the different positions could usefully engage in 'negotiation'. Finch and Mason's (1993) analysis of how family responsibilities are organized highlights the way in which family members arrive via negotiation at 'a common understanding', but there are limits to how far this process can go because within families not everything is treated as negotiable. What Jordan and his colleagues (1994) suggest is that commitment to the moral idea of 'doing the right thing' can lead to behaviour reminiscent of Durkheim's mechanical solidarity – that is, a framework within which the idea of negotiation between alternative courses of action is foreign. It is instructive that this observation is made in their discussion of 'non-standard household units', including step-families. From a Durkheimian point of view, people would be expected to experience difficulty coming to terms with the 'ambiguous, fluid and unpredictable' character of their situations. In such contexts, their behaviour will be as much concerned with the creation and reinforcement of predictable family identities as it is with the more uncertain sphere in which outcomes depend on negotiation.

Simpson's (1999: 134) analysis leads him to the conclusion that changes in family patterns 'require new ways of thinking about how, if at all, the basic currencies of social life such as trust, amity, support, care, obligation and predictability might be located in new and emergent structures of family life after divorce'. As part of this process, it is important to recognize that the consolidation of step-family identities and solidarities necessarily takes time, often considerably longer than is anticipated by the people involved. It has been observed that 'stepfamilies cannot develop affection, loyalty, traditions – their own rules of operation – instantly, which is what adults who create them wish to happen' (Robinson and Smith 1993: 193). This is confirmed by Baxter *et al* (1999), who reported that those step-families in which people sought high levels of mutual commitment from the outset were more vulnerable to subsequent fragmentation than those in which a more gradual approach was adopted. There are echoes here of Hochschild's (1990: 184) respondent whose step-father developed a strong relationship with his step-children because 'he understood that it would take some time to interject himself into our family'. The evolution of step-families into what Jordan and his colleagues (1994) call 'micro-communities of mutual commitment' can follow a number of different trajectories, and their diversity means that any search for a 'logical timescale' (Gorell Barnes *et al.* 1998) governing how step-family relationships develop would be doomed to fail. Family rituals play an important part in bringing people together, and family gatherings at Christmas are particularly potent in their capacity 'to show the warmth and solidarity inherent in the "bosom" of families . . . to make real the morality of trusting, intimate bonds of family' (Bittman and Pixley 1997: 26). Other rituals centred on the home also have the potential to contribute to the positive reinforcement of family unity, and where this occurs it has the effect of 'disguising otherwise evident inequalities' (Gillis 1997: 114). The symbol of 'home' can be a powerful integrating force.

It does not follow from this that sharing the space of a home necessarily brings step-family members together. Young's general observation made in the context of his discussion of people's routine attachments to home is that shared space can just as readily divide as unite them: 'the more frequently people interact together . . . the more positively as well as negatively charged solidarity they feel for each other' (Young 1988: 100). Daly (1996) has expressed this idea another way through the notion of families being subject to both centrifugal and centripetal forces, with 'centrifugal families' understood as ones in which competing demands for family members' time, attention and energies pull them apart. Where such centrifugal forces are in operation, they can be considered to contribute to the greater likelihood of step-children leaving home at a younger age than children in other household types (Jones 1995), as well as to the higher probability that remarriages will end in divorce compared to first marriages (Gibson 1994). Demands made by employers on family members are the principal source of centrifugal pressures identified by Daly, but other factors such as relationships with wider kin can also operate to undermine step-family solidarities. Robinson and Smith

(1993: 205) highlight the vulnerability to external influences of bonds within step-families in their suggestion that 'the most likely event to destabilise a stepfamily at later stages . . . is a will left by a parent or grandparent which excludes non-biologically related family members'. Finch (1997: 144) echoes this theme in noting about inheritance that 'different people and different families can choose to act differently from each other, for example with some families trying to treat stepchildren on completely the same terms as full-blood children, and others making a distinction between these two categories'. Bornat and her colleagues (1999: 259) found that 'people overwhelmingly resorted to the principle that blood is thicker than water' when considering issues of inheritance where step-relatives were present, and they went on to highlight the bearing that this has on the way in which care arrangements for older people are likely to develop in an era of historically high divorce rates.

Researchers have identified several further factors that influence the extent to which the members of step-families forge strong and enduring bonds with each other and 'make a go of it' (Burgoyne and Clark 1982: 295). Age of children when step-families are formed is one such factor, and Burgoyne and Clark's (1984: 192) type of step-family in which the parents were '[l]ooking forward to the departure of the children' was characterized by children having already reached their teens. Burgoyne and Clark (1982: 293) comment that 'the classic problems of adolescence are often compounded by step-relationships in which legitimate authority, mutual trust and recognised family routines have not been fully worked out'. Conversely, very young children made it easier to construct 'ordinary' family life, partly because it is more straightforward for members of such households to adopt the same family name. The birth of a further child to a remarried couple is a further variable, one portrayed by Burgoyne and Clark's (1982: 291) respondents 'in terms of the "bond", "seal" or "unity" which he or she brought to the stepfamily'. Personal characteristics also play a part. Just as 'personal liking' (Harris 1990a: 63) helps to account for why some kin ties are maintained while others are allowed to fade, so it is also the case that the position of step-parents will be shaped by 'basic factors such as whether they and the children like each other' (Sharpe 1994: 143). Contrasting degrees of integration within local community networks represents another element in the explanation of how relationships within step-families evolve, as Wallman's (1984) comparison of the two 'second family households' in her Battersea study demonstrates. Moving to a new neighbourhood was valued by those of Burgoyne and Clark's (1982) respondents who were seeking to 'start afresh' because established community ties threatened to lock them in to the past from which they were trying to move on.

Burgoyne and Clark (1982: 295) note how the accounts given to them by their respondents were 'often curiously pragmatic in tone and essentially devoid of the culturally prevalent ideologies of romantic love'. This may be explained by economic necessity, as Simpson (1998: 50) suggests in his observation that 'in the absence of resources . . . sentiment and the pragmatics of subsistence often pull in different directions', and it is certainly the case that financial constraints matter to many step-families. Step-families are 'more likely to be disadvantaged in terms of housing and income compared with couple households' (L. Clarke 1996: 79), and it has also been argued that children in step-families are not necessarily less disadvantaged than their counterparts in lone-parent households (Kiernan 1992). The conclusion that step-family solidarities need to be considered in the context of their members' economic positions as well as in relation to their emotional attachments and rivalries is of itself unremarkable. More significant are the related points to emerge from research in this area pertaining to the possibilities and difficulties of boundaries around step-families being re-drawn in a more fluid fashion than they are in conventional nuclear families, and to the processual nature of family life. Daly's (1996) analysis of individuals being pulled towards or pushed away from the centre of family life by centripetal and centrifugal forces follows in the tradition of analyses in the sociology of community which portray collectivities being split apart by centrifugal forces that are more or less effectively countered by centripetal forces that hold people together (Crow and Allan 1995). This theme will be explored further in the next chapter, following consideration in this chapter's final section of the idea that the notion of family responsibilities is undergoing fundamental re-evaluation.

Rethinking family responsibilities

Hodder's (1989) observation that many people view step-families as 'untidy' is followed by one of her respondents, a step-father, being quoted as saying about his new situation, '[t]here is no going back'. The same point could be made more generally about contemporary family life. In the age of 'the unclear family', Simpson (1999: 127) suggests that 'the confusion of boundaries, rights and obligations are apt to be a source of anxiety and insecurity', but there is no realistic prospect of a return to the orderly world described by theorists whose neat models of family life were constructed from 'the modern point of view' (Cheal 1991: 31). Cheal notes that there are good grounds for questioning how accurately such models captured the realities of family relationships of the mid-twentieth century, but there would be a difficulty even without this qualification, since it is implausible to regard developments over the subsequent period as reversible. The contribution of the process of individualization to what Cheal (1991: 133) calls the '*destandardization* of the family' (emphasis in original) is a good illustration of this point. Individuals concerned to make the most of their opportunities are liable to monitor the costs and benefits of the relationships in which they participate, and there is no reason in principle why this should not include family relationships. Individualization is corrosive of family members' preparedness to share resources with each other automatically, and replaces it with a more calculating mentality. Cheal (1996: 83) describes the contrast by saying '[i]nstead of an ethic of unlimited sharing, it is more likely that individuals in post-Fordist families emphasize the costs of sharing'. Once economistic principles become established as the basis of family relationships, it is very difficult for them to be reallocated a more minor role.

Evidence is inconclusive on how far solidaristic feelings have been eroded by the process of individualization. Brannen and Moss's (1991: 47) study of dual-earner households after maternity leave found mothers concerned to be seen to make a contribution to family finances by returning to paid work, but at the same time 'the strong *belief* in marriage as a shared and equal partnership' meant that 'women did not appear to want to calculate whether each partner was receiving fair and equal shares of household resources' (emphasis in original). The suggestion that women rarely engage in such calculation is connected to the idea that women ensure the smooth running of family life by placing their concern for the good of the group ahead of considerations of individual advantage. It is in this sense that Hutson and Jenkins (1989: 153) refer to the way in which women 'take the strain' of family relationships, and they observe that '[i]n the management of family conflict, as in the provision of support and succour, women – particularly mothers – play a pivotal role'. Other studies suggest that women's altruistic disregard of self-interested calculation in favour of the interests of others does have limits. An example of this is provided by those lone mothers in Graham's (1987) study who compared their situation to that when they were married and reckoned themselves to be 'better off poorer' because they no longer had to deal with their husbands taking a disproportionate share of resources, albeit that they continued to practise 'self-sacrifice' in relation to their children. Looked at from this angle, rising divorce rates may be interpreted as evidence that women are becoming less prepared to 'put the family first'. Another indicator of change in women's preparedness to give greater priority to their individual preferences is provided by Hochschild's study of people putting work ahead of family in their priorities. According to Hochschild, women are increasingly to be found escaping from the demands placed on them at home by spending more time at work. Work provides them with 'a source of security, pride, and a powerful sense of being valued'. The perception that 'the "male" world of work seems more honorable and valuable than the "female" world of home and children' (Hochschild 1997: 247) has, in Hochschild's account, led at least some women to challenge the model of the family constructed around the male breadwinner married to a female home-maker. It is instructive that the public response to Hochschild's thesis was to fault women 'for their selfishness in preferring the workplace to the home' (Epstein *et al.* 1999: 104).

Hochschild's analysis is made particularly interesting because it is framed in terms of emotions. She suggests that workplaces have come to compete with families as people's primary 'emotional culture', defined in deliberately Durkheimian terms as 'a set of rituals, beliefs about feelings and rules governing feeling which induce emotional focus, and even a sense of the "sacred"'. Forces that have the effect of 'pulling workers out of family life and into the workplace' are reinforced by strained relationships at home where emotional

labour is arguably more vital than ever but is undervalued and even unacknowledged. In the light of the previous section's concern with step-families,
it is noteworthy that Hochschild reports that many of her respondents 'spoke
with feeling about strained relationships with step-children and ex-wives
or husbands' (Hochschild 1996: 20, 27, 26). A similar argument has been
advanced by Lynch (1989) in her analysis of how time pressures derived from
concentration on paid work have had the effect of marginalizing the various
elements of the (unpaid) work that goes into maintaining caring relationships
that she refers to as 'solidary labour'. It would be a simplification of these
ideas to reduce them to the proposition that the growth of women's employment has been at the expense of solidary labour, but it is instructive that
Roberts's (1995: 197–8) analysis of mid-twentieth century patterns of help
given to members of the extended family found 'no evidence of women
putting their jobs before the care of their relations'. Roberts acknowledges
that it is very difficult to quantify the extent of the expression of solidarity
through caring for family members, and that it is equally difficult to disentangle the mixture of motives that prompted women to behave in this way.
In the analysis of people's accounts, it also needs to be borne in mind that
altruism and self-sacrifice are more publicly acceptable than self-interest or
the expectation that some form of reciprocal arrangement was in operation.
There are nevertheless good grounds for believing that Roberts's (1985)
scepticism about the existence of a 'calculative orientation towards kin' in
an earlier period would have continued to apply, although the proportions of
women in paid work had risen in the interim.

Consideration of the past and current state of family solidarities is difficult
to undertake in isolation, given the interconnectedness of family and community. Harris (1980: 398) has noted how the idea that families are becoming
increasingly 'privatized' is 'the logical corollary of that other ancient refrain,
the "decline of the local 'community'"'. The fact that there is a long history
of social commentators bemoaning the passing of a sense of responsibility
to others in itself provides grounds for caution, as do assessments of the
evidence that draw less dramatic conclusions such as Everingham's (1994:
128) view that 'the family still has very important links to kinship and communal forms of social organization and it continues to be largely women's
work to maintain these links'. It is also appropriate to recognize that from
some points of view the demise of the family would be something to be
welcomed. Close family ties are open to the criticism of being 'anti-solidaristic'
in the sense that 'the emphasis upon personal intimacy runs counter to
attempts to create solidarity across class, gender or other social groups'
(Bernardes 1997: 134). The family is thus open to being considered divisive
and 'anti-social' (Barrett and McIntosh 1982). At this level of analysis, firm
conclusions are hard to draw, although it can be shown that freedom from
conventional family ties is not a guarantor that alternative forms of support
will be forthcoming. Rowlingson and McKay's (1998: 196) study of lone
parents found that their common experiences did not bring them together,
and that what stands out is that 'there is relatively little solidarity among lone

parents as a group'. In contrast, solidarity among older people is a more readily identifiable form of togetherness beyond the family, at least among those who are members of the large number of organizations available for them to join (Jerrome 1992). The determinants of such community solidarities (or of their absence) is thus an appropriate topic to consider next.

4

Community solidarities

Introduction

It is only superficially paradoxical to observe that much of the strength of community solidarities is derived from their oppositional character. As was noted in the Introduction, the boundaries of any social group necessarily serve to identify outsiders as well as insiders, and studies in the field of community life furnish particularly vivid illustrations of this point (Crow and Allan 1994). Some of the most powerful community bonds have been forged among working-class people conscious of their shared opposition to employers and sometimes also to the State. Lockwood's (1975: 18) classic account of working-class images of society treats this as a defining characteristic of traditional proletarian workers: '[s]haped by occupational solidarities and communal sociability the proletarian social consciousness is centred on an awareness of "us" in contradistinction to "them" who are not a part of "us"'. Mining communities are the prime example of this outlook to which Lockwood refers, and the status of miners as archetypal proletarians has led to an enormous amount of research effort being devoted to them. The atypicality of miners reveals in a particularly stark form the features that are present to varying degrees in communities built around many other occupations. Traditional pit villages came closer than any other social arrangement to the ideal type of community in which there is a coincidence of shared place, shared interests and shared identities (Bulmer 1975), even though the precise nature of this sharing could vary considerably between regions and over time. More recent assessments of the intense solidarities generated by geographical isolation, class-based institutions and cultural conservatism have highlighted the constrained character of the lives of people encapsulated within such relationships. Women and men experienced the solidarity of mining communities in very different ways, unsurprisingly in a social world in which

Dennis and his colleagues (1969: 204) found miners spending much of their leisure time together and 'the husband is very often a comparative stranger to his home'. Accounts of traditional working-class life also suggest that solidarity could be expressed through a suspicion of innovation and a preference for ritualized familiarity (Hoggart 1958; Martin 1981), although there is a danger of such assessments incorporating romanticized images of people being 'poor but happy' and content with their lot.

Community relationships that have a strong oppositional element need to be understood in the context of their members attempting to achieve a degree of control over their lives by limiting the power that others can exercise over them. The institutions developed to this end in mining communities have some notable achievements to their credit, but their history also serves to demonstrate that solidarities cannot be captured and preserved indefinitely by institutions, and various accounts have shown such arrangements to be unstable and subject to change. To this end, Dennis and co-workers' (1969) analysis of mining communities as the product of centrifugal and centripetal forces has been taken up and developed by Warwick and Littlejohn (1992: 20) who note that it is useful in its suggestion that community life 'is maintained and will be changed by forces beyond the control of individual members and households'. These forces include national and international market conditions and political processes as well as more local factors. Historical accounts such as Williamson's (1982) reveal considerable fluidity in the extent of solidarity between members of mining communities, with levels of unemployment being one important influence on people's attitudes towards others. Strikes also figure prominently in the history of mining communities and they are particularly significant because of what they reveal about the need for community identities to be revitalized periodically. The 1984–85 miners' strike is also highly revealing about how gender relationships in mining communities are not reproduced automatically. One study of the strike concluded about women's position that in the aftermath of the strike it was possible to identify 'both significant shifts and deep continuities in their daily experiences and self-perceptions' (Waddington *et al.* 1991: 93). The strike did not lead to the wholesale re-ordering of gender relationships that was anticipated by some commentators, but it did reveal in a particularly explicit way the importance of women's contributions to the 'solidary labour' by which families and communities are held together. As a result of this, women are better able to challenge the idea that their traditional subordination is necessary for the good of the group, even if the outcomes of such challenges to date have fallen short of radical renegotiation of their position.

The atypicality of mining communities makes them especially useful in comparisons with other occupational groups and their associated communities. To some writers, traditional working-class communities like the occupational communities of miners and their families have been subject to long-term erosion due to the processes of nation-building, globalization and individualization. It is from this standpoint that Pakulski and Waters refer to 'small, homogeneous, well bounded and clearly circumscribed' social groups whose members share common experiences and territorial proximity as 'crumbling communities of fate'. According to these authors, communities in which 'patterns of exploitation and domination can easily be apprehended and class interests can readily become recognized and shared . . . have progressively disappeared from modern societies' (Pakulski and Waters 1996: 96, 90). Their place can be seen to have been taken by workers whose more individualized relationship to the world makes collective action and identification problematic. In Mills's (1951: ix) classic account of white-collar workers, he argued that 'whatever common interests they have do not lead to unity . . . Internally, they are split, fragmented . . . As a group, they do not threaten anyone'. More recent assessments of the position of white-collar workers suggest that they are able to develop the capacity to forge effective connections as a group and as a class, despite tending to be geographically more dispersed than members of place-based communities. In Lockwood's (1995: 3) view, important elements among the middle classes have been 'very well "formed" right from their inception . . . perhaps not as *a* class, but certainly corporatively, through various national associations, professional bodies and trade unions; through appointments or elections to the membership of innumerable representative and consultative bodies at local, regional and national levels; through informal local networks and cliques' (emphasis in original). It is equally important to investigate how solidarity can emerge through processes like these as it is to acknowledge the mechanisms by which traditional solidarities were generated.

The oppositional solidarity of mining communities

The strong sense of 'us' against 'them' that characterizes traditional working-class communities has often been cast in terms of a fundamental social class division between workers and employers. It is unsurprising that such class consciousness is strongly associated with mining communities, given their social homogeneity and their history of engagement in long and often bitter industrial disputes. In many of these communities, mining provided the majority of the paid work available to men at the same time as women's opportunities for employment were restricted. Horden in County Durham was typical in that it had a small middle class, 'the doctor, the top colliery officials, the managers of the three Co-operative stores and the three cinemas', but as a village it had been 'brought into being only in the service of the pit' (Hudson 1995: 304, 12) and most families living there were those of miners. A similar situation prevailed in South Wales, where '[s]heer weight of numbers ensured . . . that community interests and the interests of the miners were often perceived as identical' (Gilbert 1992: 69). In a study conducted in 1950s Yorkshire, it is recorded that 'over 60% of the male working population of Ashton finds employment at the local collieries' (Dennis *et al.* 1969: 26). Nineteenth-century legislation debarred women from working underground, with the result that '[i]n most mining communities, it was the custom for married women to stay at home and commit themselves to domesticity and housework'. Bradley (1989: 114) follows this observation by commenting that women's exclusion from pitwork did not prevent their continuing to be 'identified with the mining community', but she notes that they were outside the masculine culture of the work group by which they were treated as 'the other, threatening, polluting'. Solidarity between miners and gender solidarity did not necessarily reinforce each other, and could pull in different directions. Frankenberg's (1976: 40) reading of the Ashton study is that 'the solidarity of the male peer group reinforced by shared work hazards, shared pit language, shared clubs and shared interest in Rugby League, led to a situation in which men reacted to exploitation by fighting not as a class against capitalism, but as a gender group against women'. Women were also capable of showing 'sex solidarity', although this sometimes had the effect of reinforcing rather than challenging the solidarity of the men and the subordination of the women. This could happen, for example, when the community structures into which gender segregation had been built were taken to constitute a natural order whose members had an 'organic' unity reminiscent of Tönnies's *gemeinschaft* (Ennis 1999).

Further dimensions to the complexity of the solidarities and divisions operating in coal mining communities can be identified besides those that ran along the lines of class and gender. Dennis and his colleagues (1969) recorded how miners performed a variety of different tasks for which there were varying rates of pay, and noted that a corresponding status hierarchy existed in which it was the better-paid and more demanding jobs that were most prized. Solidarity between men in these different status positions can be explained by reference to the 'common interest' of workers who can expect to occupy most positions in this hierarchy over the course of their working lives. This solidarity does not readily extend to people working in the industry as representatives of the employers, as Gilbert's (1992) account of the enduring social divisions associated with the butty system illustrates. Long-lasting divisions could also be generated by people taking different positions with regard to strikes and other industrial action, and Dennis *et al.* (1969: 79) describe the prevailing philosophy in Ashton as one in which '[a] miner's first loyalty is to his "mates" . . . The "blackleg" miner must be made a social outcast in every way'. Similar attitudes were found among some of the respondents of Waddington *et al.* (1991) with regard to relations between strikers and non-strikers in the 1984–85 dispute. Local loyalties sometimes led to suspicion of miners from elsewhere, and Williamson (1982: 199) describes how in the inter-war period when unemployment rates were high a 'strong sense of locality and community' led to 'lodges seeking to protect the employment of Throckley men against those defined as "strangers"'. In each of these cases, shared economic interests provided a potential basis for people to join together, although the groups that they formed did not necessarily extend to all members of the communities in which people lived, or to all members of the working class.

The experience of people in mining communities offers powerful support to the Durkheimian proposition that common economic interests are not in themselves sufficient to generate social solidarity. Gilbert's historical account notes that '[c]ollective interests could be acted upon only where there was a clear sense of collective identity', and while trade union organization could do much to promote this, it was most effective when it meshed with wider social solidarities. This was particularly apparent in the South Wales coalfield, where '[t]he solidarity of Welsh villages during the lock-outs came not from the formal direction of the lodge, but from the complete character of the local social formation and the way in which local communal interests and the class interests of the miners were fused' (Gilbert 1992: 255, 249). Bulmer (1975: 87–8) makes a similar point about the interconnectedness of the various facets of mining community life by saying that '[t]he social ties of work, leisure, neighbourhood and friendship overlap to form close-knit and interlocking locally based collectivities of actors. The solidarity of the community is strengthened . . . by a shared history of living and working in one place over a long period of time'. Neighbourhood ties in such circumstances are likely to include a significant proportion of links to kin, and Warwick and Littlejohn (1992) report finding 74 per cent of men and 84 per cent of women respondents in their study having kin living locally. In general terms, what is being suggested is that members of mining communities feel themselves to be bound together by a shared 'way of life' (Beynon *et al.* 1991) in which familiar institutions are reinforced by customs and established local practices, or what Warwick and Littlejohn refer to as 'local cultural capital'. This term is used to suggest that mining communities are united not only by shared economic interests, but also by the fact that their members share a common culture built upon 'their kinship networks and their local skills, and memories of past individual and collaborative efforts to improve the quality of their lives, their churches, clubs and co-ops' (Warwick and Littlejohn 1992: 205). Without such a common culture, collective endeavour of the forms that have emerged would not have been possible.

Warwick and Littlejohn's account of how 'local cultural capital' holds together mining communities is sensitive to the subtleties and variations of the process. Their reference to 'the set of dominant values which characterise relationships and activities in the locality' (Warwick and Littlejohn 1992: 84) is made in recognition that adherence to community norms is not absolute and may be contested, for example by people of a more idiosyncratic cast of mind. Those communities in which people are held together most tightly are, they suggest, ones in which various factors have been more favourable to the development of such solidarity. Prominent among these factors are the number of kinship ties people have locally, their length of local residence, and the proportion of households reliant on mining for their incomes. Because mining communities differ according to these 'subtle and important variations in the social structure of each locality' (Warwick and Littlejohn 1992: 189), they are vulnerable to fragmentation by centrifugal forces to varying degrees. The impact of forces for change can be affected in turn by what particular individuals contribute to the maintenance of the cultural framework within which people live. According to Warwick and Littlejohn (1992:

85), 'the dominant local culture is held as a kind of capital which is trans-
mitted and sometimes modified from generation to generation . . . in each
generation there are key people who become significant reproducers of this
local cultural capital, who define its limits and to some extent create modi-
fications'. There are echoes here of the role attributed to 'old families' in a study
of insider/outsider relations in Leicestershire, among whom there existed
'[g]reater cohesion, solidarity, uniformity of norms and self-discipline', and
whose members prized 'orderliness, circumspection, foresight and group
cohesion' (Elias and Scotson 1994: 152–3). In mining communities in the past,
these values often had a religious foundation, particularly among those groups
within them that aspired to 'respectability' (Moore 1974).

From Moore's point of view, what stands out is the conservatism of the
miners of County Durham, whose strong sense of occupational community
did not automatically translate into the oppositional class-consciousness of
Lockwood's ideal-type proletarian worker. Indeed, Moore (1975: 52) suggests that 'working-class culture can institutionalise a kind of parochialism
that can undermine or prevent class solidarity'. In similar vein, Williamson
(1990: 109) describes working-class culture as 'deeply conservative and
defensive' with 'a strong emphasis on the maintenance of boundaries'. The
boundary between 'us' and 'them' could be cast in terms of workers and
employers, but it could just as readily be used to differentiate between men
and women, different occupational statuses, different localities or different
religious affiliations. That religious attachments can be a mark of distinction
is indicated by Moore's (1974: 220) description of chapel attendance as 'a simple
rite of solidarity, the Methodists collectively asserting to themselves and to
the rest of the village who they are'. Language could also be used to distinguish different sections of the community, and one of Hudson's informants
recalled this being a feature of Horden life: 'the village was divided into two
parts, the top and the bottom, and we were told not to play with children
from the bottom of the village . . . We were told not to talk to them. We
weren't allowed to talk pitmatic (the dialect of the pits)' (Hudson 1995: 22).
Skill hierarchies and the desire to preserve local autonomy in trade union
organization have been interpreted as further impediments among miners to
the development of class-wide solidarities, just as in other industries 'intense
craft loyalties can inhibit the growth of any wider class solidarity' (Roberts
et al. 1977: 97).

The argument about the operation of various centrifugal forces within
mining communities making wider solidarity difficult to create and maintain
can therefore draw on a substantial amount of supporting evidence. The fact
that mining communities were nevertheless characterized by solidarities of
various sorts, including intense and enduring ones, indicates that the centrifugal forces that threatened to generate fragmentation were more or less
effectively counteracted by centripetal forces bringing and keeping people
together. Shared poverty, what Hoggart (1995) calls 'common hardship',
has often been advanced as a fundamental basis of solidarity in traditional
working-class communities, and might be expected to figure prominently in

any explanation. According to Abrams, the networks of 'collective attachment, reciprocity and trust' that characterized working-class community life in the past were by and large the product of 'constraint, isolation and insecurity'. Abrams goes on to comment that these are wrongly perceived as 'natural helping networks' because they 'developed as a response to certain highly specified social conditions which one would not wish to see reproduced today' (Bulmer 1986: 92). Poverty, or at least the ever-present threat of poverty, is understood from this standpoint to compel people into mutually supportive arrangements, and it is in this sense that Jackson (1968) refers to mutuality as 'that necessary habit'. Roberts's (1995: 201) research also points towards this conclusion, in the light of her finding that 'neighbourliness and neighbourhoods were strongest in the poorest areas'. The association of solidarity with poverty would appear to be further supported by Stead's (1987: 4) comment in relation to the Polmaise pit in Stirlingshire, '[t]he harder the times, the greater the solidarity', but it is important to note that the hard times referred to here are those of the 1984–85 strike, not the more distant past. The history of miners and their families is one of economic privation and material hardship, but on its own poverty is unlikely to promote mutual aid. For this to happen trust also has to be present, and the lesson of mining communities' history is that this development was far from automatic.

The making and unmaking of mining community solidarities

The history of mining communities in the nineteenth century is marked by concern among people in authority over their disorderly character. Against a background of rapid expansion in mining ventures, Samuel (1977: 67) has commented that '[t]he mining population at mid-century was notoriously restless and unsettled'. He goes on to note that the large-scale movement of miners continued, citing the case of Bolden Colliery in the 1890s, which had 'a polyglot population drawn from Lancashire, Staffordshire, Cornwall, Ireland, Scotland, Wales, Northumberland and Durham'. In South Wales prior to the First World War, the Abercrave Colliery met its labour needs through 'a large influx of Portuguese, Germans, Frenchmen, Belgians and Spaniards, along with the native Welshmen' (Francis and Smith 1998: 11). The new settlements in which coal and other miners lived were anything but traditional to observers at the time, who expressed anxiety 'that a new working-class community was emerging in which traditional mechanisms of social control were absent' (Nicholson 1997: 143). Prompted by the prospect of unruliness, mine owners often played an active role in the promotion of paternalistic schemes to create 'community'. Williamson (1982: 60) provides an illustration of such actions by noting how shareholders in the Throckley coal company 'had built a Wesleyan chapel and a school in the village' and 'donated money to the pit brass band'. At the same time Williamson (1982: 6) is at pains to point out that community life was not simply the creation of employers, and that the contribution of the miners themselves was crucial: '[t]hrough their unions and co-operative societies they built their own institutions distinct from those of the coal company. Through family and kinship they built defensive walls against chance and circumstances, constructing a way of life which was theirs and not simply a reflection of the coal company's plans'. With the passage of time, employers' paternalism became increasingly anachronistic as miners and their families developed new collective identities, not least as a result of the experience of the industrial disputes that punctuate their history.

The General Strike and miners' lock-out of 1926 figure prominently in Williamson's account of the history of the Throckley community in which his grandfather had been a miner. Industrial action over several months had the effect of 'testing severely the quality of community and family life. The solidarity, ingenuity, tolerance and strength of Throckley people were brought to the forefront of the struggle' (Williamson 1982: 168). During such disputes, horizons were widened and strikers were encouraged to develop 'a feeling of common cause with other working men, perhaps, even, to the abstraction of a working class as a whole' (Williamson 1982: 7), but the local identifications that prevailed at other times were not readily compatible with such abstractions. A similar picture of industrial disputes radically affecting collective identities emerges from Gilbert's research into Ynysybwl in South Wales. In the two decades prior to the outbreak of the First World War, '[t]he old order in which the chapels were the integrative and controlling institutions, and in which the company had an influential place, was replaced by a new order, with the lodge the dominant local institution' (Gilbert 1992: 120). Founded during the strike of 1898, the local union lodge adopted a more oppositional stance than previous workers' representatives had, and challenged the formerly powerful notion that employers and workers were parts of a larger organic community. In subsequent disputes, the lodge continued to be effective at coordinating support for members and their families, for example through the provision of food, the collection and distribution of relief money, and the organization of activities and entertainments. Gilbert (1992: 140) attributes the strength of the lodge to 'the social density of the community; the ways in which various institutional networks enmeshed with networks of kinship and of friendship', but he notes that the other side of this powerful solidarity was its essentially inward-looking character. He concludes that strikes revealed 'the limitations of such power, reactive and contained within its local crucible'. Strikes reinforced notions of community as 'us here against them out there' (Gilbert 1992: 100), and in doing so highlighted the double-edged effect that the assertion of group distinctiveness can have.

Strikes and their associated struggles have had an enduring effect on life in mining communities. Dennis and his colleagues (1969: 14) observed that '[c]ommon memories of past struggle have undoubtedly helped to bind a community such as Ashton', and Warwick and Littlejohn (1992: 65) refer to the way that disputes with employers 'indelibly marked the working class in mining localities'. Memories of the inter-war period were still strong in the 1950s when the original Ashton study was conducted, the 1926 strike being remembered as a time when 'the men of the village could see themselves as one unified force, facing a common enemy and a common fate'. Similarly, the period following the strike's defeat was recalled as years of hardship that created between miners' families 'a bond of suffering'. This perspective even led some older miners who had first-hand experience of the inter-war years to lament that the younger generation of miners who had joined the industry more recently took their improved position for granted and to conclude that 'a little hardship would do them good' (Dennis *et al.* 1969: 80, 60). A more sceptical view of such memories is offered by Pahl (1984: 95–6), who quotes the description of an inter-war Rhondda village 'which used to be famous for its working class solidarity' but which had seen this eroded in the context of mass unemployment as evidence that every generation looks back to a lost 'golden age of solidarity'. Pahl implies that such retrospection might be interpreted as just one more example of the habit familiar to community sociologists, identified by Williams (1975: 21), 'of using the past, "the good old days", as a stick to beat the present', but this is insufficient to explain the particularly enduring association that mining communities have with the idea of solidarity. An alternative explanation offered by Benney is that mining and mining community life have little room in them for individualism. The legacy of the past that Benney (1978: 58) identifies is that '[t]he mining community . . . makes its demands on life *as* a community, and not as a collection of individuals' (emphasis in original), a tradition rooted in members' everyday interdependence. Without such foundations in everyday life, strikes could not have drawn upon the reserves of solidarity that they did.

Comparisons between the 1984–85 strike and earlier disputes in the coal industry are instructive. Williamson (1990: 249–52) refers to the strike of 1984–85 as 'the greatest industrial struggle people in Britain had ever known', and locates it in the tradition of conflicts pursued in the name of 'the values of solidarity, justice and community'. He cites a young miner's comment that the 1926 strike 'is something you never forget and is passed on from generation to generation' to drive home the point that mining communities have remarkably enduring collective memories. Alongside these echoes of former disputes are other aspects of the 1984–85 strike that made it different from the past, and Williamson suggests that 'the central role played in it by women' is prominent among these. Miners' wives had been actively involved in previous strikes (Leonard 1991; Gilbert 1992), but their contribution in 1984–85 gained a much higher profile: '[t]hrough their work in support groups, in communal kitchens and on the picket lines, many women expressed their solidarity with their men and organized the means through which communities could sustain themselves without pay and under conditions of great stress' (Williamson 1990: 252). In similar vein, Warwick and Littlejohn (1992: 170) report how women and the groups they formed were valued 'for their contribution to household and community survival'. They go on to note that the experience of participation in the strike was perceived by these women to have had a lasting impact on their lives: '[t]he women who had participated in support groups not only reported being more conscious politically, they also said they were more self-confident and more socially aware' (Warwick and Littlejohn 1992: 191). This echoes Leonard's (1991: 139) conclusion that '[t]he politicization of thousands of women was one of the most tangible, positive outcomes of the 1984–85 miners' strike', and the sense of change associated with this led a number of commentators to anticipate a permanent shift in the nature of solidarity in mining communities.

The 1984–85 strike may have acted as a catalyst for the expression of new forms of solidarity in which women played a more prominent role than they had in previous disputes, but these developments need to be placed in the context of wider social changes. The nineteenth-century legacy of patriarchal relations found in the Durham colliery villages described by Massey (1994: 193) in terms of 'male solidarity and female oppression' were being challenged long before the strike, not least because of the increased permeability of community boundaries. Inward geographical mobility has made settlements in mining areas more open, and mining communities have also been influenced by the growth of married women's paid work. As Warwick and Littlejohn (1992: 165) note, '[w]omen are now much more likely to have paid employment than in the early twentieth century, and this has an effect on the domestic division of labour'. These and other centrifugal forces have been in operation over a period of several decades, and the gradual loosening of the bonds that tied women to traditional domesticity were an indispensable precondition for the upsurge of community consciousness during the strike to take the form it did. Gibson-Graham's (1996: 208) critique of conventional '[a]nalyses that highlight the mercurial nature of miners' wives political behaviour as it moves between quiescence and intense activism' is relevant here because it emphasizes that many of the women's actions to which attention is drawn during strike periods are simply more visible expressions of the social support that is regularly given at other times. Strikes encourage community identities to crystallize, particularly where they involve 'flashpoints' that can be interpreted by those present as stereotypical confrontations between 'us' and 'them' (Waddington *et al.* 1989). Bauman (1992: xix) has noted that spontaneous eruptions of community solidarity, such as those that occur during industrial disputes, may be characterized by 'literally breath-taking intensity' at 'the moments of condensation', but he also points out that this level of identification with the group is difficult to sustain beyond the short term. The return to more routine expressions of solidarity once disputes are over is only to be expected.

The course of the 1984–85 strike and its aftermath varied considerably between different areas, although common patterns could be identified. Waddington and his colleagues found broad agreement that 'the dispute imbued the strikers and their supporters with an unforgettable sense of solidarity', which one of their respondents likened to being a member of 'a massive family, all pulling together'. In the years that followed 'the heightened sense of community generated during the course of the strike . . . dissipated' (Waddington *et al.* 1991: 49–50) and people reverted to more normal routines. There could be no straightforward reversion to the pre-strike order, however, particularly in districts in which the numbers of people employed in mining fell dramatically. Miners' frequent 'nostalgic references to a halcyon period when local youths were systematically recruited down the mine' served merely to emphasize the loss of the unifying effect that had been present when mining provided the main source of local employment. Youth unemployment constituted a particular problem to which moving away appeared to many people to offer the best solution, even if it did threaten to contribute to 'the disappearance of existing culture and tradition' (Waddington *et al.* 1991: 158, 162). The attraction of local culture and tradition in turn provides a reason why the young people on the margins of the labour market in areas formerly dominated by mining may be resistant to the idea of moving elsewhere. The respondents in Coffield and his colleagues' (1986: 142) study of young adults in North East England 'were proud of their origins and traditions, and had a genuine affection for their place of birth . . . They were so much a part of extensive social networks and local associations . . . that the quality of their lives would have been lowered by leaving'. In the longer term, the legacy of the past in former mining communities can be expected to wane, and Warwick and Littlejohn's (1992: 206) prediction is that 'local cultural capital . . . is likely to be eroded within a generation as the reality of coal mining as employment and that basis for social and political organisation disappears'. In the absence of this unifying force, the prospect of community fragmentation looms large.

The run-down of the coal industry in recent decades, expressed most dramatically in the steep fall in the number of miners employed (Fieldhouse and Hollywood 1999), has created numerous 'residual communities' (Taylor 1979) in which traditions outlast the conditions that gave them their rationale. Wight's research in the ex-mining village of 'Cauldmoss' in central Scotland found that the community 'had many of the characteristics Durkheim described as "mechanical solidarity" . . . where cohesion is based on the similarities between individuals and the common moral sentiments binding them together'. The power of the collective memory of the village's past was illustrated by the finding that '[m]ost locals were conscious of their mining legacy and even the young sometimes described themselves as mining folk'. Various features of mining culture survived the closure of local pits, including the status attached to activities (such as hard drinking) considered by local people to embody masculinity. Extensive kin ties gave a degree of plausibility to the claim made by some inhabitants that the community was 'almost one big family', imagery that was used to reinforce the idea that community members were friendly and cooperative but at the same time tight-knit and exclusive. Conversely, in-migrants were considered by established residents to pose a threat to 'the "integrity" of the village' (Wight 1993: 35, 31, 30), and one result of this was the reinforcement of the sense among the long-standing villagers that they shared a distinct identity rooted in the past. Such reinforcement of traditional identities can also come from other sources. Dicks and her colleagues drew this conclusion from their investigation into health, welfare and education service providers whose work brought them into contact with people in areas of declining mining employment. Interviews with doctors, social workers, teachers and related professionals revealed that 'the community of yesterday remained very much a reference point for their current assessments'. The way of life of mining communities was understood by these workers as one revolving around male breadwinners and female carers, and their 'assessments of the decline in community well-being turned on the loss of the family wage, previously provided by men'. Despite evidence that 'more and more women turn to paid work as the mining industry declines' (Dicks *et al.* 1998: 290, 291), there was little appreciation that this would be bound to have an adverse effect on their capacity to provide care and to service support networks in the wider community.

The conditions that made the solidarity of mining communities such a powerful force have been subject to increasingly rapid erosion in recent decades, but the culture continues to show resilience. Coal mining has long been vulnerable to changes in international market conditions (Beynon *et al.* 1991), and mining communities' solidarity reflects people's experience of the struggles to which that vulnerability exposed them. The solidarity was necessarily oppositional in character because miners were pitted against employers who themselves were well-organized as a class (Benwell Community Project 1978). The attempt to achieve a degree of order and predictability through the observation of traditions and their associated rituals also gave mining communities a conservative character that survives to some extent even after the closure of a pit (Bostyn and Wight 1987). Traditions continue to be influential as well in the alternative scenario of mines taken over and run by their workforces (Francis and Smith 1998; Waddington *et al.* 1998). Both situations in different ways confirm the existence of 'the deep-running and deeply-imbued mystique of coal mining to those involved in it' (Parker 1986: 194). This is captured in the words used by a miner from the Rhondda Valley, who described his job as 'a struggle against nature' that provided members of mining communities with 'a sense of a shared epic' (Seabrook 1978: 59). Yet while the rhetorical appeal of this tradition still carries weight, it is important, as Salaman (1986: 93) notes, to look beyond rhetoric to what he calls 'the problem of *capacity* – to the question of the power of groups to act in furtherance of their interests, as well as their willingness to do so' (emphasis in original). Comparisons with the situations of miners in other countries and workers in other industries have the potential to reveal the extent to which the characteristics of British mining communities are distinctive and how far similar patterns can be found among members of different occupational groups.

Mining solidarities in comparative perspective

Studies of mining in a number of countries confirm that the industry is strongly associated with solidarity and conflict, although not always in the same fashion. The combination of oppositional solidarity among workers and a male-dominated culture shaping family and community life has been found to be a feature of mining in Australia (Williams 1981), as has a growing self-confidence among women there to challenge their subordination (Gibson-Graham 1996). A somewhat different perspective is provided by Salaman's account of the introduction of new technology at Moonidih mine in Bihar, India, which identifies two groups of people involved in the operation whose solidarity with members of their respective groups and mutual mistrust of the other group are superficially reminiscent of the British experience of conflict between employers and workers. What makes the situation different is the fact that the two groups in question are the Indian coal company and the British manufacturers and consultants who supplied them with and advised them on the installation of the new technology. The relationship between the two groups was marked by 'distrust, solidarity and estrangement', because the different interests of the two groups led to assumptions about the untrustworthiness of the other party by both sides. Even though individuals could develop good working relationships across the divide, it was not possible for the two sides of the dispute to reach agreement about how best to understand the problem of coal production not reaching specified targets, let alone concur on how to resolve it. Both groups attributed motives to the other in terms of their interests, and distrust was fostered because these interests were understood to be in conflict. Salaman (1986: 71) concludes that the groups were 'locked into a pattern of unreciprocal dependence', the development of the dispute merely serving to reinforce each group's solidarity and their stereotyped understanding of the other group's shortcomings.

Solidarities associated with other occupational communities do not necessarily take on the character of those found in mining, although there are several interesting parallels. Differences are to be expected, given that mining communities (at least in their ideal-typical form) stand out because they fuse geographical separateness, an unusually high dependence on a single type of employment, and cultural distinctiveness. Put another way, it is exceptional for shared place, shared interests and shared identities to be meshed together to the extent that they are in mining. Salaman's (1974: 21) analysis of occupational communities takes this as a starting point, focusing on those aspects 'which are the result of features of members' work and not simply of the geographical isolation of the area . . . Some "true" occupational communities – such as those of fishermen or coalminers – sometimes also tend to involve geographical or spatial separation; but . . . they would occur without this'. This means that occupational communities can in principle be either 'cosmopolitan' or 'local', the former involving individuals who associate and identify with all others in their occupation, as opposed to the latter whose members' connections are more restricted to immediate work-mates. Architects and railwaymen are used respectively by Salaman to illustrate the contrast, and also to make the point that in both cases what was vital in holding people together was a shared culture: '[a]s a result of their shared commitment to an occupational culture, members of both occupations experienced feelings of solidarity and similitude with their occupational colleagues' (Salaman 1974: 104). These cultures embodied codes of behaviour that defined what it meant to be a good architect or a good railwayman, involving such characteristics as reliability, helpfulness, responsibility and trustworthiness. These were regarded as traits that established members had an obligation to nurture in people joining the group in order that they would perpetuate the group's common sense of identity.

Salaman's analysis emphasizes the point that the shared culture of an occupational community has a crucial bearing on the way in which its members express and pursue their common interests. His research among London fire service workers uncovered surprisingly little evidence of work groups seeking 'to advance their shared interests through *strategies* (which carry the impression of organized and far-sighted steps in pursuit of goals)'. There were stronger grounds to support the view that '[o]pposition is conducted at the level of language', that is, 'talk, muttering, gossip, theory' (Salaman 1986: 92, emphasis in original). Solidarity among firefighters was engendered and sustained to a significant extent by emotional appeals to the shared values and characteristics that (as they saw it) set them apart from others. Numerous similarities between the solidarity of firefighters and of miners can be identified, including the use of language to maintain group cohesion and to exclude others (Dennis *et al.* 1969). Both occupations involve workers in difficult and dangerous tasks that are undertaken by small teams whose members are necessarily interdependent. These teams are isolated in that they have relatively little contact with other teams or with managers, with whom there is nothing like the same amount of trust that exists among group members. Shift-working also enhances group solidarity, as does the homogeneity of members' backgrounds. Salaman (1986: 45–6) found that 'firemen, and fire officers, were remarkably homogeneous in social origins, previous occupational experience, social attitudes, and general social characteristics and culture, i.e. white, working class, often with a services background'. This homogeneity reflected past recruitment practices in which word of mouth between relatives, friends and neighbours more or less effectively closed off opportunities to 'outsiders'. The response of existing firefighters to an equal opportunities initiative designed to increase the numbers of female and ethnic minority members of the service was to reassert the 'traditions' of the culture, particularly those constructed around masculinity and 'fairness', and to portray the *status quo* as a situation of 'family-like' mutual supportiveness that change threatened to undermine. What stood out was the imagery of solidarity as the defence of a shared culture, rather than the calculation of how solidarity was necessary for the achievement of material benefits.

The general conclusion to which Salaman is led is that a division between 'them' and 'us' is a regular feature of workplace relationships, but that it is more unusual for this to develop into consciousness of broader class interests. On the basis of the cases he considers, he observes that 'the development of full-blown consciousness . . . is rare. What is more common is a lower order form of opposition'. Solidarity between workers is 'only rarely related to the *experience* of shared interests, and the *determination* to act to advance them' (Salaman 1986: 91, emphases in original). Where it does produce such outcomes it is quite possible that what will be promoted are sectional interests, with the result that workers may 'actually fragment class solidarity'. Echoing the point made by Weber about social closure that was discussed above in Chapter 1, Salaman (1986: 105–106) notes that 'exclusion strategies often involve attempts to exploit pre-existing social categories of low esteem, or low social prestige and power – the old, women, minority ethnic groups, immigrants, children'. Tilly and Tilly (1998: 80) add religion to this list of categorical distinctions, which are frequently used to exclude 'strangers' from work groups, having earlier argued that 'employers and senior workers build existing network boundaries by race, gender, or ethnicity into distinctions among jobs, while both male and female workers sustain same-sex solidarity by means of jokes, gossip, teasing, and sharing of personal styles on the job'. Pringle's (1989: 231) remark about how 'a group of women in, say, a typing pool may enjoy a certain group solidarity in bitching about outsiders' provides another illustration of how cohesion in the workplace can be contributed to by the deployment of informal cultural tactics. It also serves to show that solidarity among work groups is not the exclusive preserve of male employees working in dangerous occupations, although it is the case that the shared danger of miners, firefighters, construction workers and people working in maritime occupations has generated particular research interest among these groups (Applebaum 1984).

The longshoremen who work in the San Francisco docks are one such group, and David Wellman's (1995) study of them develops the argument that solidarity among workers can be particularly effective when built around the language of 'community'. The familiar distinction between 'us' and 'them' reminds dockworkers in the longshore community 'that loyalty and trust are important for the organization of opposition to domination' (p. 81). The language of workers being 'brothers' (p. 64) who constitute a 'fraternity' (p. 64), and of gang members being 'typically "family" for each other' (p. 104), is reminiscent of Tönnies's views on community as the embodiment of the values of kinship, but the echoes of Durkheim's work are just as strong in Wellman's observation that '[t]heir experience of community teaches San Francisco longshoremen to be moral, not just economic actors' (p. 308). The culture of 'doing the *right* thing, not the expedient thing . . . means thinking in terms of group, not individual, needs' (p. 305, emphasis in original), with the result that limitations are placed on how far people can follow 'the selfish principles of self-interest and me-first' (p. 305). Everyday working life is full of reminders that '[a]n injury to one is an injury to all' (p. 70) and '[n]one of us is smart as all of us' (p. 57), reinforcing members' sense of being part of a community in which the principles of liberty, equality, fraternity and reciprocity are understood to come as a package. In this way, solidarity extends across ethnic and racial divisions, because the experience of being part of this community teaches members that 'tolerance . . . is an especially necessary quality for fashioning unity and solidarity out of heterogeneity' (p. 81). The overall picture was summed up by Wellman's respondent who remarked '[w]e're part of a way of life . . . we're an emotional, economic and political entity' (p. 57). Wellman argues that class consciousness is clearly present within this occupational community, but that solidarity has to be seen as part of members' way of life and not something that can be separated out from the other aspects of their experience of community.

Approaching this issue from a more theoretical angle, Harris explores the reasons why occupational communities take the form that they do and links this to the discussion of how community relationships are connected to place. In his view, '[p]luralities of persons residing in the same place or having the same occupation are social *categories* . . . and the term community implies something more than category membership . . . to use the term "community" of territorial or occupational categories is to claim that their members share something in addition to their category membership' (Harris 1990b: 190, emphasis in original). Not all categories of people become communities in the sense that Harris is using the term, namely a group of people who develop 'a distinctive way of life on the basis of that category membership'. He suggests that such communities emerge through 'association', and that face-to-face interaction continues to be the most important form of association despite the scope for interaction between people in different places that the development of communications technology has brought. It follows that an individual's association with others will be likely to be dominated by 'persons the proximity of whose residence renders face-to-face interaction possible' (Harris 1990b: 191), that is, by those living nearby. Harris is careful to avoid suggesting a deterministic model to explain people's patterns of association; propinquity makes association possible, but on its own it will not generate meaningful interaction, let alone solidarity. In his earlier work with Rosser, Harris detailed how at the turn of the twentieth century the Morriston district of Swansea had conformed to the image of the traditional working-class community, 'small in scale, limited and narrow in its social horizons, homogeneous in its social composition, familiar and familistic, with a strong community consciousness generated by common residence and common necessity'. In addition to its inhabitants having where they lived in common, Morriston was also '[a] community . . . of work with the men engaged in identical or similar occupations, a community of worship in the chapels, a community of basic cultural uniformities in language, in housing and material possessions, and in moral values'. Taken together these various elements constituted 'a distinctive way of life' (Rosser and Harris 1965: 15–16).

By the 1960s, this situation had changed dramatically. What Rosser and Harris refer to as 'the Cohesive Society' had been replaced by 'the Mobile Society' in which the old ties were undermined by industrialization and geographical mobility. The account that they go on to develop differs from conventional 'loss of community' narratives in that the past is not mourned. They note that on the whole the change was positively welcomed by respondents, on the grounds that '[t]he cohesive society was stable and enduring and "people knew where they were", but it seems also to have been the stagnant society. It is simply out of date, for all its old-fashioned cultural virtues' (Rosser and Harris 1965: 299). Two decades later in South Wales, industrialization had been replaced by de-industrialization, and Harris's research against this background identified processes of social polarization akin to those reported by Warwick and Littlejohn (1992) in the Yorkshire mining communities that they studied. In place of broad adherence to 'the traditional pattern of social life focused on local communal institutions', it was primarily the unemployed and other disadvantaged groups that sought to preserve such arrangements, while the beneficiaries of economic restructuring were developing new modes of 'network maintenance and participation' constructed around altered senses of identity that set them apart from the traditional working class. The new situation is one in which 'club/pub, church/chapel and various forms of associational life' still exist as public institutions; what has changed is that they are no longer '*common* features of the networks of individuals' (Harris and Brown 1987a: 217, emphasis in original). The former situation fits Bauman's (1992: xix) description of 'Tönnies-type "communities by inertia" (communities that lingered effortlessly, as if merely by dint of physical proximity and absence of movement)', whereas contemporary conditions require individuals to be more active in the maintenance of their networks. Familiar patterns of community relationships appeared to be stronger in the affluent commuter villages, while unemployment was 'associated with the decline of communal sociability and reciprocal flows of aid which were once the very essence of working-class culture and solidarity' (Harris and Brown 1987b: 225). Rees's more recent account confirms that change has brought 'winners and losers'. Among the latter group, 'long-term unemployment has become a way of life not just for some individuals but for whole families and communities, particularly in the hard-hit south Wales valleys and in the farming communities of rural Wales' (Rees 1999: 5–6).

The contrast between traditional working-class communities of the past characterized by a geographically stable population sharing a common culture and the more fragmented social relationships of people living in an age of greater mobility has been taken up and developed in the literature concerned with the local impact of globalization. O'Byrne's (1997) findings in South London echo the conclusions reached by researchers in areas once dominated by mining, that people with fewer resources will lead lives constrained by locality, while it is the more affluent groups that are most able to take advantage of new opportunities for developing wider networks. His working-class respondents exhibited 'a fierce loyalty towards locality and community in Roehampton' (p. 74), often reinforced by 'nostalgic or imagined perceptions of solidarity' (p. 81). The 'limited world view' (p. 82) that he describes includes strong consciousness of 'us' and 'them', expressed through the distinction between 'insiders' and 'outsiders'. As he says, '[o]n the surface, we have a "traditional" community based on solidarity and locality' (p. 87), but it is a community that people might have reservations about joining. Among young people, for example, this culture requires physical presence and involvement, and anyone guilty of 'spending too much time away from the centre of activities' (p. 83) risks exclusion by being branded 'no longer truly "one of us" because the estate no longer dominates that person's social activities' (p. 83). Newcomers to the area whose position in global middle-class and ethnic minority networks makes them less dependent on, or attracted to, the 'cultural capital' of established residents are more cosmopolitan than local in their outlook, and relations between the two groups are, O'Byrne suggests, as likely to be marked by conflict as by solidarity.

Whether their arguments are couched in terms of de-industrialization, globalization or some other broad trend, the general conclusion that emerges from the findings of Harris, O'Byrne and many other researchers into community change is that the balance of locals and cosmopolitans is bound to change over time. Writing long before anyone had coined the terms 'de-industrialization' and 'globalization', Homans put forward the view that it has always been the case that 'cohesion has been achieved at a price. Intelligent men have always found small-town life dull, and the internal solidarity of the group has implied a distrust and hatred of outsiders' (1951: 454). His study of the small New England settlement of 'Hilltown' identified a number of processes leading to 'social disintegration', and their cumulative effect was 'centrifugal rather than centripetal' (p. 360). Among these processes were the process of secularization whereby the controlling influence of the churches declined, the opening up of communications with other places, the spread of the individualistic culture within which every person was encouraged to 'make something of himself' (p. 359), and the growth in household self-reliance as a result of which 'the need for neighbors to work together became much less than it had been' (p. 359). The decline in 'mutual good feeling' (p. 361) (and also in 'mutual bad feeling') (p. 361) and the growth of 'indifference' between the town's residents over the hundred years to 1945 simply reflected the fact that Hilltowners had progressively less to do with each other and had by the time of Homans's study ceased to be, 'except in the most trivial sense, a community at all' (p. 367). Homans attributed this change to 'civilization' (p. 367), and regarded it as problematic only if other institutions than the local community failed to generate the social support that it once provided.

Rayside's research in the small Canadian town of Alexandria provides an interesting contrast to Homans's earlier study. Carrying out his investigations a generation later than Homans in a broadly comparable environment, Rayside might have been expected to find that the disintegration of community relationships had proceeded further. Several bases of fragmentation could be identified, including social divisions along class lines and between French and English speakers. Counteracting these centrifugal forces were centripetal forces that offset their fragmentary momentum and generated cohesion. One of these related to family connections, it being the case that 'most who remain have elaborate kinship ties within the town and surrounding countryside' (Rayside 1991: 291). Another related to the links that existed between the various occupational communities in the town, and a third factor was the enduring influence of local culture. In addition to these internal relationships, Rayside notes that the sense of community among the town's residents is influenced by their relationship of dependency with the institutions of the wider society: 'Alexandria's subordination to distant authorities . . . generates a certain cohesion in the community, as well as a reluctance to "rock the boat" in any way' (Rayside 1991: 292). Dependence on government and on local employers who could move their operations elsewhere 'reinforces a form of protective solidarity . . . There is a strong sense of "we" and "they" in the town residents' perception of their relationship to the outside world, one that not only encourages the development of a sense of community, but also marginalizes protest and mutes open division' (Rayside 1991: 293). A similar observation is contained in Dempsey's (1990: 268) analysis of the 'Smalltown' community in Australia, where workers 'are not looking to engage in any collective action that may frighten away existing employers or discourage new ones to start up a business'. This ties in with Dempsey's more general observation that the extent to which communities are characterized by solidarity is something over which their members have no more than partial control.

Communities are bounded but they are not isolated entities. Dempsey's remarks on this point are apposite: 'a local social system is neither self-generating nor self-perpetuating; it is an integral part of the wider society; it is in close contact with that society; and it is greatly influenced by the structures, ideas and values of that society' (Dempsey 1992: 251). The same point applies to other communities besides those that are place-based, such as the occupational communities that exist among middle-class professional groups, the collective organization and identity of which cannot be understood without reference to their relationship to the State (Savage *et al.* 1992). Dickens notes that the wider connections of members of middle-class communities also include those fostered by their 'extensive memberships . . . in, for example, sporting, charitable, educational and political associations' and that the State has also been instrumental in the promotion of informal relations of this sort that can be identified as integral parts of 'civil society'. Dickens defines 'civil society' as 'the range of social and collective activities outside paid work', and he argues that it is in the sphere of civil society rather than in the sphere of employment that 'some of the most basic social relations are now being contested between groups with fundamentally opposed views about how contemporary society should be organised'. In contrast to the essentially defensive solidarities of traditional working-class communities discussed earlier in this chapter, Dickens suggests that civil society is a realm of diverse social movements whose members are seeking 'to generate a degree of social transformation'. Civil society can be described as 'a relatively malleable area of social life' (Dickens 1988: 129, 3) within which new social movements can challenge rather than defend traditions. These social movements are characterized by a distinct sort of solidarity in which people come together through an active engagement with the *status quo*, and they often cultivate a broad appeal through the development of a programme that is 'amenable to idiosyncratic interpretation by the members in the light of their own circumstances and experiences' (Cohen 1985: 108). Of all the examples that are available to illustrate the distinctive features of this form of solidarity, the one selected as the focus of the next chapter is the movement that adopted the word as its name: *Solidarnosc*.

5

The solidarity of *Solidarity*

Introduction

Social solidarity can take many forms, but the Polish *Solidarity* movement is arguably the most dramatic expression of its potential to effect change and of the difficulty of embodying it in sustainable institutional arrangements. *Solidarity* has been referred to as 'one of the biggest social movements to have stirred a country at the end of the twentieth century' (Touraine *et al.* 1983: 2), 'the most impressive and significant working-class movement of our period' (Barker 1986: 7), and even 'the greatest political movement of modern history' (Sztompka 1999: 157). Perhaps the most remarkable feature of its rise, survival in the face of attempted suppression, electoral success and subsequent loss of power is the speed with which this sequence of events took place. Within a matter of months from its inception in the summer of 1980, the movement grew to a point at which it had 10 million members (inclusion of members of *Rural Solidarity* took the figure to 12 million) and could call on support from three-quarters of the country's workforce (Lane 1996; Zirakzadeh 1997). The declaration of martial law in December 1981 required 'the most extensive internal military operation in Polish history' (Ekiert 1996: 257), but this attempt to suppress the *Solidarity* movement failed and in the process served to highlight the limits of state power in the state socialist system. As disillusion with the Soviet model of economic and social development set in and increasing numbers of people within eastern Europe came to regard the system as 'the future that failed' (Arnason 1993), so the prospect of post-communist arrangements emerged more explicitly onto the political agenda. Even so, neither the scale of the success of *Solidarity* in the 1989 elections nor the rapid collapse of the communist regime was anticipated (Kowalik 1994), and accession to power deepened divisions within the movement that shared opposition to the communist authorities had formerly held in check. *Solidarity* can be regarded as a prime illustration of Ray's (1996: 205) more general observation that '[t]he social movement organizations that appeared in later communism were perhaps what Weber called *Schicksalsgemeinschaften* (communities of fate), retaining little cohesion once their common enemy was vanquished'. Deep bitterness and animosity grew up between former partners, and the history of the *Solidarity* movement confirms Weber's (1978: 28) remark that 'a political relationship once based on solidarity may develop into a conflict of interests' and also to conflicting subjective interpretations of that relationship.

The fragmentation of *Solidarity* into warring factions is one of a number of ways in which the movement's history is marked by paradox. Besides the point that the movement came to be characterized more by strife than by the solidarity that its name proclaimed, there is the paradoxical nature of workers challenging a communist political party that claimed to rule on their behalf. The Polish United Workers' Party had been founded in 1947 but had in the intervening period become increasingly detached from its nominal constituency. The further paradox exists that trade union members who had been instrumental in challenging the state socialist system were prominent among the groups subsequently to lose out. *Solidarity* exemplifies the way in which 'trade unions were at the frontline of change' (Frydman *et al*. 1998: 79), only to see their interests marginalized and their vision of an alternative society pushed to one side. Prominent among these trade unionists were groups like the shipyard workers of Gdansk, 'the workers of the largest industrial enterprises, those most obsolete dinosaurs of the failed communist industrialization, least capable of entering the dream of Europe and marked for extinction' (Bauman 1992: 162). There is also something paradoxical about the way in which the attempts to suppress *Solidarity* during the period of martial law had the unintended effect of pushing some of its leaders in the direction of free market economics. Following their arrest and detention, leaders of the movement 'were prohibited from working in state-owned enterprises. To survive, they formed independent businesses during the 1980s. Rewarded for their own entrepreneurial skills and constantly thinking about market conditions, they were gradually transformed into bourgeois theorists' (Zirakzadeh 1997: 154). The thesis that these leaders betrayed the rank and file members of the *Solidarity* movement is a widely held one, but it does need to be noted in this context that there were from the outset differences of opinion about the movement's objectives and the most appropriate tactics to use to achieve them. The Gdansk strikers in 1980 identified their position as one of 'Solidarity and Prudence' (Zirakzadeh 1997: 135) and 'prudence' was one of the *Solidarity* leader Lech Walesa's watchwords (Ascherson 1982: 23). This indicates that even in the earliest stages of the movement, there were important differences of opinion about what course of action to pursue. As the movement developed and incorporated increasingly diverse constituencies, so the potential for fragmentation also grew, and the history of the post-communist period is dominated by the forces holding members together being overwhelmed by other forces leading to the disintegration of the movement.

All sorts of comparisons and contrasts have been made between the *Solidarity* movement and social movements in other countries, with diverse conclusions drawn about the capacity of such movements to effect or to resist change. Therborn has drawn a parallel between the defensiveness of the British miners and *Solidarity*'s trade union objectives, arguing that both 'fought for basically the same things, certain short-term protective devices in a world where bosses were not trusted'. The different outcomes of the 1984–85 miners' strike in Britain, defeated by the Thatcher government, and of the failure of martial law in Poland to suppress *Solidarity*, meant that '[t]he admiration which a number of frustrated Polish officials of the 1980s had for Mrs Thatcher is understandable' (Therborn 1995: 328). Admiration for Thatcher was also subsequently expressed by Walesa following his conversion to the case for the privatization of state-run enterprises (Zirakzadeh 1997). There are further echoes of the history of Britain's miners in the observation that '[t]he men and women who in the socialist past worked in the coal pits of Siberia and eastern Ukraine, the shipyards of Poland's Baltic Sea, the steel mills of Slovakia – depending on one another to survive – often had no choice but to learn community' (Frydman *et al*. 1998: 78). The extent to which these ties to each other have survived the closure of the factories and pits around which the communities grew up is one indicator of how successful *Solidarity* and related movements were in fostering sustainable networks of informal social relationships referred to by many analysts as 'civil society'. According to Keane's (1998: 22) analysis of *Solidarity*, '[i]ts ultimate goal was the cultivation of solidarity among a plurality of self-governing civil associations capable of pressurising the state from without and enabling various groups to attend peacefully to their non-state affairs'. A degree of tension was bound to be generated by the development of civil society within a state socialist system built around centralized political and economic control, but the way in which this tension was played out varied significantly from one country to another. Misztal and Jenkins (1995) and Elster *et al*. (1998) suggest that the comparison of Poland and Hungary reveals how the configuration of the economic and political dimensions of reform was crucial in determining the outcome of the transition to post-communism. Other writers attach greater importance to different national traditions, for example the strength of romanticism in Poland (Wesolowski 1995), and Arnason (1993) cautions against drawing general conclusions about civil society from the case of *Solidarity* because of the uniqueness of Poland's circumstances. As well as having relevance to the debate about the role of civil society in the transition to post-communism, *Solidarity* has also been discussed in relation to the question of the capacity of trade union movements to achieve their objectives without direct involvement in political activity. The combination of political and economic demands has been found throughout the industrializing world, albeit with diverse results (Kilminster 1992). This comparison is given particular relevance by the fact that Poland's history of economic weakness and international indebtedness and dependence played a key role in the emergence of the social forces that were to create *Solidarity*.

The rise of *Solidarity*

The mercurial rise of the *Solidarity* movement has been widely acknowledged as a remarkable sequence of events, which, like the collapse of state socialism to which it contributed, occurred in ways that were more or less unexpected. The immediate background to the emergence of the movement was a series of strikes in the summer of 1980 in a range of enterprises and regions across Poland. One of these enterprises, the Lenin Shipyard in Gdansk on Poland's Baltic coast, was to become the focal point of this wave of popular protest against the government's austere industrial and economic policies and the negative stance it adopted in relation to political opponents. The plans for this particular strike had been laid at a small gathering of 'a dozen or so local workers and intellectuals' (Zirakzadeh 1997: 127), but the demands made by the strikers and the tactics used to secure them rapidly became radicalized as the conflict with the authorities unfolded and new elements were drawn in. Included among these was Walesa, who had been sacked from the shipyard in 1976 and who quickly established himself as the leader of the strikers. Workers' initial demands for the reinstatement of a more recently sacked worker, Anna Walentynowicz, together with a pay rise, were extended to the demand for 'free trade unions, independent of the party' and redress for a number of other broad grievances. These 'Twenty One Demands' were issued on 17 August, only 3 days after the occupation of the shipyard by the workers had commenced and barely a week after Walentynowicz's sacking.

The extended demands struck a chord with workers in other parts of the country, and exactly one month later a meeting in Gdansk of delegates from thirty-eight Inter-Factory Founding Committees founded 'The Independent, Self-Governing Trade Union Solidarity'. This union 'already had promises of membership from 3,000,000 people in 3,500 factories. By November Solidarity had 7,500,000 members, and by June 1981 the figure was 9,486,000, which constituted 70 per cent of all workers in the social (i.e. state) sector of the economy' (Fowkes 1995: 158, 160). By the end of November 1981, *Solidarity* 'represented 10 million workers in more than 8,000 enterprises' (Zirakzadeh 1997: 139). Efforts to establish a counterpart organization in the countryside for independent farmers, *Rural Solidarity*, were met by police violence against *Solidarity* activists in Bydgoszcz, but despite this and the fragile nature of the unity between them 'the farmers' Solidarity and several smaller farmers unions represented a considerable social force with 3.5 million members' (Ekiert 1996: 241). *Solidarity*'s membership figures dwarfed those of the Communist Party, which had peaked at around 3 million in 1980 (Sułek 1992: 249). *Solidarity*'s aim had not been to seize control of the state, but the challenge it posed to the existing order was taken by the authorities to be so serious that, within 15 months of the movement coming into existence, martial law had been declared, justified by those who introduced it on the questionable grounds that 'extremists . . . were misusing Solidarity for political ends' (Ascherson 1982: 278). This was the prelude to the attempted 'abolition' of *Solidarity* by the government the following October, a measure that proved impossible to enforce. The rest of the 1980s was characterized by further political and economic manoeuvring for advantage that culminated in what Sztompka (1999: 159) refers to as 'the sweeping electoral triumph of Solidarity in June 1989' and the subsequent post-communist transformation.

The course taken during the rise of the *Solidarity* movement could not have been anticipated, not least because of the speed with which events unfolded. As Pelczynski (1988: 363) has said, '[t]he suddenness must be strongly emphasised'. At the same time as noting that developments moved faster and further than previous experience of pressure for change in the Soviet bloc had led observers to expect, some form of eruption of oppositional forces was predictable. In the context of the economic crisis and widespread scepticism over the government's claims to legitimacy that characterized Polish society in 1980, the traditions of popular protest that had been developed during that country's three decades of state socialism were bound to be drawn upon in one way or another. Older traditions of thought and action also fed into the process, for example ideas rooted in Roman Catholicism, romanticism and nationalism. Wesolowski (1995: 113) has described what he calls 'the Solidarity ethos' as an outlook 'focused on certain fundamental values . . . [that] included national independence, human dignity, societal solidarity and fair industrial relations'. Polish nationalism had for several centuries been a channel through which antipathy towards the country's larger and more powerful neighbours could be expressed. Popular dissatisfaction with the ruling party was intimately connected to anti-Russian feeling because of the role that the Soviet Union had played in establishing Poland's communist regime in the aftermath of the Second World War. The strong position of the Roman Catholic Church in Poland had similarly deep roots, and the uneasy relationship between church and state became more tense with the visit to his homeland of Pope John Paul II in the summer of 1979, which provided an inspiration to 'thousands of opponents of the regime' (Zirakzadeh 1997: 121). Nationalism and religion ran alongside what Wesolowski (1995: 112) calls Poland's communitarian tradition of thought, which 'insists that society is, or should be, bound together by the principles of cooperation, mutual aid and the organized provision of basic goods for every member of the society'. Ordinary Poles' experiences of the realities of state socialism ran counter to this tradition of solidarity. By 1980, it had become increasingly apparent that difficulties in relation to any one of a range of issues could provide a spark to ignite a wider conflagration.

According to Touraine and his colleagues, *Solidarity* was born as a result of three forces coming together in Gdansk and another of Poland's Baltic ports, Szczecin: 'the demands of the workers, the affirmation of national identity and a call for democracy and free political expression' (Touraine *et al.* 1983: 51). The background to each of these forces is worthy of consideration to place the events of 1980 in context. Workers were central to the state's claims to legitimacy as the name of the ruling party indicated, and they were also crucial in the plans for the country's industrialization strategy. More than half of the workforce had been employed in agricultural production in 1950, but successive phases of development shifted the balance of the economy in favour of the industrial sector (Zirakzadeh 1997). The expansion of industrial activity was biased towards large state-run enterprises, and by the 1980s two-thirds of the country's industrial workers worked in enterprises that employed over a thousand people (Barker 1986). The Lenin Shipyard had 17,000 employees, for example (Ascherson 1982). Ironically, the large scale of these enterprises facilitated the organization of workers independently of official trade union channels, and at various moments of economic difficulty in the country's history strikes by urban workers were effective in securing the reversal of cuts in their standard of living. The availability of affordable food was a particularly important issue in 1956, when 'as tens of thousands of workers in Poznań marched through the city's streets, they shouted "We want to eat" and "we want bread for our children"' (Zirakzadeh 1997: 102). Food was again a flashpoint in 1970 and 1976 when price increases of staples such as meat and sugar were announced. The strong interconnections of town and country made it difficult to pursue the classic communist policy of squeezing the rural sector to bestow privileges on industrial workers, and instead the authorities placed their faith in their ability to create rising living standards through economic growth based on foreign loans. For a time in the early 1970s this policy appeared to be paying off, as Poland's gross national product grew by 10 per cent a year on average, but it was unsustainable. Foreign debt rose astronomically from $100 million in 1971 to $6 billion in 1975, $17 billion by the end of 1979 and $23 billion by the end of 1980 (Zirakzadeh 1997). The capacity of the authorities to buy off the workforce by rising living standards financed through borrowing had reached its limits.

The prominence of economic objectives in the initial *Solidarity* programme is unsurprising. Against a background of economic difficulties, the nascent trade union was bound to attach special importance to workers' pay, rights and conditions of work. More explicitly political demands were initially not given the same priority, and it was only later that *Solidarity* 'developed into a political opposition' (Lane 1996: 66). Fear of Soviet military intervention that would reassert the dominance of hard-line communist authorities was a major reason why there was caution about making direct challenges to the regime's right to exist, given that this had happened on other occasions (most famously in Hungary in 1956 and Czechoslovakia in 1968). The movement's leaders exercised a degree of restraint on the unfolding events of 1980–81, reflecting the fact that 'a majority of the national leaders of Solidarity opposed any violent or militant action that Soviet leaders might construe as anarchistic' (Zirakzadeh 1997: 137). These pragmatists were nevertheless not in complete control of the movement's development, and various indications of the strength of nationalist feeling surfaced. *Solidarity*'s first national Congress, which met in Gdansk in September 1981 against the backdrop of Soviet fleet manoeuvres offshore, published an open letter to Poles living abroad that declared 'Solidarity is not only a trade union, but also a social movement of thinking citizens wishing to work for Poland's independence' (Touraine *et al.* 1983: 140). The delegates also identified among the movement's aims the goals of promoting 'the moral rebirth of the people' in order 'to rebuild a just Poland' (Zirakzadeh 1997: 145). *Solidarity* thus had 'the aspect of a moral crusade', grounded in the widely held view of Communism as 'evil in so far as it violated the national, pluralistic and Catholic traditions of the country' (Pelczynski 1988: 372). Pope John Paul II's statement, made during his 1979 pilgrimage to the country, that '[t]he future of Poland will depend on how many people are mature enough to be non-conformists' (quoted in Ash 1983: 29), reinforced these sentiments. More generally, his visit revitalized the public mood, not least through the crowds' experience of a sense of their collective strength and wider purpose, reflected in their greater preparedness to criticize the authorities. According to Sztompka (1999: 157), '[t]here was a tremendous outburst of national pride, religious emotion, and interpersonal solidarity. The quality of trust found so far only within the close networks of family and friends extended to wide segments of the population'. Surveys indicated that the Church 'was the institution in which Poles "placed most trust"' (Lewis 1983: 450) and that there was a corresponding distrust of the party and state.

Like the two other forces identified by Touraine and his colleagues as contributing to the rise of *Solidarity*, pressure for the democratization and liberalization of the political system had also been building for some time. Zirakzadeh (1997: 116) notes that '[t]he ongoing warfare between workers and the party-state – especially the strike waves of 1956–58, 1970, and 1976 – played a key role in the political education of the future leaders of Solidarity'. For example, Walesa's membership of a strike committee at the Lenin shipyard in 1970 gave him first-hand experience of the wiliness of the authorities in negotiations, while the future vice president of *Solidarity*, Stanisław Wadołowski, recalled how he had been politicized by the street fighting that accompanied the Szczecin strike in the same year. More generally, it was the case that 'the strikes of 1970 and 1976 were etched on the collective memory of Poland's proletariat' (Zirakzadeh 1997: 115), again echoing a theme of the previous chapter's discussion of British miners. Political opposition also developed among intellectuals, who were becoming increasingly disenchanted with attempting to change the system from within. Their desire for greater freedom of expression gave them common ground with workers attempting to extend their rights to strike and organize independently, and the Workers' Defence Committee that they founded together in 1976 grew from small beginnings into a powerful force for change. As a result of such collaboration, '[b]onds of trust were gradually and informally built between workers and intellectuals' (Zirakzadeh 1997: 127). In contrast to this growth in trust among the various opposition groups, the state itself 'became the object of deepest distrust. It was seen as a foreign imposed power oppressing the nation, as an atheist conspiracy suppressing religion, and as a greedy employer exploiting the workforce' (Sztompka 1999: 157–8). Separate actions by various opponents of the regime might be defused more or less effectively as they had in the past, but the prospect of concerted pressure for change by a united movement promised to move developments onto another plane.

The fact that *Solidarity* developed as a loose confederation of numerous different groups was both a strength and a weakness. The common ground of its members was their shared dissatisfaction with the existing state of affairs in the country and their understandable desire to see improvements. The principles affirmed at *Solidarity*'s first national Congress were inclusive, given that a large majority of the population could be expected to be '*against* injustice, *against* abuses of power, *against* monopolisation of the right to speak in the name of the nation, *against* a state that treats its citizens as its own property, *against* workers lacking means of their own defence, *against* leaders able to decide how much freedom their subjects should have, *against* rewards for political obedience, *against* duplicity in national life and *against* the squandering of the results of the nation's hard work'. The other side of this agenda lay in being '*for* a just Poland, *for* respect for the person, *for* a state that serves rather than dominates people, that is not monopolised by a single party, and that really belongs to the whole nation, *for* labour that corresponds to human needs and that is for the whole people' (Barker 1986: 115, emphases in original). These worthy but vague sentiments were recognized to contain elements that appealed to a wide variety of constituencies, and the document produced by the Congress acknowledged that the movement embraced 'many social currents'. Put another way, 'Solidarity's first official programme was not very coherent. It can perhaps be described as a quilt of clashing colours. Almost all factions at the congress had their ideas mentioned. The result was an often inconsistent-sounding document' (Zirakzadeh 1997: 145). In the space of a year, the movement had expanded its agenda as well as its membership, but it embraced contradictory goals as well as conflicting ideas about how to bring about change. The fact that its 10 million members included one million from the ruling party (Pryce-Jones 1996: 195) was indicative of its eclectic character. The movement's growing heterogeneity reinforced the 'endless process of negotiation and cross-fertilisation among factions with different values and beliefs' (Zirakzadeh 1997: 130) that had characterized its development from the outset.

The decentralized nature of the movement was a prized and jealously guarded feature of *Solidarity*. This reflected the movement's origins. The workers who occupied their shipyard in Gdansk in August 1980 had in less than a fortnight prompted workers in 380 local factories and other enterprises to follow their lead; by the end of the month the figure had reached over 600, plus another 130 factories in Szczecin and miners elsewhere. The spirit of the Gdansk workers was captured in the newsletter that activists circulated to publicize the unfolding drama, the logo of which 'was simply the word *Solidarity* written in red (the traditional symbolic colour in Europe for workers' struggles) with the letters evocatively leaning against one another, as if they were a group of people engaged in helping and encouraging'. The logo went on to emblazon the posters, banners, badges and other insignia of groups across the country. Its popularity can be explained by the fact that 'it connoted mutual aid, strength through unity, and the possibility of an alternative to the current practices of state domination and citizen subordination' (Zirakzadeh

1997: 134). It also suggested a marching crowd, and had further connotations of national unity through the choice of the same colours as the national flag, red and white (Laba 1991). By the end of November 1980, *Solidarity*'s organizational structure had been established, whereby '[t]he union was designed as a federation of largely autonomous regional chapters coordinated by the National Coordinating Committee'. Ekiert's (1996: 239–40) description of this as 'a huge, well-designed organizational structure possessing massive human and material resources as well as a massive and disciplined following, supported by all segments of society' is at odds with other accounts in which the bases for various tensions within the movement are highlighted. Lewis (1993: 295), for example, notes that *Solidarity* was a movement wedded to the idea of direct democracy, 'unmediated mass participation in political life', and one that was valued precisely because it had developed 'outside and in opposition to the bureaucratized power structures which spread throughout the communist system'. Channelling the widespread resentment against the state into a dialogue with those holding the reins of state power was bound to be difficult for a movement whose members had been brought together by disappointment with and hostility towards the communist world view and who were motivated by 'the spirit of "anti-politics"'. In other words, *Solidarity* 'triggered off ambitions that elsewhere looked more like idle utopias' (Bauman 1992: 161), and it is against this backcloth that subsequent dissatisfaction with the movement's achievements must be seen.

The 'many social currents' within the *Solidarity* movement included several that widened the agenda well beyond the establishment of an independent trade union. White-collar workers sought 'a new economic system in which elected workers' councils would make workplace policies, replacing the incompetent party functionaries' (Zirakzadeh 1997: 137). Others strove for a broad coalition of oppressed social groups within a national umbrella body. The strikes in the summer of 1980 had generated 'an unusual display of inter-class solidarity' in which 'striking workers expressed their concern about the deprivations of other segments of society: intellectuals, office workers, students, and peasants' (Misztal and Jenkins 1995: 330–1). This had paved the way for long-standing intellectual critics of the regime such as Karol Modzelewski and Jacek Kuroń to participate in the foundation of *Solidarity* (Fowkes 1995), as well as for the emergence of organizations like *Rural Solidarity*. In addition to disagreements about what they were seeking to achieve that such a diverse coalition inevitably threw up, *Solidarity*'s members were divided over the best strategy to adopt in dealings with the authorities. The cautious and pragmatic approach to negotiations with representatives of the state that was followed by leaders like Walesa and other self-styled 'realists' (Ash 1983) was a source of frustration to more radical elements of the movement that sought faster progress towards the achievement of their objectives. In turn, Walesa and like-minded leaders felt that their credibility as 'responsible' figures at the head of a self-disciplined organization would be undermined by frequent recourse to strikes or threats of strikes. The Catholic Church also had a moderating influence on *Solidarity*, for example through the advice proffered by Cardinal Wyszyński, whose favourite motto was 'not everything at once' (Pelczynski 1988: 373).

Divisions of opinion over whether to cooperate with or to continually challenge the party-state, and over the related question of how to determine the mandate of the leaders in their discussions, were already serious before the issues were resolved by the imposition of martial law at the end of 1981. Blue-collar workers remained sceptical of proposals for factory self-management that originated with white-collar workers, and were fearful that it might lead to 'the self-exploitation of the workers' (Touraine *et al.* 1983: 125). Morale was sapped by the resignation of prominent leaders such as Modzeleweski over disagreements with Walesa's mode of conducting negotiations. Disillusion also set in among ordinary *Solidarity* members whose economic situation had not improved (but was on the contrary deteriorating). Their expressions of protest such as hunger marches by and large went unsupported by their national leaders, who were concerned not to provoke the authorities. There was also dissatisfaction that only two of the twenty-one demands of a year before had been achieved in full (Zirakzadeh 1997). It was all too apparent that 'the government refused to accept Solidarity as a partner', and the appointment in October of General Jaruzelski as the country's new leader signalled the adoption of a more uncompromising stance on their part. The mood of disillusion among *Solidarity* members helps to explain why, when martial law was declared, '[r]esistance to the coup was far weaker than expected' and 'the majority of Poles returned to silence and withdrew from public life' (Fowkes 1995: 165, 167–8). The Catholic Church's call for calm also contributed to this outcome, as did *Solidarity*'s 'ethos of a nonviolent struggle' (Ekiert 1996: 266). The *Solidarity* movement proved unable to coordinate opposition to Jaruzelski, and the scene was set for a war of attrition in which the movement survived the attempt to suppress it but was in the process transformed. During the period of martial law, '[t]he once-mighty Solidarity . . . was reduced to small local resistance groups putting out clandestine publications and endlessly feuding over goals and tactics' (Zirakzadeh 1997: 149), as might be expected in a situation characterized by mutual suspicion rather than trust (Sztompka 1999). Martial law was lifted in 1983, but it took several more years before all of the various repressive measures with which it had been associated had been removed, and the re-legalization of *Solidarity* did not take place until 1988. These years of repression took their toll. Efforts to re-capture the momentum of the first 15 months of *Solidarity* were subsequently to enjoy some success, but in ways quite different to those that had been envisaged when the movement had been founded.

The fragmentation of *Solidarity*

The course of events leading to *Solidarity*'s triumph in the 1989 elections and the subsequent transition to post-communism was a tortuous one. Following its re-legalization in April 1988, membership of *Solidarity* grew to 2 million by 1990 (Etzioni-Halevy 1993), but this was a far cry from the situation at the start of the 1980s, when 'most of the industrial workers, most of the private farmers, most of the humanistic intelligentsia and most of the students belonged to or supported Solidarity or one of its allied organizations' (Pelczynski 1988: 370). More important than the question of numbers was the fact that *Solidarity* now stood for a radically different programme from that which had been championed in 1980–81. The movement had undergone 'slow regrouping and revival' (Sztompka 1999: 158), during the course of which the gap between those who brooked no compromise with the regime and those who saw cooperation as the best way forward became unbridgeable. One of the reasons for this polarization into opposing camps was the conversion of leading figures in the latter group to the case for a market economy. As Zirakzadeh (1997: 153) has noted, '[b]y 1988 most of Solidarity's national leaders were extolling free market economies and had jettisoned earlier goals of factory councils, a powerful trade union that would help the state make economic policies, and other visions of an alternative to both the Soviet command-economy and western capitalism'. This shift in orientation was justified by those who adopted it on pragmatic grounds. The Polish economy had continued to founder. By 1988, the country's international debt had grown to $39 billion, while real wages had declined by 20 per cent over the decade. The country's international trade had also been re-oriented, so that by 1989 the majority was conducted with trading partners in the advanced capitalist countries rather than with other state socialist partners (Fowkes 1995).

The disastrous performance of the Polish economy also convinced those in charge of the party-state of the need for reform, as did the steep decline in party membership. Young workers were particularly prominent among the mass exodus from the party that took place during the early 1980s, when a million members left. By the later 1980s, membership had fallen to a little over 2 million, further weakening the regime's legitimacy (Fowkes 1995). Change elsewhere in Eastern Europe provided an additional spur to reform-oriented members of the communist party's leadership, with the result that by the late 1980s pressure from moderate *Solidarity* leaders for 'round-table' talks was pushing on an open door. Walesa's response to the wave of strikes that took place in 1988 was to argue 'that by returning to work and temporarily accepting low wages, striking workers could facilitate long-term economic reforms that would benefit all Poles' (Zirakzadeh 1997: 156). This stance strengthened the possibility of power-sharing between the communist authorities and Walesa's group of *Solidarity* moderates, but it also intensified the struggle with what Misztal and Jenkins (1995: 331) call 'a new generation of younger, more radical activists' who sought to steer the movement in a different direction. A number of these 'withdrew from Walesa's increasingly market-oriented Solidarity and established their own rival labour organizations, among which were those evocatively named Workers Group, Fighting Solidarity, and Solidarity '80', by which they indicated that they 'declared themselves the genuine descendants of pre-martial-law Solidarity' (Zirakzadeh 1997: 154, 155). This process of fragmentation was to go much further after the election of a *Solidarity* government, but it is important to note that it pre-dated the movement's coming to power.

The agreement between General Jaruzelski's regime and *Solidarity* regarding the latter's participation in the June 1989 elections stacked the odds against the eventual outcome. The proportion of seats in the new Polish parliament for which *Solidarity*'s candidates could run was restricted by reserving the majority of seats in the Sjem, the more powerful of the parliament's two chambers, for the communist party and its traditional allies like the United Peasant Party. The timing of the elections was also inauspicious for *Solidarity* because it gave their candidates little opportunity to prepare, but despite having none of the institutional advantages of their established opponents the *Solidarity*-sponsored Citizens' Committees won all but one of the seats available to them. Poland thus became 'the first communist regime actually to collapse' (Lewis 1997: 404). In the light of the fact that *Solidarity* had 'overwhelmingly won the elections, drawing support from a broad cross-section of industrial workers, peasants, the urban middle class, and Catholics' (Misztal and Jenkins 1995: 331), the communists' former partners deserted them and the way was opened for a non-communist government in which *Solidarity* members would play the leading role. Despite not having run for office himself, Walesa used his influence to ensure that his preferred candidate for prime minister, Tadeusz Mazowieck, headed a broadly based coalition government that included communists but which had pro-market *Solidarity* members in most of its key positions (Zirakzadeh 1997). As a result, '[t]he real force in the government was Solidarity; the programme was Solidarity's; and the policy was the progressive dismantling of the communist system of control over the state and the economy' (Fowkes 1995: 180).

This government's assessment of the situation was that radical measures were required to reverse the continuing deterioration in the economic sphere. The introduction in January 1990 of 'shock therapy' in the form of the Balcerowicz Plan alarmed trade unionists, who sought unsuccessfully to reassert working-class control over the selection of candidates representing *Solidarity*, a process which had been by-passed by 'the largely middle-class Citizens' Committees' (Zirakzadeh 1997: 158). The fears of the *Solidarity* trade unionists that the effects of 'shock therapy' would be more severe and longer-lasting than the pro-market reformers suggested were realized when gross national product shrank by approximately 10 per cent in 1990 and again in 1991, with industrial and agricultural output disproportionately badly affected. Real incomes fell by as much as a third in the first year as inflation outpaced earnings, and unemployment rose, particularly in areas of heavy industry (Kowalik 1994; Zirakzadeh 1997). These developments 'brought Solidarity's latent fault lines to the surface' (Frydman *et al.* 1998: 109). Sztompka (1999: 160) wrote that '[t]he enthusiasm and celebratory atmosphere that accompany a revolution never last for long', but in the Polish case it was particularly short-lived. The severe economic dislocation and austerity ushered in by the new government's 'shock therapy' quickly undermined any sense of unity derived through moving together into a post-communist future. *Solidarity*'s success in the 1989 election owed much to the movement's broad appeal, apparently offering something to almost all social groups and promising as well to revitalize the Polish society that together they made up. Like other movements in eastern Europe, *Solidarity* 'served to integrate those who shared the widespread disillusion with and antipathy against communist authority, and provided a distinctive vehicle for the expression of opposition' (Lewis 1993: 295). After years of adversity and struggle, it was understandable that people's expectations would include improvement in their material circumstances as well as the opportunity for freer political expression, but such optimism was swiftly replaced by more pessimistic assessments of the changes underway.

Workers were among the staunchest critics of *Solidarity*'s record in government. Strike waves continued to be a prominent feature of Polish economic life, reflecting workers' refusal 'to accept that they should pay a high price for their glorious victory over the communists' (Wesolowski 1995: 115). In the early days of *Solidarity*, Walesa had declared 'we are anti-materialistic and capable of sacrifice' (quoted in Ash 1983: 280), but the appeal of such rhetoric could not last indefinitely. In the countryside, the post-communist regime also generated frustration and disappointment, and 'peasants were among the first social groups to stage massive opposition to the reforms . . . Once thought to be allies of the postsocialist transition, peasants turned out to be among its main foes'. The drop in real incomes was, if anything, more severe for peasants than it was for workers, and they reacted angrily to the fact that 'they carried disproportionately the transition's high costs' (Zbierski-Salameh 1999: 191, 196). Young people constituted a third group among whom there was disillusion with *Solidarity* in government (Zirakzadeh 1997), and a fourth group was Polish women. Female workers had made up almost a half of *Solidarity*'s early membership, although women constituted fewer than 10 per cent of the delegates to the 1981 Congress. They had seen some benefits brought by the movement, but by 1989 'women in the union were being urged not to introduce issues that could produce . . . divisiveness'. In the wake of the 1989 elections, the positions adopted by the *Solidarity* Women's Section on abortion and gender inequality in the home 'were not welcome in Solidarity' and in 1991 the Women's Section was dissolved. Its former members 'had begun to oppose the Solidarity leadership and to think about a women's party' (Hauser *et al*. 1993: 261, 263). Women's experiences of postcommunism led them to ask 'Solidarity for Whom?' (Reading 1992: ch. 7), just as male workers, peasants and young people were struck by the uneven distribution of the costs and benefits of change.

The process of fragmentation now proceeded apace. The unexpectedly harsh impact of the policy of shock therapy was the focus of intense disagreements that proved impossible to contain; in Zirakzadeh's words (1997: 159), '[d]ivided over the reasonableness of continued free-market reform, the Solidarity movement rapidly splintered into rival profarmer, proworker, and promarket factions'. Some of this factionalism was conducted by setting up competing groups within *Solidarity*, whereas others left the movement altogether to set up distinct and competing organizations. By the time of the October 1991 elections, *Solidarity* 'had fragmented into dozens of post-Solidarity parties, each addressing distinctive constituencies'. Zirakzadeh goes on to give just some of the names of the parties that contested the election to illustrate the extent of this fragmentation: 'Catholic Election Action, Peasant Party–Programmatic Alliance, Peasant Accord, Solidarity, Labour Solidarity, Solidarity '80, German Minority, Movement for Silesian Autonomy, Great Poland and Poland, Friends of Beer, Women Against Life's Hardship, Union of Political Realism, and Party X' (Zirakzadeh 1997: 159, 161). Parliamentary seats were won by more than 80 parties, among which it was difficult to find much common ground, and as a result 'the Polish parliament was made up of 29 factions' (Wesolowski 1995: 120). What emerged was 'a conservative regime influenced by a handful of entrepreneurs, the petite bourgeoisie, and the Catholic Church but without the legitimacy to reorganize the economy' (Misztal and Jenkins 1995: 337). Only 43 per cent of the electorate had voted in the 1991 elections (Holmes 1997). The electorate's negative reaction to worsening relations between the various elements that had formerly been united under *Solidarity*'s banner doomed them to a disastrous performance in the September 1993 elections when just over half of voters turned out, still a long way short of the 60 per cent turnout in 1989 (Zirakzadeh 1997). After 4 years in which *Solidarity*-led governments had sought to transcend the communist legacy, they were replaced by a government in which former communists played a leading role. This government did not propose returning Poland to its pre-1989 arrangements, but it did criticize the 'shock therapy' programme for being unnecessarily harsh (Zbierski-Salameh 1999), and in doing so it appealed to many people who felt that they had lost out under post-communism. In the light of the 1993 election result, Wesolowski (1995: 125) lamented that '[t]he Solidarity ethos, which was once considered to be a powerfully integrating force, clearly no longer exists'. As if to emphasize this point, Walesa's bid for re-election as President of the country in 1995 failed when he was beaten by the former communist Aleksander Kwaśniewski (Zirakzadeh 1997).

The fortunes of one strand of the *Solidarity* legacy were revived in the September 1997 parliamentary elections, which resulted in Solidarity Electoral Action forming part of a coalition government committed to 'renewed decommunization' (Sakwa 1999: 78). Such developments could not disguise the fact that the fragmentation of the movement earlier in the decade had reduced it to 'a hollow shell' (Misztal and Jenkins 1995: 337), a process from which it could not recover. The years after 1989 in Poland suggested that 'the vision that brought about the downfall of communism found no solid ground in which to put down roots' (Bauman 1994: 19), and subsequent events have confirmed this conclusion. Reasons for this can be sought in the way in which the leaders involved deported themselves. Zirakzadeh (1997: 163) commented that the 'parties tied to the Solidarity movement were partly responsible for their own demise' because of their viciousness towards one another during campaigning, echoing Bauman's (1994: 18) observation that '[t]oday, the gallant heroes are occupied as much as anything with defaming and vilifying their brothers-in-arms of yesterday'. It is also possible to identify more fundamental differences of principle underlying the fragmentation of *Solidarity*. Wesolowski's account distinguishes between three contrasting elements in 'the Solidarity ethos', thereby revealing how the movement sought to promote a combination of 'associative ties', 'communal ties' and 'communitarian ties' that turned out to be highly unstable. Associative ties are characteristic of groups whose members are free to join and to leave, and have the rational character of relationships between people who come together to pursue their common interests. In contrast, communal ties are characterized by individuals being 'integrated into the group by a set of symbols, values and beliefs that produce a high degree of loyalty and devotion to the group'. Membership of communal groups or 'spiritual communities' is not a reflection of individuals' rational choice but of their supposedly natural affiliations, and the examples he cites are of ethnic and religious groups. He goes on to observe that communal groups are more tightly held together than are associative groups, and also more likely to view other groups as threatening. Communitarian ties involve a mixture of the first two types of relationships, combining respect for tradition with concern for people's welfare in the simultaneous pursuit of 'such fundamental values as solidarity, liberty and democracy' (Wesolowski 1995: 111–12). Communitarians stress the importance of cooperation between as well as within groups, and emphasize the importance of shared norms within the broader society.

Wesolowski's analysis of *Solidarity* highlights the tensions that eventually tore the movement apart. The movement drew on the idea of associative ties in its promotion of a loose network of autonomous and self-governing associations independent of the state, but it also drew on traditions enshrined in the Catholic Church and in Polish nationalism and romanticism, which were more communal in character. There were also within *Solidarity* currents that counterposed 'society' and 'the state' as 'us' against 'them' in a broadly communitarian fashion. When combined, '[t]his amalgam of principles created a force which proved, in its confrontation with the dependent and oppressive party-state, to be indestructible' (Wesolowski 1995: 114). By the 1980s, the communist regime in Poland had managed to alienate diverse associative, communal and communitarian groups, the combined strength of which it was unable to match. The combination of these various elements as an effective opposition movement proved difficult to transfer into the realm of government. Following their 1989 electoral success, *Solidarity*'s leaders concluded that 'the Solidarity ethos did not provide a workable set of principles for the future organization of society' (Wesolowski 1995: 114), not least because it was at odds with their pursuit of 'a rational economy' (Sakwa 1999: 93). The adoption of a programme of 'shock therapy' for the economy was made possible by the fact that, among the movement's leaders, 'during the 1980s there was a radical questioning of Solidarity's syndicalist past, and the ideal citizen as entrepreneur came to replace the parliamentary delegate' (Ray 1996: 204). The notion of individual responsibility that is central to free market economics met with a hostile reception from the broad mass of people whose preference was for collective affiliation of some sort. Political appeals to 'the common people' were deliberately anti-individualistic, and based on the recognition that many Poles showed 'no desire to become self-motivated individuals taking responsibility for their own lives' (Wesolowski 1995: 115). In addition, leaders of the Roman Catholic Church were critical of ' "individualistic" tendencies to put private happiness above the collective good' (Einhorn 1993: 67), and in the process they drew implicitly on Tönnies's model of traditional gender roles in *gemeinschaft*, as Einhorn notes.

The role of *Solidarity* in Poland's transition to post-communism has been drawn on by several commentators to make more general observations about civil society. The weakness of the institutions of civil society in state socialist societies gave *Solidarity* significance far beyond Poland both because of its strength as an opposition movement that successfully challenged the communist regime and because of the lessons that might be learned about its failure to survive the transition to post-communism. Arnason is one commentator who doubts that *Solidarity* has much relevance to these wider debates, except in a negative sense. For him, the Polish case was one in which 'a mass movement of industrial workers found an ally in the Catholic establishment and became a vehicle for national aspirations. A conjunction of class, church and nation can hardly be regarded as an embodiment of the ideals that have traditionally been linked to the concept of civil society' (Arnason 1993: 188). This may be considered a harsh judgement on a movement whose members sought to remake their world in adverse circumstances. Religion, nationalism and trade unionism were prominent among the traditions that were available to be drawn upon, but this is not an exhaustive list of the bases on which *Solidarity* developed. It says nothing, for example, of the institution of the Środowisko that Wedel (1992: 12) defines as 'the "social circle" of family, friends, colleagues, and acquaintances brought together by some combination of family background, common experience, or formal organization that surrounds each individual'. Such informal relationships outside and beyond the centrally controlled formal institutions of the Polish economy and state had the potential to generate 'spontaneous cohesion' (Konrad 1992: 56) and a regionally distinct form of civil society that had parallels elsewhere in state socialist eastern Europe, albeit ones that attracted relatively little international attention.

Solidarity in perspective

Poland's transition to post-communism had a number of distinctive features, but it also had parallels with other eastern Europe countries undergoing the same broad process. The most obviously distinctive feature was the prominence of *Solidarity*, for nowhere else did such a mass movement emerge and hold centre stage for such a prolonged period. This may be attributed, at least in part, to the especially severe economic difficulties faced by the Polish state socialist regime, and to the high degrees of religious and ethnic homogeneity of the population. All of these factors provided bases for people to find common ground against a system that came to be perceived as inefficient, economically and spiritually bankrupt and subordinate to a foreign power. Poland thus stood out as 'the weak point in the communist system', and it is unsurprising that it became the first country to elect a post-communist government. The repetition of this process in neighbouring states shortly after *Solidarity*'s pioneering achievement in 1989 suggests that the Polish case was not particularly unique. Common to all of these states was 'a loss of legitimacy and declining capacity for internal reform' (Misztal and Jenkins 1995: 325, 327), although their trajectories varied according to how the different regimes handled the economic and political reform processes, as Misztal and Jenkins's comparison of Poland and Hungary illustrates. Another common feature was the way in which 'the closer oppositional movements came to power-sharing or a negotiated transition, the more earlier visions of social re-organization were revised to accommodate market ideologies' (Ray 1993: 119). Such readjustment coincided with the revival of divisions that shared opposition to the communist regime had temporarily put on hold. It is instructive that Kovács's (1998: 113) comment, that 'the rapprochement of the national(ist) and liberal strains of anticommunism was due to the common enemy rather than to normative cohesion', was made with reference to Hungary but could apply equally well to Poland and to several other states in which anti-communist alliances fragmented following democratization. The solidarity of those who made common cause against the communist order evaporated when they considered more closely what alternative arrangements might replace it. As Bryant (1995: 144) notes, 'the notion of "civil society against the state" . . . made sense as an oppositional strategy to the party-state, but is unhelpful in conditions of democratic reconstruction' when the party-state is being replaced.

Comparison of different countries undergoing the transition to post-communist regimes throws up the broad conclusion that democratization is less problematic where material resources are more readily available. It is in the more affluent societies such as Hungary and the Czech Republic that the transition has been smoothest, while countries in which living standards are lower have generally been characterized by more friction and conflict. There is, as Lewis (1997: 410) has observed, a distinct 'association of democratization with higher levels of socio-economic development', although he goes on to remark that there are no simple causal linkages in operation here. Lane's argument is that the populations of state socialist societies were characterized by declining loyalty and commitment to the system and that this was a consequence of 'the modernization of the social structure' as the effects of urbanization, industrialization and the expansion of education worked their way through. The result was that 'significant groups of people felt that the rewards (material and psychological) did not match the required expenditure of energy and commitment'. Of particular importance as an indicator of 'changes in the loyalty and solidarity of the population' (Lane 1996: 156, 161) was increased dissatisfaction among the expanding intelligentsia or professional middle class, among whom there was a growing receptiveness to new ideas, especially among its younger members. Other writers have directed more attention to the way in which the relaxation of centralized control over economic decision-making prompted what Szelenyi (1988) refers to as a pattern of '[s]ocialist embourgeoisement' quite distinct from the path of development followed in western capitalist societies. Szelenyi's account focuses on the emergence of small-scale rural entrepreneurs in Hungary as the state socialist system there moved in the direction of allowing freer rein to market forces, and notes how their 'silent revolution from below' was as much backward-looking as it was forward-looking. The period of state socialism was characterized by resistance to attempts to impose change from above, and Szelenyi posits that ordinary people typically 'bounce back to old, familiar ways' as opportunities open up for them to do so.

Szelenyi's ideas tie in with the wider argument that disillusion with the promise of communism to usher in a fresh start in economic and social life revitalized appeals to the pre-communist past, most obviously in the guise of nationalism. Kovács (1998), for example, notes that in Hungary the post-communist period has witnessed a revival of populist and nationalist politics, while Elster and his colleagues (1998) point to the religious, linguistic and ethnic identities that have come to the fore throughout much of eastern Europe. The strong nationalist elements in Poland's *Solidarity* movement and some of its successors provide a further example. Kideckel's study of Romanian villagers during and after communism shows that appeals to the past could take other forms at a more local level. The leaders of the Socialist Republic of Romania purported to be presiding over the development of 'new interpersonal relations of collaboration, mutual assistance and reciprocal respect – corresponding to the principle of "all for one and one for all" ' (Kideckel 1993: 101). Such rhetoric was a far cry from the impoverished reality of life for its citizens who were, he argues, more likely to experience mistrust and solitude than solidarity and who consequently retreated into survival strategies at the household level. A popular joke of the early 1980s was '[i]f we had Solidarity [the trade union] here, every Romanian would have their own' (Kideckel 1993: 173), signalling the extent to which state socialism under Ceauşescu was perceived to have fragmented social relationships. This fragmentation generated a situation in which the distinction between 'us', the people and 'them', the state and its agents, produced a unity that 'was neither permanent nor a goad to action'. Before, during and after state socialism, Romania has remained 'a society centred on the household' (Kideckel 1993: 24) because of the capacity of family and kinship ties to modify the impact of uncertainty and because wider bases of collective action have not materialized. This conclusion is echoed by Almond (1992: 74), who argues that in an 'atomized society' trust is most likely to be found in 'the network of extended family relations, bound by blood and mutual obligations'.

These debates about the transition to post-communism in eastern Europe are informed in various ways by the writings on social solidarity of the founding figures of sociology, whose ideas were explored in Chapter 1. Referring back to Marx, Kideckel (1993: 3) notes that in the Romanian countryside the state socialist system 'produced a class *in* itself – that is, a structured and dominated social group – but prevented the emergence of a class *for* itself, one able to organize for purposes of collective resistance' (emphases in original). Offe's conclusion about post-communist societies is that they are also character- ized by the absence of effective organization along class lines. As he expresses it, '[p]ostcommunist social structures are often described as "amorphous" or "atomized"'. In consequence, people's life chances are shaped less by 'individual engagement in collective associational efforts on the basis of the assumption of broadly shared interests' and more by factors such as whether they know the right people. He goes on to suggest that people in post-communist societies 'tend to relate to each other as might passengers travelling on the same bus, rather than as members of the same class' (Offe 1996b: 243). Where collective identities are formed, he notes, they are more likely to be regional or ethnic ones than ones formed on the basis of class. Alongside these echoes of the debates between Weber and the followers of Marx a century ago, there are echoes of Tönnies's concept of *gemeinschaft* in Wesolowski's (1995) account of the strength of communal ties in Poland. Tönnies's account of *gesellschaft* in terms of 'the atrophy of moral commun- ities, isolation, atomization, and individualization of social life' (Sztompka 1999: 6) also has a bearing on the analysis of social relationships where trust is weak. The absence of trust generates uncertainty, and Burawoy and Verdery (1999: 12) suggest that the 'uncertain transition' to post-communism is an important part of the explanation of the potency of the 'appeal to "the good old days"', for example among Polish peasants. In a similar vein, Wedel (1992: 13) argues that the reinvigoration of Poland's Środowiska reflects the search for a reliable form of mutual assistance in 'an environment of uncertainty and indeterminacy'.

The attempt by people in conditions of uncertainty to 'escape to commun- ity' can also be read in Durkheimian terms, as is the case with Lewenstein and Melchior's (1992) analysis of the rise of the religious youth movement 'Oasis' in Poland during the period of martial law. Their account puts forward the thesis that young people joined the movement in search of 'community', keen to escape the disordered state of 'anomie' into which the country's travails had plunged them. Ferge's broader assessment of post-communism also has Durkheimian echoes. She portrays the most vulnerable groups as living 'in continuous uncertainty about their future' and being concerned to achieve 'existential security' (Ferge 1993: 280, 281) as well as an adequate income. Offe highlights the obstacles that stand in the way of civil society developing in post-communist countries to the extent that they can provide their mem- bers such security. The 'atomized' nature of post-communist social relation- ships makes it difficult to envisage the formation of robust and sustainable 'intermediary bodies' between the individual and the state that could draw on people's sense of moral commitment, obligation and solidarity. Offe's (1996a: 49) question of how to foster 'the forces of a civil self-organization beyond market, state and ethnic "community"' bears a strong resemblance to Durkheim's concern with the range of 'secondary groups' linking individuals to the wider society. It is worth remembering in this context, as Barker (1999) reminds us, that Durkheim was also concerned with the phenomenon of 'collective effervescence'. The *Solidarity* movement can be thought of as a prime example of how collective action can develop a momentum that has the potential to transform social relationships. The years of *Solidarity* stand out as one of 'those signal epochs of crisis when some great collective movement seizes us, lifts us above ourselves, and transfigures us' (Durkheim 1974: 59). It remains to consider the more general conclusions that may be drawn about social solidarities as a result.

PART THREE

---------(6)

Making sense of
social solidarities in
unsettled societies

◯————————————————————

Introduction

The presence or absence of social solidarity is an important dimension of
social relationships in a wide range of settings, but it takes on a particular
significance in societies in which existing arrangements are being actively
unsettled. In the contemporary world a number of unsettling forces can be
identified, among which individualization, globalization and democratization
are especially prominent. The preceding three chapters have shown that such
forces present a challenge to established social arrangements and in the process
raise fundamental questions about the possibility and desirability of bringing
people together in mutually supportive and enduring relationships at the level
of intimate family life, at the level of 'community' and at the level of national
'society'. Simpson's (1999) analysis of family life in 'insecure times', Bellah
and his colleagues' (1996) account of community responses to anxieties in
'our restless and mobile society', and Bauman's (1999) perspective on nationalist politics that are fed by appeals to 'clean and quiet, orderly and familiar,
native backyards', all in their different ways illustrate how the conscious
pursuit of solidarity and the difficulties of achieving it can be considered as
two related aspects of life in unsettled societies. Numerous other examples
could be drawn upon to support the broad conclusion that solidarity continues
to be a widely sought after characteristic of people's social relationships
despite the existence of many obstacles to its achievement and maintenance.
The parallels between this situation and that confronting the early sociologists are worth noting, not least because they help to explain why the ideas
of Durkheim and his contemporaries still figure as major reference points.
Industrialization, democratization and individualization provided the backdrop to the emergence of the sociological tradition (Nisbet 1970), and much
of the ensuing debate within the discipline revolved around the question of

whether it was either feasible or worthwhile to preserve elements of the old order as the social world was radically recast. The continued controversy over 'family', 'community' and 'nation' as viable bases of social reconstruction necessarily involves reconsideration of this same question, albeit in somewhat changed circumstances.

Durkheim's analysis of the social changes of his time in terms of the breakdown of traditional social orders continues to have relevance to contemporary discussions because of what he has to say about social solidarity's shifting foundations. Durkheim understood the impact of unsettling change as a process of 'declassification' and he recognized that it would take time for new ways of thinking about and organizing the social world to be developed (Lockwood 1992). The breakdown of established distinctions between 'us' and 'them' provides a good illustration of the general point that social change often undermines inherited understandings of who we are before alternative classifications have emerged to take their place. Kideckel (1993: 3) has noted how '[u]s/them distinctions were rife throughout socialist East Europe', reflecting the potential for shared identities to develop among people who were brought together by antipathy towards the communist state. It was remarked in the previous chapter that fragmentation and atomization were prominent consequences of the subsequent removal of opposition groups' common adversary in the post-communist era. Similar observations can be made about the re-working of 'us/them' distinctions as they apply to the areas of family and community life discussed in Chapters 3 and 4. The increases in divorce and re-partnering have created the context in which it is appropriate to refer to the 'unclear family' (Simpson 1998), just as the growth of geographical mobility and the proliferation of different types of communities have complicated the delineation of 'insiders' and 'outsiders' (Crow and Maclean 2000). Such outcomes are not necessarily consistent with what Durkheim predicted, and Cohen (1985: 110) has even suggested that the continued prominence of community solidarities is 'almost the entirely opposite effect' to that which Durkheim's analysis would lead us to expect. Alexander (1992) is one among a group of other writers who present a more favourable assessment of Durkheim's legacy, putting forward the view that he did recognize the significance of the informal relationships of civil society in the promotion of 'fellow feeling' and social solidarity.

Durkheim's writings have provided a starting point for subsequent debates on social solidarity in several respects, but they inevitably left a number of issues unresolved. Alexander argues that it was only in his later work that Durkheim concentrated on the connections between solidarity and subjectivity, the implication being that his earlier analyses, in which the distinction between mechanical and organic solidarities was discussed, were insufficiently sensitive to 'the close interrelation between symbolic classifications, ritual processes and the formation of social solidarities' (Alexander 1988: 2). Whether this line of development in Durkheim's thought and its focus on 'collective effervescence' has the potential to be taken much further is the subject of continued disagreement. Barker's (1999) view is that Durkheim's approach would be worth pursuing only if it gave greater acknowledgement to the inherently political nature of collective action and recognition to the likelihood that some individuals will lose out as a result of the strengthening of collective identities. Durkheim's attention was much less focused on how the enhancement of social solidarity reinforces the exclusion of outsiders than it was on the promotion of the inclusion of insiders. The association of social solidarity with exclusivity is given greater prominence in other approaches, such as that put forward by rational choice theorists. As Hechter (1987: 10) notes, '[t]he starting point of this theory is the assumption that actors initially form groups, or join existing ones, in order to consume various *excludable jointly produced* goods' (emphasis in original). In contrast to Durkheim's emphasis on cooperation and shared values, there is in the rational choice approach much more attention paid to competing interests and social closure. The extent to which it is appropriate to posit a rational basis for social solidarity has in consequence become a crucial aspect of contemporary debates. One view is that 'rational choice theory founders upon the problem of solidarity' (Fardon 1999: 226) because (from the point of view of its critics, at least) it cannot deal with people who put the good of the group before the satisfaction of their own individual interests. Against this Hechter (1987: 11) claims that '[t]here is nothing in rational choice that denies that individuals can pursue altruistic or prosocial ends', even if such actions are not the primary focus of this approach.

On-going disagreement over the extent to which it is possible to identify rational bases of social solidarity ties in with the related debate about social solidarity and time. It is a theme of much of the literature on globalization that people's time horizons have shrunk, and that long-term trust has become more difficult if not impossible to achieve. Beck (2000), for example, refers to globalization having produced 'the unsettled, friable world in which we live', while Bauman (1991) speaks of the provisional and contingent nature of relationships that are characterized by 'until-further-notice certainty'. Bauman's oxymoron and his other writings on the fleeting nature of contemporary solidarities present a challenge because relationships characterized by short-term solidarities appear to be poorly placed to resist the processes of social fragmentation and disintegration that have been central concerns of commentators on social solidarity from the outset. The resort by communitarians to the promotion of non-governmental institutions to revive more atavistic collective identities and obligations built around 'family' and 'community' echoes Durkheim's emphasis on the importance of the development of 'intermediary bodies' between the individual and the state. This agenda is arguably more backward-looking than Durkheim's vision, however, given the sorts of arrangements that he thought would be required to secure social solidarity in modern conditions in which individual differences are positively valued. The communitarian agenda has responded to individualism by invoking what Phillips refers to as 'an undifferentiated and uniform community' that is in many ways closer to Durkheim's model of mechanical solidarity than it is to his image of organic solidarity. There is also an echo of

Durkheim's thought in Phillips's statement that 'the resuscitation of dying forms of communal solidarity is neither possible nor desirable. People are not going to return to unquestioned loyalties of family or religion or locality', although it remains to be seen precisely how the alternative scenario of solidarities 'forged out of alliances between people who are different' (Phillips 1999: 108) will emerge and how the solidarities generated in this way will fare. Giddens (1994a: 125) was making essentially the same point when, in criticism of communitarians and others, he observed that '[t]he renewal of social solidarity is a conservative problem . . . but it does not admit of conservative solutions'. He argued instead that whatever form contemporary solidarities take, if they are to be at all robust they will have to be compatible with the forces of individualization, democratization, globalization and detraditionalization that rule out a return to past ways of life. As Albrow (1996: 5) notes, living in the global era has highlighted that ideas like '"community" . . . never acquire a final meaning'. It follows from this that research into the various manifestations of social solidarities and their attendant causes and contexts is necessarily a comparative project, and that only when such research has been undertaken can the wider consequences be gauged.

The causes of social solidarities

The search for the causes of social solidarity has been at the heart of the sociological enterprise ever since the founding figures of the discipline challenged the idea that solidarity had a 'natural' basis. The discussion in Chapter 1 noted that fundamental disagreements existed between the founding figures over the respective importance of shared place, shared interests and shared identities as the bases of people coming together in a solidaristic fashion. Taking these debates as a point of departure, Collins (1975: 298) distinguished between the different sorts of sanctions that people have available to bind others to them, the main types being 'coercive threats, material rewards and loyalty to ideals'. Expressed alliteratively, the point is that solidarity may be based on an appeal to one or more classes of incentives: 'coercion, compensation and commitment' (Tilly and Tilly 1998: 74). Using this framework to capture the essence of Durkheim's position, it might be said that societies characterized by members' similarity have greater potential to be held together by coercion (referred to by Durkheim as the repressive law of mechanical solidarity) but that societies in which differences between individuals become more pronounced require something other than a Hobbesian threat of punishment to provide the basis for their social cohesion. Durkheim's comments about the fleeting nature of shared interests were made in criticism of Spencer's proposition that economic relationships could provide a solution to the problem of order, and he argued instead that trust had to be underpinned by a positive moral commitment. This standpoint was combined with scepticism towards the idea that appeals to traditional loyalties would be sufficiently strong in modern conditions in which individualism had taken root, and he therefore regarded organic solidarity in a very different way to writers like Tönnies. Durkheim's remark that the ties binding people to territorial groupings 'become daily more loose and tenuous . . . and no longer arouse deep emotions within us' set him apart from those who placed greater store in such traditional loyalties. At the same time, he was mindful of the need for some form of social organization at a less abstract level than the whole society, arguing that '[a] society made up of an extremely large mass of unorganised individuals, which an overgrown state attempts to limit and restrain, constitutes a veritable sociological monstrosity' (Durkheim 1984: liv). Those who detect a parallel between this latter image and the all-encompassing state socialist regimes described in the previous chapter also suggest that Durkheim's contribution to the study of civil society has continuing contemporary relevance (Sztompka 1999), although this is by no means a view that is universally held.

Durkheim's approach to explaining the bases of social solidarity has certainly been subject to a number of criticisms. One of the most important of these relates to the way that Durkheim's assessment of the social problems of his era led him to advocate the development of occupational associations 'which would provide a new basis of social cohesion, and hence the framework within which individuals would be bound by ties of interests, ideas and feelings', thereby becoming 'the heirs of the family' (Eldridge 1973: 89). In practice, such arrangements have not prospered to anything like the extent that Durkheim anticipated, and Giddens's (1994a: 124) judgement on Durkheim's belief 'that community could to some extent be re-established in the occupational sphere' is that it has proved to be 'an impractical dream'. The related lesson to be drawn from the discussion of occupational communities in Chapter 4 is that people's loyalties and identities are connected just as closely to the informal culture that links members of the group as they are to its formal organizational structures. Church and Outram's (1998: 121) finding that in coal-mining communities 'much local solidary behaviour was unorganized' reflects the strength of local cultural capital as an immediate influence on people's actions that national trade union organizations achieved only rarely. The survival of 'community' more generally is at odds with Durkheim's anticipation that it 'would be swept away by the political and economic logic of large-scale systems of production' (Cohen 1985: 110). Institutions provide a framework within which social solidarities may emerge, but it is questionable to assume (as Durkheim seems to have) that patterns of interaction arising out of the division of labour 'form the basis upon which moral beliefs spontaneously develop' (Gouldner 1962: 26). In Gouldner's (1980: 218) view, 'Durkheim mystified the reasons why men submit to moral norms' because he was engaged in a polemic against explanations framed in terms of economic interests. This led him to underestimate the potential for people to be more actively involved in the formation of their moral codes in the light of their perceived interests and the embodiment of these codes in informal as well as formal structures.

Writers approaching the subject of social solidarity from the perspective of rational choice theory have developed the point that the explanation of people's active engagement in solidaristic behaviour requires more than reference to the social structural forces that bear down on individuals. Hechter (1987: 9), for example, has noted that structural explanations tend to predict 'far more group solidarity . . . than the historical record reveals', and he goes on to argue that people who share a common location within a social structure do not necessarily come together as a united force, even where they can be identified as having common interests. Hechter's critique of structural analyses of the bases of solidarity draws on his own (1975) research into nationalism, which shows that the extent to which people come together as nationalist movements fluctuates in ways that cannot be accounted for in purely structural terms. The structural approach may do 'a good job of predicting those areas that have the potential to develop nationalist movements', but 'it is virtually mute about the conditions under which nationalism erupts, rather than lying dormant' (Hechter 1987: 5). Hechter (1987: 6) is particularly emphatic on the point that structural theories are weak in explaining how people react to their circumstances, and overlook the ways in which '[i]ndividuals typically have some choice-making discretion' in relation to the solidaristic ties that they develop. It follows from this that attention needs to be paid to the processes whereby members are attracted to and retained within groups.

Hechter argues that people may seek to become members of groups because of the individual benefits that they will enjoy as a result, but that their sense of obligation to the group is an equally important part of explaining why groups persist and why individual members exhibit solidarity in situations where it is not immediately obvious how they stand to gain personally from doing so. He suggests that individuals calculate that solidarity in such circumstances is the necessary price of group membership from which they can expect to benefit in general terms. Such solidarity can be predicted to be stronger in situations where group members are highly interdependent and where the group is able to impose sanctions against 'free riders' – that is, against people who seek to reap the benefits of the group's actions without incurring any of the costs themselves. In other words, groups in which relationships are characterized by solidarity are more than simply 'collections of rational individuals' because they also require 'encompassing control institutions shaping interactions between members'. Group solidarity can thus be defined within this framework as '*the extent to which members comply with their corporate obligations to contribute to the group's joint goods*' (Chai and Hechter 1998: 35–6, emphasis in original), and for solidarity to be realized it will be necessary for group members to be aware of their interdependence and of the bounded nature of their group. This approach focuses attention on 'the extent to which group membership determines individual life chances', its underlying premise being that individuals will be more committed to a group (such as an ethnic group) the more their welfare is tied up with the fortunes of that group. Conversely, 'when one's life-chances are seen to be independent of inclusion in a particular ethnic group, the subjective significance of membership in that group will tend to recede or to disappear altogether' (Hechter and Levi 1994: 185), a conclusion that it is possible to extend to other groups besides the ethnic and nationalist ones on which Hechter's research has concentrated.

This approach goes some way towards meeting Durkheim's objections to the focus on the individual that was characteristic of Spencer and the other utilitarians. There is agreement, for example, over the point made by Durkheim about solidarity involving something more than self-interested behaviour, narrowly conceived. In *The Division of Labour in Society*, Durkheim (1984: 173) had advanced the general proposition that people 'cannot live together without agreeing, and consequently without making mutual sacrifices, joining themselves to one another in a strong and enduring fashion'. Social life was for Durkheim based fundamentally on 'altruism', and this theme also informs Douglas's (1987: 4) observation that 'solidarity is only gesturing when it involves no sacrifice'. An important difference remains, however, in that Durkheim's explanation of people's preparedness to be altruistic or self-sacrificing looks beyond any calculations that individuals may make of how altruism will be beneficial to them, of how 'altruists are made better off by their altruism' (Hechter 1987: 71). Instead of treating people's preparedness to act solidaristically as the product of individuals making rational assessments of the various options open to them, the Durkheimian approach places much greater store on people's collective experiences that reinforce moral norms through emotion. This is particularly the case in relation to societies in which individuation and individualization have undermined the capacity of the state to use repressive laws to coerce members into acting in accordance with the interests of the group, but what is crucial for Durkheim is that both mechanical and organic solidarity are the product of shared rituals rather than of calculation of advantage. Hechter (1987: 63) acknowledges this as an important point of divergence between Durkheimian and rational choice theory when he notes that Durkheim was 'at pains to emphasize [that] much ritual and religious behaviour . . . cannot be regarded as the outcome of benefit/cost calculation in any meaningful sense of the term'. Rituals are treated by Durkheim as a necessary part of the reproduction of collective identities, and they have significance because they generate what Moore (1978: 143), in deliberately Durkheimian terms, refers to as 'at least a temporary surge of social unity' among group members. Durkheim's analysis of the issue of how 'to integrate the individual into the collective life' (Lemert 1997: 82) identified rituals as central to this process.

The symbolic significance of rituals is relevant to the discussion in earlier chapters at several points. In relation to domestic life, for example, mealtimes figure prominently in accounts of how the shared identity of family members is replenished. In addition to the physiological need that they meet, mealtimes that bring family members together can also be considered to be 'an expression of solidarity, of the greater importance of the community over the individual' (Wood 1995: 19). Wood's acknowledgement of Bourdieu's influence on his analysis of food is echoed in Warde's analysis of the potential for shared consumption more generally to reinforce a sense of community. Warde argues that the attraction of shared consumption is that 'it is comforting to know appropriate ways to act, to have aesthetic judgements affirmed by like-minded people, to share in a consensus on what comprises a decent and good life'. Warde stresses that this sense of community 'cannot be stage-managed, but rather evolves piecemeal over time . . . Participation in community is less a matter of personal zeal, more the becoming immersed in a Bourdieuvian habitus – deep-rooted, subconscious, informal, given, persistent' (Warde 1997: 183). Bourdieu's influence is also present in Warwick and Littlejohn's account of the 'local cultural capital' found in mining communities. It is particularly significant that the 'collection of local skills, communication networks, social values, and shared prestige and status rankings' to which this term refers are treated as 'a means of maintaining the distinctiveness of one locality from another'. Warwick and Littlejohn's research was conducted in an area of Yorkshire in which community consciousness was contributed to by enduring memories of 'the Featherstone massacre' of 1893, in which two striking miners had been killed by troops, their deaths symbolizing to members of mining communities 'past individual and collaborative efforts to improve the quality of their lives' (Warwick and Littlejohn 1992: 15, 61, 205). Significance was attached to such events because of the way in which they embodied the ideal of mutual supportiveness.

There is a strong similarity between the commitment to solidarity that can be called upon by reference to such sacrifice for the common good and the powerful sentiments that were generated among *Solidarity* supporters in Gdansk in 1980 by remembrance of the strikers killed in earlier conflicts with the Polish authorities. One of the elements in the chain of events that produced the *Solidarity* movement was the resistance of the authorities to pressure from workers to erect a memorial to the victims of the conflict in Gdansk in December 1970, when troops had killed 46 demonstrators and injured a further 1165 (Fowkes 1995; Zirakzadeh 1997). On the ninth anniversary of this episode, Walesa spoke to people who had gathered to remember the shootings, and anticipated the events of the following year by encouraging the crowd 'to organise yourselves in independent groups for self-defence. Help each other' (quoted in Ash 1983: 31). His subsequent appeals to *Solidarity* supporters to exercise restraint and to be prudent rested on his belief that his followers were prepared to make material sacrifices. These appeals were effective for a time, but the movement fragmented in the context of disappointment at its failure to deliver the benefits that had been anticipated. Walesa's rhetoric and his skilful use of the emotional appeal of ritual occasions could not indefinitely deliver solidarity as the world changed around him, and this became particularly apparent in the era of post-communism. In another context, Douglas (1987: 35) has observed that 'we have no reason for believing that . . . public statements about solidarity will promote it', from which it might be concluded more generally that rituals and their associated beliefs have to have some resonance in the lives of group members if group solidarity is to be reinforced by them.

The relative significance attributed to rationality and to emotions in the analysis of social solidarity varies according to whether the approach being adopted is that of 'political economy' or that of 'moral economy', to use Cheal's distinction. Cheal develops this distinction to highlight the limitations of political economists' tendency to assume that 'individuals rationally pursue their self-interests' and to make the related point that '[i]n the contemporary world system, moral economies exist alongside political economies'. It is within moral economies that 'trust is generated as a result of members sharing a common way of life', especially where the system of obligations is founded on the belief 'that it is part of the natural order of things'. Relationships within the moral economy are governed more by sentiment than by precise calculation of individual benefit, and 'for certain purposes the boundaries between self and other are denied, and a collective identity is defined *vis-à-vis* outsiders' (Cheal 1988: 7, 15–6, 18). The mutuality found within such groups cannot readily be attributed to self-interested behaviour, but at the same time it is difficult to envisage how appeals to members' loyalty can be framed without at least some reference to how commitment to the group is connected to people's interests and well-being. Hechter (2000: 188–9) makes this point in his criticism of writers who represent nations as 'interestless', arguing instead that '[p]eople may be willing to sacrifice for nations because they encompass collective rather than individual interests, but this does not distinguish them from other kinds of groups'. To the extent that it focuses attention on people's interests, the political economy approach may not offer a complete explanation of the causes of social solidarity, but it would be equally one-sided to discount the role of interests altogether, particularly if the material content of solidaristic relationships is explored alongside their symbolic significance.

The contexts of social solidarities

Social solidarity involves members of a group being able to identify something that they have in common which provides a shared basis for their collective endeavour, but they do not need to be equal in every respect before they can come together as an effective entity. As Gillis (1997: 114) has noted, one of the remarkable things about the ideology of 'the homeland' is that it has, like the ideology of the home, 'effectively collapsed difference into similarity, thereby disguising otherwise evident inequalities . . . between women and men, old and young, rich and poor'. In both cases, 'home' as the location of 'family' and 'homeland' as the location of 'nation' or 'society' are capable of being constructed as the bases of interests and affinities that take precedence over other claims to an individual's loyalties. The same point can be made about the capacity of 'community' to override class, gender and other lines of social cleavage that may be present among members. The potential that exists to construct such solidarities around families, communities and nations despite their members' myriad differences is by no means always realized in practice. Moore's (1978: 507) observation that '[r]eciprocity and cooperation do not develop spontaneously' has particular relevance to this point because of his additional comment that such relationships where they do develop are made vulnerable by the 'continual tendency for selfish individual and group interests to break through'. The ideal of voluntary cooperation and solidarity is repeatedly pursued because it has a number of advantages over other bases of social relationships such as coercion, but it is difficult to create and sustain solidaristic ties in the context of social forces that operate to pull members apart from each other.

The Polish *Solidarity* movement was notable for the ambitiousness of its attempt to build an inclusive solidarity out of diverse constituents. Mason (1985: 89) has noted how 'Solidarity was a huge coalition, encompassing almost the whole of Polish society', and his comment that '[m]anaging such a coalition would prove a difficult task' was confirmed by subsequent events. The unity of the *Solidarity* movement forged in the context of its members' shared opposition to the communist regime was always vulnerable to fragmentation according to the very different interests and ideals of those who composed it, particularly once the transition to post-communism had been effected. The same point can be made about other instances of what Hechter and Levi (1994) refer to as 'reactive group formation'. Giddens (1994a: 125), for example, suggests that a connection can be identified between 'Solidarity at home, clear-cut enemies abroad', and the implication of this analysis is that nation-states that can no longer identify external threats will be vulnerable to 'disintegrative tendencies'. Another example is provided by Gilroy's account of how centuries of exploitation and discrimination along racial lines have generated a defensive solidarity among members of the Black diaspora, but he goes on to argue that 'camp mentalities' based on appeals to race are undermined by contemporary economic and social change. Supposedly natural solidarities are fragmented by the social class cleavages that result from 'deindustrialization and brutal economic differentiation', and at the same time 'struggles arising from family, gender and sexuality have also been clearly visible within the same groups that used to be identified as unitary racial communities' (Gilroy 2000: 83, 38). The difficulty of maintaining the unity of community is also remarked upon by Cheal, whose account of 'the dialectic of intimacy and community' proposes that there is something of a trade-off between the two. His argument is that 'the mutual gaze of intimates separates them from the community and its collective activities, whereas the formal organization of communal occasions leaves little room for the unique interactions of a personal relationship' (Cheal 1988: 117). The connection between 'intimacy' and 'community' is a problematic one in that the two are not always compatible. Situations in which they come into conflict test the loyalties of individuals by requiring them to identify one or other as a priority. Cheal's (1988: 120) view is that 'intimacy and community can be effectively combined only under special conditions', thereby raising the more general question of how easy it is to reconcile the different sets of solidaristic relationships in which people are located.

Family relationships provide an appropriate starting point for Cheal's analysis. The basic sociological observation that '[s]ome relationships are stronger and last longer than others' can be explained by the fact that 'some relationships have higher levels of presence-availability, attachment, sentimentality, sociability, and economic cooperation for longer periods of time than do others'. He goes on to remark that '[t]hese elemental social bonds are nowhere more powerfully combined than they are among individuals who have chosen to live together in the same household' (Cheal 1988: 150). Other relationships like those of community cannot generally match those of the family in terms of the levels of intimacy, trust and reciprocity that they entail, but they are nevertheless important because families are not self-sufficient units, at least not in the contemporary world in which they are locked into wider networks of social and economic interdependence. Mutual support may be at its strongest between family members, and this helps to explain people's preparedness to endorse the ideology of 'putting the family first' (Jordan *et al.* 1994) when forced to identify priorities, but interdependence is found in many other contexts beyond the household, for example in kinship ties, in friendships and in wider community relationships. Instances can be found in all of these areas of what Cheal (1988: 39) calls 'the struggle to institutionalize feelings of solidarity as the basis for social interaction'. Cheal is sceptical of arguments derived from the political economy tradition of analysis which interpret solidarity as something founded upon the calculated expectation of reciprocity, noting that this goes against people's accounts of their participation in solidaristic relationships in which emotions such as love and a commitment to the well-being of others generally have greater prominence. Solidarity is nurtured by a social framework in which there is an explicit 'disavowal of reciprocal expectations of giving and receiving in balanced relationships' (Cheal 1988: 86). Put another way, an instrumental orientation to social exchange is not readily compatible with social solidarity, at least not when it is understood as involving the expression of altruism (Widegren 1997).

Cheal's observation that altruistic motives are prominent in people's accounts of their participation in solidaristic action is confirmed in a number of other studies besides his own investigation into gift-giving. Chapter 3 noted that Roberts's research into the history of kinship ties pointed towards this conclusion, as did her related finding that it is 'very difficult to unravel relationships solely in terms of instrumentality or reciprocity' (Roberts 1995: 182). This theme echoes that in Abrams's study of neighbours in which he was persistently presented with 'assertions of the intrinsic value of helping and giving' (Bulmer 1986: 103). Fantasia's (1988) analysis of the almost year-long strike of workers at a corn processing plant in Iowa interprets the preparedness of strikers and their families to 'look out for one another' as an expression of altruism, and of the 'moral economy' that bound them together. This echoes the discussion in Chapter 4 of solidarity in mining communities that also included mention of how people's involvement in solidaristic action such as a strike rested on other bases besides their expectation of reciprocal benefits. As Church and Outram note, rhetorical appeals to the good of the group and to the values embodied in the way of life of the community were also important in 'the construction of social solidarity', and this was a process in which religious organizations played an important part. The construction of solidarities around local communities was sometimes in tension with the construction of solidarity at the national level in which the idea of miners' common class position had greater prominence. Church and Outram (1998: 104) contrast the 'automatic responses to appeals for aid reflecting shared experiences and shared values' of the former with the latter in which 'calculatedness' about interests was more in evidence. They go on to conclude that the solidarity of local mining communities was particularly intense in conditions characterized by 'a dense network of kin and neighbours' and a set of attitudes and values that could be 'taken for granted'. Likening this to Durkheim's model of mechanical solidarity, they argue that it could not go on 'defying the forces of modernity' (Church and Outram 1998: 262, 261) and that the mythology surrounding the solidarity of miners and their families needs to be revised accordingly. Dicks's (1997) research on how the heritage industry in South Wales has portrayed the mining communities of the past as populated by people who were especially 'resilient, solidary and disciplined' suggests that such mythology may paradoxically be strengthened by the decline of the industry.

The theme of the decline of traditional solidarities like those of traditional working-class communities has been encountered at various points in earlier chapters. According to Beck-Gernsheim, the process of individualization has undermined the 'obligation of solidarity' and 'mutual dependence' that characterized traditional family relationships. What has emerged in place of this 'community of need' is the 'personally chosen togetherness' of the 'post-familial family', in which ties are less extensive in scope and weaker in the 'degree of obligation and permanence' to which members are committed (Beck-Gernsheim 1998: 57, 61, 67). The logic of individualization, if taken to its extreme, would, according to Beck (1992: 116), produce a society of single individuals ' "unhindered" by a relationship, marriage or family'. The inability of family relationships to provide certainty and security has become apparent long before this hypothetical point has been approached. Beck and Beck-Gernsheim (1995: 149) refer to the situation of children whose parents have separated as 'fundamentally ambiguous' as they 'move quietly across the boundaries of new partnerships and families', a point that is echoed in Simpson's (1998) account of these 'unclear families'. A parallel to these ideas exists in the discussion of community relationships, where Putnam's (2000) image of a society of individuals 'bowling alone' is presented as the outcome of the failure of community organizations to be revitalized and the decline in the ethic of reciprocity. The transformation in eastern Europe can also be understood in terms of the demise of an established framework of social relationships, the removal of which has left something of a vacuum in terms of people's orientations and organizations. Ost's (1991: 4) assessment of the new situation was that '[s]ocial groups in post-communist society do not have a clear sense of what is in their interest and what is not', a view that was emphatically confirmed by the proliferation of political parties in Poland. It is also consistent with Offe's (1996b: 242) description of post-communist societies as ones in which 'people find it difficult to detect reliable clues as to their own position in society, their relation to relevant others, and their likely future'.

One response to the decline of traditional solidarities has been the super-ficially paradoxical one of seeking to restore them in some fashion. Beck-Gernsheim (1998: 67) argues that 'individualization also fosters a longing for the opposite world of intimacy, security and closeness'. The family thereby 'represents a sort of refuge in the chilly environment of our affluent, imper-sonal, uncertain society', even if there is some recognition among people that the impossibility of a return to traditional family arrangements means that new family relationships will have to be founded on 'a different kind of com-mon ground' (Beck and Beck-Gernsheim 1995: 2, 4). A similar theme can be detected in the field of community relationships, in which globalization's corrosive effects have been responded to by 'defensive community forma-tions' (Smith 2001: 102) that seek to re-establish local control in the face of impersonal forces. The trend towards 'gated communities' offers a vision of 'homogeneity and "tranquillity"' (Amin and Graham 1999: 20) secured at the expense of the social exclusion of other members of 'unsettling cities' unable to meet their membership criteria. Bauman (2000: 180) describes these com-munities in nightmarish terms as 'cut-off and fenced-off, truly exterritorial residential areas equipped with intricate intercom systems, ubiquitous video-surveillance cameras and heavily armed guards on twenty-four-hours-a-day beats'. In post-communist societies, the resurgence of nationalism provides a further illustration of how traditions are re-worked, and for Sibley (1998: 382) this reflects how 'the dominant and conforming majority needs to con-firm its boundaries with reference to a group which represents its antithesis'. In the context of economic and political uncertainty, 'regional or ethnic codes may be taken to be the most likely ones resorted to in organizing collective action' (Offe 1996b: 243). In all of these areas, the attraction of the security offered by the familiar institutions of family, community and nation helps to account for their enduring appeal.

It is widely acknowledged that the irreversibility of the processes of indi-vidualization, globalization and democratization rules out any straightforward pattern of people in unsettled societies resurrecting traditional arrangements. As Warde has noted, '[a]ttempts are constantly being made to restore, recreate or invent communities' and these are understandable as the products of 'a search for institutional patterns of action that will provide security and assur-ance in the management of everyday life'. At the same time, it needs to be recognized that 'most people touched by modern experience are inherently suspicious of the viability of primordial community', such as the traditional solidarities that are 'associated with place, with nation, with ethnic group and with social class'. Tradition is all the more difficult to reproduce to the extent that people 'recognize the rapidity of change, expect mobility, anticip-ate diversity of opinion, search for novel experiences' (Warde 1997: 183–4).

In such circumstances, it is appropriate to reconsider the possibility that solidarity is incompatible with the development of individualization and other unsettling trends. Beck and Beck-Gernsheim are led by their analysis to pose the question, 'is it still at all possible to integrate highly individualized societies?' Their answer is that recourse to solutions rooted in the past are unacceptably repressive, unstable or exclusive, and that the best prospects for integration arise where people 'try to forge new, politically open, creative forms of bond and alliance' (Beck and Beck-Gernsheim 1996: 45) that are more readily compatible with a reflexive age. It has been left to others to chart the detail of these new forms of solidarity, of which several potential candidates have been identified. In relation to family relationships, Silva and Smart (1999: 9) have speculated that 'individuals may be shifting their locus of intimacy and support away from kin towards other people', among whom friends are particularly prominent. This theme is also present in Pahl's exploration of the question of whether friendship is emerging as 'the social glue of contemporary society'. His conclusion is that 'as people focus more and more on sustaining and maintaining distinctive identities that are not formally provided by family or employment, so the social meaning of friendship will continue to increase in salience' (Pahl 1998: 115). It is also possible to conclude, he suggests, that 'friends are becoming more important than family and kin in certain respects' (Pahl 2000: 87), among which emotional support can be highlighted.

The forces responsible for creating unsettled societies can be seen to have a potentially more far-reaching impact on a global scale. Beck (1997: 12) posits that the emergence of world-wide communication networks means that 'global social movements are becoming a possibility'. Among the many new social movements to have emerged in recent years, one of the most remarkable is that which has developed among disabled people. The speed of its growth, the international reach of its influence and the heterogeneity of its members' situations all make the disability rights movement worthy of attention (French 1994). Charlton has chronicled the growth of the movement around the shared philosophy 'that people with disabilities must have their own voice and have control in their lives', a democratic ethos encapsulated in the slogan 'nothing about us without us'. Charlton's account of the movement's development since the 1970s charts how people were brought together by a growing awareness of their shared oppression. This process was accelerated by congregating in conferences, rallies, demonstrations and other expressions of collective strength that contrasted with members' other experiences of individual isolation and disempowerment. Self-help groups have also contributed to disabled people's 'peer relationships and friendships, material aid and support, and sense of control', even though they tend to be difficult to maintain over time. Charlton's comment that '[m]any local self-help groups appear spontaneously and as quickly disappear' (Charlton 1998: 129, 137, 139) provides a useful illustration of Bauman's remarks considered in Chapter 2 on the impermanent character of many contemporary solidarities.

One response to this impermanence has been the attempt to establish more formalized organizational structures. Among the various obstacles that exist to the unity of the disability movement, there is the difficulty familiar to all efforts to achieve solidarity of how to deal with difference. Charlton identifies this as an especially important issue, arguing that '[t]he contradiction between the individual and the collective is particularly complex among people with disabilities because of our isolation, stigmatisation, and fragmentation into categories . . . [such as] deaf, late-deaf, hard-of-hearing, blind, visually-impaired, and so on'. Further lines of potential cleavage rest on the 'wide spectrum of experiences among people with disabilities that are filtered by class, gender, and race', all of which threaten to weaken the challenge to the *status quo* that the disability movement is able to make. Charlton's conclusion is that only when inherited classifications of disabled people are contested will the disability rights movement be able to 'unite all who can be united on the principles of empowerment and self-determination' within 'a broad constituency' (Charlton 1998: 155, 165). This is no easy task, not least because it is unclear how far the subversion of conventional categories will be taken in what Barton calls the 'new politics of diversity and difference'. A defining characteristic of the contemporary disability movement is that its organizations 'are run by disabled people on behalf of disabled people', among whom 'a very difficult position has to be achieved with regard to the importance of *both* points of commonality and difference' (Barton 1996: 185–6, emphasis in original). The implication is that the potential for fragmentation along lines of race, gender, sexuality and age needs to be borne in mind at the same time as the members of the movement seek to escape from the undifferentiated conception of 'disability' to which they were previously subject.

Monks has described 'the membership's recognition of peculiarities of experience being coupled with a commitment to collective political action' as 'a current major dilemma for the movement'. She argues that the solution to this dilemma is to challenge 'the exclusivity of "communities"' through the encouragement of 'the recognition, if not the celebration, of difference' and thereby the promotion of 'a radical and inclusive citizenship' (Monks 1999: 75, 66, 70). This debate extends far beyond the disability movement to the more general search for what Dean (1996) refers to as 'solidarity based on a respect for difference' and what Lister (1997) calls '[a] politics of solidarity in difference'. According to Lister, the field of gender politics provides 'countless examples around the world of women forging bonds of solidarity across their differences in the pursuit of specific common goals'. In the process, a challenge is thrown up to 'conventional conceptualisations of community which treat it as a natural organic whole with given boundaries in which people enjoy a sense of belonging and a commitment to those with shared interests, positions or goals' (Lister 1997: 80, 83). A similar theme is developed by Phillips (1993: 161), for whom 'a politics of solidarity, and challenge, and change' is at odds with the 'expectation of future homogeneity and consensus'. Campbell and Oliver's (1996: 195) remark in relation to disability that '[d]ifferences are very important and conflicts have been creative for the move-ment' has a much wider applicability. Solidarity is as likely to be associated with conflict and change as it is to consensus and order, and arguably more so.

The consequences of social solidarities

Social solidarity is a complex and often paradoxical phenomenon. One theme running through the discussions above is that concern for the well-being of others may be prompted to some extent by individuals' consideration of how solidaristic action will be to their own advantage, although self-interest cannot provide more than a partial explanation of what unites people in a common endeavour. The altruism that figures prominently in people's accounts of their behaviour is not reducible to a subtle form of using the language of sacrifice for personal gain, but it is the case that it is often 'hard to distinguish intrinsic and instrumental motivations' (Mulgan 1997: 122), as various analyses of relations of reciprocity have shown. Secondly, it has been argued that the bases of social solidarity are not fixed, although claims framed in terms of the 'naturalness' of collectivities are among the most power-ful influences on group formation and maintenance. Individualization, globalization, democratization and other unsettling forces may have under-mined the 'traditional' solidarities of family life, place-based communities and projects constructed around national 'societies', but among the effects of such processes there has been a powerful reaction against them by counter-vailing forces. Warde presents 'communification' as a countervailing force to the process of individualization, commenting that '[t]o be part of a community is an aspiration widely held in modern societies, in part because modernity is perceived to destroy the natural rootedness and uncomplicated sense of belonging which village life in traditional societies engendered'. This is linked to the paradoxical character of 'projects consciously designed to create com-munity' (Warde 1997: 183) that at the same time are understood to be the expression of 'natural' predispositions.

A third general theme relating to the analysis of social solidarity concerns the problematic relationship between social inclusion and social exclusion. The desirability of social solidarity may be brought into question on two counts, because social inclusion can be experienced as oppressive as well as because of the more widely acknowledged issue of the exclusion of those to whom solidarity does not extend. According to Smith (1982: 44–5), the 'enclave mentality' of traditional working-class communities produced a situ-ation in which there was 'widespread toleration of physical sanctions against anyone who disobeyed the norms of the local community', and Chapter 4 contains a number of other examples of the ways in which community mem-bers may be subject to the requirement to conform. Traditional family rela-tionships are treated by Beck, Beck-Gernsheim and others as similarly constraining, as was noted in Chapter 3. The extent to which such control continues to be exercised over group members continues to be an important issue when considering the consequences of social solidarity, along with the issue of whether heightening the consciousness of 'us' necessarily places 'them' as inferior outsiders. The answer to both questions hinges on the way in which people in groups deal with difference and, in particular, the extent to which they practise exclusionary social closure that requires internal homogeneity. As Sibley (1995: 81) notes when remarking that 'families, communities and institutions are all implicated in the construction of deviance and the exclusion of deviant individuals and groups', these issues thus lead back to the consideration of the Durkheimian theme of classification and declassification.

Durkheim's legacy to the study of social solidarity is problematic in all sorts of respects, but it has also been a source of profound insight. His presentation of mechanical and organic solidarities as a dichotomy and his implication that the two are linked in an evolutionary process is an unnecessarily narrow framework of analysis due to its neglect of the complexity of historical change and the existence of important national differences (Mann 1986; Morgan 1999). His approach may also be said to have shortcomings resulting from its underlying premise that occupational associations had the capacity to replace families, local communities and other bases of traditional solidarity. His vision of the transformative power of these associations as institutions that have the capacity to generate 'sentiments of solidarity as yet almost unknown' (Durkheim 1970: 381) is uncharacteristically speculative, and it was noted above that the historical record has not borne out his confidence concerning their potential to bring people together. If Durkheim's legacy were restricted to the detail of his distinction between two types of solidarity and of the institutions likely to emerge to secure cohesion under modern conditions, then his writings would have little contemporary significance. What gives them continuing relevance is his recognition that traditional solidarities are weakened by the impact of various unsettling forces, and that attention deserves to be focused on the resultant 'declassification' and how people respond to it. If processes such as individualization are irreversible, then the problem of finding common ground among people conscious of their individual differences necessarily comes to the fore. The perceptiveness of Durkheim's central point about the compatibility of individualism and solidarity has not always been appreciated by individualization theorists who treat the relationship between the two phenomena as inherently problematic, and it is for this reason that Durkheim's ideas have been given such prominence in this book.

The question 'can we live together?' (Touraine 2000) remains a crucial one, as does the consideration of whether any alternative exists. There are two dimensions to this issue. The first concerns relationships between group members. It is a theme in much of the literature considered above that social change has given people a greater degree of choice over the collectivities of which they are a part. This is the thrust of arguments about 'families of choice', for example, and also of arguments concerned with the way that geographical mobility has freed people from dependence on place-based communities. The extent to which membership of a group is voluntary has an important bearing on relations between members, as was suggested in the discussion of 'communities of fate' in Chapter 4. Various studies have indicated that individualization, understood as the growth in people's choice over the extent and nature of their involvement in collective activity, does not necessarily spell the end of 'community'. Lichterman's findings from his research among members of the Green Movement in the USA go against the expectations of communitarians who 'have often argued that communities formed out of a convergence of personal preferences will amount only to a collection of individuals pursuing private ends, not a broad public good'. This does not mean that voluntary associations are completely open. Lichterman reports how 'Green activists with their lengthy debates over platform statements, their consensus decision-making process, and their frequent go-arounds of participation at meetings depended on shared cultural skills more readily available to and comfortable for highly-educated middle-class people than other strata'. Such 'cultural capital' was not deployed as part of any 'conscious attempts to impress or exclude others' (Lichterman 1996: 10, 155, 153–4), but it does illustrate the point that it is not only compulsory solidarities that have a potentially oppressive dimension to them. The difficulties of learning to live with each other's differences are not avoided simply by virtue of group members coming together voluntarily.

The second dimension of the problem of difference is the exclusive nature of social solidarity. If relations within social groups are frequently problematic, those between social groups are more often so because of the way that the other face of social solidarity can be experienced as social exclusion. The position adopted by Young on this point has been particularly influential, since she is critical of '[t]he striving for mutual identification and shared understanding' not only on the grounds that it can lead 'to denying or suppressing differences' within a social group but also because of the exclusiveness of 'communities'. Her conclusion that the ideal of community has the effect of reproducing inequalities of race, class, gender and sexuality leads her to argue instead for 'social relations without domination in which persons live together in relations of mediation among strangers with whom they are not in community' (Young 1995: 244, 234). There is, as McDowell (1999) has noted, a utopian flavour to Young's position that serves to challenge the assumption of the inevitability and desirability of community solidarities.

One response to Young's argument has been to reassert the importance of what Harvey calls 'that realm of political-economic action so often marginalized in post-structuralist accounts'. Harvey posits that people in relatively weak bargaining positions stand to lose a great deal if existing solidarities such as those between members of the working class are to be superseded by more indefinite arrangements. Grounding the analysis of social justice in a political economy framework allows recognition to be given to the point that 'respect for identity and "otherness" must be tempered by the recognition that although all others may be others, "some are more other than others"' (Harvey 1993: 61, 63). Harvey (1989: 235) acknowledges that community solidarities may involve a pattern of social bonding that 'goes far beyond that tolerable to pure individualism', but his point is that the analysis of such situations and the search for alternatives will not get far without consideration of the material forces that bring people together in this way. If the alternative to solidarity is the disaggregation, fragmentation and atomization of people into a more narrowly individualistic society, then the likely result is that social class and other inequalities will be reinforced. Furlong and Cartmel's (1997) study of the impact of individualization on young people is one of many pieces of research that could be cited in this context.

Other assessments are more optimistic about the prospects of combining solidarity with social inclusion. Putnam's thesis is that community relationships 'can be directed towards malevolent, antisocial purposes' such as 'sectarianism, ethnocentrism, [and] corruption', but that this does not have to be the case. The 'social capital' embodied in community ties has the potential to promote 'mutual support, cooperation, trust, [and] institutional effectiveness', and to support this argument Putnam distinguishes between '*bridging* (or inclusive) and *bonding* (or exclusive)' forms of social capital. The former 'are outward looking and encompass people across diverse social cleavages' in contrast to the latter that are 'by choice or necessity, inward looking and tend to reinforce exclusive identities and homogeneous groups'. Mindful of the scope that exists for contrasts like Durkheim's mechanical and organic solidarity or Tönnies's *gemeinschaft* and *gesellschaft* to be treated as binary oppositions, Putnam goes on to observe that 'bonding and bridging are not "either–or" categories into which social networks can be neatly divided, but "more or less" dimensions along which we can compare different forms of social capital' (Putnam 2000: 22–3, emphasis in original).

The varying degree to which different social relationships are inclusive or exclusive is one of the central reasons why it is appropriate to speak of social solidarities in the plural. Preceding chapters have been designed to convey how relationships within families, communities and societies are enormously diverse in the extent to which they are characterized by the strong inclusion of their members and the exclusion of outsiders. Similar lessons can be drawn about the diversity of other types of social relationships in which people come together for a common purpose. The argument developed above has also sought to show that there is great variation over time in the level of solidarity to be found. Solidarity can be a remarkably mercurial phenomenon, but in many circumstances it will not be forthcoming until relationships of trust have been established, a process that can be very lengthy in relation to the creation of step-families, to the generation of the bonds of community, or to transcending the legacy of mistrust bequeathed by state socialism. A related aspect of solidarity concerned with time is that, once trust and mutual supportiveness are established in relationships, they can be remarkably enduring. The best example of this point in the material considered above is provided by the persistence of solidarities in former mining communities despite the disappearance of the original basis of their existence, but the point also has relevance to the enduring nature of family solidarities and of loyalties to political movements such as *Solidarity* (which, it should be remembered, survived the years of repression of martial law). Douglas's remarks about solidarity involving the preparedness of individuals to suffer in order to further the common good of a group are pertinent here.

The contribution of social scientists to the development of our understanding of social solidarities has been brought into question by Ignatieff (1990: 141), who has expressed the view that 'painters and writers' have been more effective at capturing modern life's 'fleeting and transient solidarity'. But the language of nostalgia for lost community that Ignatieff finds wanting does not exhaust that available to the social scientific analysis of social solidarities. Old forms of solidarity may be in irreversible decline and it is part of the task of social scientists to draw this uncomfortable truth to the attention of wider public audiences. The other, arguably more important, part of the task confronting social scientists researching in this area is to engage in critical assessment of the various claims that are made about the prospects for the emergence of new or revitalized forms of solidarity. These claims deserve attention just as much as do arguments that solidarity has an increasingly marginal place in the contemporary world. The position taken in this book is that traditional forms of solidarity have greater durability than is suggested in some of the more despairing assessments of contemporary social relationships, and that new forms of solidarity continue to emerge as they have done in previous generations. Social scientists have an active role to play in this process, and the book has been written in the spirit of Bauman's (1990: 16–17) belief that 'sociological thinking may well promote solidarity between us' through the systematic and imaginative exploration of the issues around which people make common cause.

References

Abrams, P. (1982) *Historical Sociology*. Shepton Mallet: Open Books.
Abrams, P. and McCulloch, A. (1976) *Communes, Sociology and Society*. Cambridge: Cambridge University Press.
Aitken, S. (1998) *Family Fantasies and Community Space*. New Brunswick, NJ: Rutgers University Press.
Albrow, M. (1990) *Max Weber's Construction of Social Theory*. Basingstoke: Macmillan.
Albrow, M. (1996) *The Global Age: State and Society Beyond Modernity*. Cambridge: Polity Press.
Albrow, M. (1999) *Sociology: The Basics*. London: Routledge.
Alexander, J. (1982) *Theoretical Logic in Sociology, Vol. Two: The Antinomies of Classical Thought: Marx and Durkheim*. London: Routledge & Kegan Paul.
Alexander, J. (1988) Introduction: Durkheimian sociology and cultural studies today, in J. Alexander (ed.) *Durkheimian Sociology: Cultural Studies*. Cambridge: Cambridge University Press.
Alexander, J. (1992) Citizen and enemy as symbolic classification: On the polarizing discourse of civil society, in M. Lamont and M. Fournier (eds) *Cultivating Differences: Symbolic Boundaries and the Making of Inequality*. Chicago, IL: University of Chicago Press.
Almond, M. (1992) *The Rise and Fall of Nicolae and Elena Ceaușescu*. London: Chapmans.
Amin, A. and Graham, S. (1999) Cities of connection and disconnection, in J. Allen, D. Massey and M. Pryke (eds) *Unsettling Cities*. London: Routledge.
Applebaum, H. (ed.) (1984) *Work in Market and Industrial Societies*. Albany, NY: State University of New York Press.
Arnason, J. (1993) *The Future that Failed: Origins and Destinies of the Soviet Model*. London: Routledge.
Aron, R. (1968) *Main Currents in Sociological Thought 1*. Harmondsworth: Penguin.
Aron, R. (1970) *Main Currents in Sociological Thought 2*. Harmondsworth: Penguin.
Ascherson, N. (1982) *The Polish August*. Harmondsworth: Penguin.
Ash, T. (1983) *The Polish Revolution, 1980–82*. London: Jonathan Cape.
Baldwin, P. (1990) *The Politics of Social Solidarity: Class Bases of the European Welfare State 1875–1975*. Cambridge: Cambridge University Press.

Barbalet, J. (1983) *Marx's Construction of Social Theory*. London: Routledge & Kegan Paul.

Barker, C. (1986) *Festival of the Oppressed: Solidarity, Reform and Revolution in Poland 1980–81*. London: Bookmarks.

Barker, C. (1999) Empowerment and resistance: 'Collective effervescence' and other accounts, in P. Bagguley and J. Hearn (eds) *Transforming Politics: Power and Resistance*. Basingstoke: Macmillan.

Barnes, B. (1995) *The Elements of Social Theory*. London: UCL Press.

Baron, S., Riddell, S. and Wilkinson, H. (1998) The best burgers? The person with learning difficulties as worker, in T. Shakespeare (ed.) *The Disability Reader: Social Science Perspectives*. London: Cassell.

Barrett, M. and McIntosh, M. (1982) *The Anti-social Family*. London: Verso.

Barton, L. (1996) Citizenship and disabled people: A cause for concern', in J. Demaine and H. Entwistle (eds) *Beyond Communitarianism: Citizenship, Politics and Education*. Basingstoke: Macmillan.

Bauman, Z. (1990) *Thinking Sociologically*. Oxford: Blackwell.

Bauman, Z. (1991) *Modernity and Ambivalence*. Cambridge: Polity Press.

Bauman, Z. (1992) *Intimations of Postmodernity*. London: Routledge.

Bauman, Z. (1994) After the patronage state: A model in search of class interests, in C. Bryant and E. Mokrzycki (eds) *The New Great Transformation? Change and Continuity in East-Central Europe*. London: Routledge.

Bauman, Z. (1995) *Life in Fragments: Essays in Postmodern Morality*. Oxford: Blackwell.

Bauman, Z. (1996) Morality in the age of contingency, in P. Heelas, S. Lash and P. Morris (eds) *Detraditionalization*. Oxford: Blackwell.

Bauman, Z. (1998a) *Work, Consumerism and the New Poor*. Buckingham: Open University Press.

Bauman, Z. (1998b) *Globalization: The Human Consequences*. Cambridge: Polity Press.

Bauman, Z. (1999) *In Search of Politics*. Cambridge: Polity Press.

Bauman, Z. (2000) *Liquid Modernity*. Cambridge: Polity Press.

Baxter, L., Braithwaite, D. and Nicholson, J. (1999) Turning points and the development of blended families, *Journal of Social and Personal Relationships*, 16(3): 291–313.

Beck, U. (1992) *Risk Society: Towards a New Modernity*. London: Sage.

Beck, U. (1994) The reinvention of politics: Towards a theory of reflexive modernization, in U. Beck, A. Giddens and S. Lash (eds) *Reflexive Modernization: Politics, Tradition and Aesthetics in the Modern Social Order*. Cambridge: Polity Press.

Beck, U. (1997) *The Reinvention of Politics: Rethinking Modernity in the Global Social Order*. Cambridge: Polity Press.

Beck, U. (1998) *Democracy without Enemies*. Cambridge: Polity Press.

Beck, U. (2000) *What is Globalization?* Cambridge: Polity Press.

Beck, U. and Beck-Gernsheim, E. (1995) *The Normal Chaos of Love*. Cambridge: Polity Press.

Beck, U. and Beck-Gernsheim, E. (1996) Individualization and 'precarious freedoms': Perspectives and controversies of a subject-orientated sociology, in P. Heelas, S. Lash and P. Morris (eds) *Detraditionalization*. Oxford: Blackwell.

Beck-Gernsheim, E. (1998) On the way to a post-familial family: From a community of need to elective affinities, *Theory, Culture and Society*, 15(3–4): 53–70.

Bellah, R., Madsen, R., Sullivan, W., Swidler, A. and Tipton, S. (1996) *Habits of the Heart: Individualism and Commitment in American Life*. Berkeley, CA: University of California Press (updated edition).

Bendix, R. (1966) *Max Weber: An Intellectual Portrait*. London: Methuen.

Bendix, R. (1984) *Force, Fate and Freedom: On Historical Sociology*. Berkeley, CA: University of California Press.

Bendix, R. (1996) *Nation-building and Citizenship: Studies of Our Changing Social Order.* New Brunswick, NJ: Transaction Publishers.

Benney, M. (1978) The legacy of mining, in M. Bulmer (ed.) *Mining and Social Change.* London: Croom Helm.

Benwell Community Project (1978) *The Making of a Ruling Class: Two Centuries of Capital Development on Tyneside.* Newcastle Upon Tyne. Benwell Community Project.

Bernardes, J. (1997) *Family Studies: An Introduction.* London: Routledge.

Beynon, H., Hudson, R. and Sadler, D. (1991) *A Tale of Two Industries: The Contraction of Coal and Steel in the North East of England.* Buckingham: Open University Press.

Bittman, M. and Pixley, J. (1997) *The Double Life of the Family: Myth, Hope and Experience.* St Leonards, NSW: Allen & Unwin.

Bornat, J., Dimmock, B., Jones, D. and Peace, S. (1999) The impact of family change on older people: The case of stepfamilies, in S. McRae (ed.) *Changing Britain: Families and Households in the 1990s.* Oxford: Oxford University Press.

Bostyn, A.-M. and Wight, D. (1987) Inside a community: Values associated with money and time, in S. Fineman (ed.) *Unemployment: Personal and Social Consequences.* London: Tavistock.

Bradley, H. (1989) *Men's Work, Women's Work.* Cambridge: Polity Press.

Bradley, H. (1996) *Fractured Identities: Changing Patterns of Inequality.* Cambridge: Polity Press.

Bradshaw, J., Stimson, C., Skinner, C. and Williams, J. (1999) *Absent Fathers?* London: Routledge.

Brannen, J. and Moss, P. (1991) *Managing Mothers: Dual Earner Households after Maternity Leave.* London: Unwin Hyman.

Bryant, C. (1976) *Sociology in Action.* London: George Allen & Unwin.

Bryant, C. (1995) Civic nation, civil society, civil religion, in J. Hall (ed.) *Civil Society: Theory, History, Comparison.* Cambridge: Polity Press.

Bulmer, M. (1975) Sociological models of the mining community, *Sociological Review*, 23: 61–92.

Bulmer, M. (1986) *Neighbours: The Work of Philip Abrams.* Cambridge: Cambridge University Press.

Burawoy, M. and Verdery, K. (1999) Introduction, in M. Burawoy and K. Verdery (eds) *Uncertain Transition: Ethnographies of Change in the Postsocialist World.* Lanham, MD: Rowman & Littlefield.

Burgoyne, J. and Clark, D. (1982) Reconstituted families, in R. Rapoport, M. Fogarty and R. Rapoport (eds) *Families in Britain.* London: Routledge & Kegan Paul.

Burgoyne, J. and Clark, D. (1984) *Making a Go of It: A Study of Stepfamilies in Sheffield.* London: Routledge & Kegan Paul.

Byrne, D. (1999) *Social Exclusion.* Buckingham: Open University Press.

Calhoun, C. (1982) *The Question of Class Struggle: Social Foundations of Popular Radicalism during the Industrial Revolution.* Oxford: Blackwell.

Calhoun, C. (1983) Community: Toward a variable conceptualization for comparative research, in R. Neale (ed.) *History and Class: Essential Readings in Theory and Interpretation.* Oxford: Blackwell.

Calhoun, C. (1987) Class, place and industrial revolution, in N. Thrift and P. Williams (eds) *Class and Space: The Making of Urban Society.* London: Routledge & Kegan Paul.

Calhoun, C. (1995) *Critical Social Theory: Culture, History and the Challenge of Difference.* Oxford: Blackwell.

Campbell, B. (1993) *Goliath: Britain's Dangerous Places.* London: Methuen.

Campbell, J. and Oliver, M. (1996) *Disability Politics: Understanding our Past, Changing our Future.* London: Routledge.

Campbell, T. (1981) *Seven Theories of Human Society*. Oxford: Oxford University Press.
Castells, M. (1996) *The Rise of the Network Society*. Oxford: Blackwell.
Castells, M. (1997) *The Power of Identity*. Oxford: Blackwell.
Castells, M. (1998) *End of Millennium*. Oxford: Blackwell.
Chai, S. and Hechter, M. (1998) A theory of the state and of social order, in P. Doreian and T. Fararo (eds) *The Problem of Solidarity: Theories and Models*. Amsterdam: Gordon & Breach.
Chandler, J. (1991) *Women Without Husbands: An Exploration of the Margins of Marriage*. Basingstoke: Macmillan.
Charles, N. (1990) Food and family ideology, in C.C. Harris (ed.) *Family, Economy and Community*. Cardiff: University of Wales Press.
Charles, N. and Kerr, M. (1988) *Women, Food and Families*. Manchester: Manchester University Press.
Charlton, J. (1998) *Nothing about Us Without Us: Disability, Oppression and Empowerment*. Berkeley, CA: University of California Press.
Cheal, D. (1988) *The Gift Economy*. London: Routledge.
Cheal, D. (1991) *Family and the State of Theory*. Hemel Hempstead: Harvester Wheatsheaf.
Cheal, D. (1996) *New Poverty: Families in Postmodern Society*. Westport, CT: Greenwood Press.
Church, R. and Outram, Q. (1998) *Strikes and Solidarity: Coalfield Conflict in Britain, 1889–1966*. Cambridge: Cambridge University Press.
Cladis, M. (1992) *A Communitarian Defense of Liberalism: Emile Durkheim and Contemporary Social Theory*. Stanford, CA: Stanford University Press.
Clark, D. and Haldane, D. (1990) *Wedlocked? Intervention and Research in Marriage*. Cambridge: Polity Press.
Clarke, J. (1996) Public nightmares and communitarian dreams: The crisis of the social in social welfare, in S. Edgell, K. Hetherington and A.Warde (eds) *Consumption Matters*. Oxford: Blackwell.
Clarke, L. (1996) Demographic change and the family situation of children, in J. Brannen and M. O'Brien (eds) *Children in Families: Research and Policy*. London: Falmer Press.
Coffield, F., Borrill, C. and Marshall, S. (1986) *Growing Up at the Margins: Young Adults in the North East*. Milton Keynes: Open University Press.
Cohen, A. (1985) *The Symbolic Construction of Community*. London: Tavistock.
Collins, R. (1975) *Conflict Sociology: Toward an Explanatory Science*. New York: Academic Press.
Collins, R. (1994) *Four Sociological Traditions*. Oxford: Oxford University Press.
Cornwell, J. (1984) *Hard-Earned Lives: Accounts of Health and Illness from East London*. London: Tavistock.
Coser, L. (1956) *The Functions of Social Conflict*. London: Routledge & Kegan Paul.
Coser, L. (1965) Introduction, in L. Coser (ed.) *Georg Simmel*. Englewood Cliffs, NJ: Prentice-Hall.
Craib, I. (1997) *Classical Social Theory: An Introduction to the Thought of Marx, Weber, Durkheim and Simmel*. Oxford: Oxford University Press.
Craig, G. and Mayo, M. (eds) (1995) *Community Empowerment: A Reader in Participation and Development*. London: Zed Books.
Crouch, C. (1999) *Social Change in Western Europe*. Oxford: Oxford University Press.
Crow, G. and Allan, G. (1994) *Community Life: An Introduction to Local Social Relations*. Hemel Hempstead: Harvester Wheatsheaf.
Crow, G. and Allan, G. (1995) Community types, community typologies and community time, *Time and Society*, 4(2): 147–66.

Crow, G. and Maclean, C. (2000) Community, in G. Payne (ed.) *Social Divisions*. Basingstoke: Macmillan.

Daly, K. (1996) *Families and Time: Keeping Pace in a Hurried Culture*. London: Sage.

Daniels, C. (ed.) (1998) *Lost Fathers: The Politics of Fatherlessness in America*. Basingstoke: Macmillan.

Davidoff, L., Doolittle, M., Fink, J. and Holden, K. (1999) *The Family Story: Blood, Contract and Intimacy, 1830–1960*. London: Longman.

Dawe, A. (1979) Theories of social action, in T. Bottomore and R. Nisbet (eds) *A History of Sociological Analysis*. London: Heinemann.

Dean, J. (1996) *Solidarity of Strangers: Feminism after Identity Politics*. Berkeley, CA: University of California Press.

De'Ath, E. (1992) Stepfamilies in the context of contemporary family life, in E. De'Ath (ed.) *Stepfamilies: What Do We Know and What Do We Need to Know?* Croydon: Significant Publications.

Dempsey, K. (1990) *Smalltown: A Study of Social Inequality, Cohesion and Belonging*. Melbourne: Oxford University Press.

Dempsey, K. (1992) *A Man's Town: Inequality between Women and Men in Rural Australia*. Melbourne: Oxford University Press.

Dempsey, K. (1997) *Inequalities in Marriage: Australia and Beyond*. Melbourne: Oxford University Press.

Dennis, N., Henriques, F. and Slaughter, C. (1969) *Coal is Our Life: An Analysis of a Yorkshire Mining Community*. London: Tavistock.

De Swann, A. (1988) *In Care of the State: Health Care, Education and Welfare in Europe and the USA in the Modern Era*. Cambridge: Polity Press.

Dickens, P. (1988) *One Nation? Social Change and the Politics of Locality*. London: Pluto Press.

Dicks, B. (1997) The life and times of community: Spectacles of collective identity at the Rhondda Heritage Park, *Time and Society*, 6(2/3): 195–212.

Dicks, B., Waddington, D. and Critcher, C. (1998) Redundant men and overburdened women: Local service providers and the construction of gender in ex-mining communities, in J. Popay, J. Hearn and J. Edwards (eds) *Men, Gender Divisions and Welfare*. London: Routledge.

Dobash, R. and Dobash, R. (1992) *Women, Violence and Social Change*. London: Routledge.

Doheny-Farina, S. (1996) *The Wired Neighbourhood*. New Haven, CT: Yale University Press.

Doreian, P. and Fararo, T. (eds) (1998) *The Problem of Solidarity: Theories and Models*. Amsterdam: Gordon & Breach.

Douglas, M. (1987) *How Institutions Think*. London: Routledge & Kegan Paul.

Douglas, M. (1996) *Thought Styles: Critical Essays on Good Taste*. London: Sage.

Douglas, M. and Ney, S. (1998) *Missing Persons: A Critique of Personhood in the Social Sciences*. Berkeley, CA: University of California Press.

Durkheim, E. (1970) *Suicide*. London: Routledge & Kegan Paul.

Durkheim, E. (1972) *Selected Writings*. Cambridge: Cambridge University Press.

Durkheim, E. (1973) Individualism and the intellectuals, in N. Bellah (ed.) *Emile Durkheim on Morality and Society*. Chicago, IL: University of Chicago Press.

Durkheim, E. (1974) *Sociology and Philosophy*. New York: Free Press.

Durkheim, E. (1976) *The Elementary Forms of the Religious Life*. London: George Allen & Unwin.

Durkheim, E. (1980) *Contributions to L'Année Sociologique*. New York: Free Press.

Durkheim, E. (1982) *The Rules of Sociological Method*. Basingstoke: Macmillan.

Durkheim, E. (1984) *The Division of Labour in Society*. Basingstoke: Macmillan.

Edwards, R., Gillies, V. and Ribbens McCarthy, J. (1999) Biological parents and social families: Legal discourses and everyday understandings of the position of step-parents, *International Journal of Law, Policy and the Family*, 13: 78–105.

Einhorn, B. (1993) *Cinderella Goes to Market: Citizenship, Gender and Women's Movements in East Central Europe*. London: Verso.

Ekiert, G. (1996) *The State Against Society: Political Crises and Their Aftermath in East Central Europe*. Princeton, NJ: Princeton University Press.

Eldridge, J. (1973) *Sociology and Industrial Life*. Sunbury-on-Thames: Nelson.

Elias, N. (1991) *The Society of Individuals*. Oxford: Blackwell.

Elias, N. and Scotson, J. (1994) *The Established and the Outsiders: A Sociological Enquiry into Community Problems*, 2nd edn. London: Sage.

Elster, J. (1985) *Making Sense of Marx*. Cambridge: Cambridge University Press.

Elster, J., Offe, C. and Preuss, U. (1998) *Institutional Design in Post-Communist Societies: Rebuilding the Ship at Sea*. Cambridge: Cambridge University Press.

Ennis, F. (1999) Sexual segregation and community, in H. Beynon and P. Glavanis (eds) *Patterns of Social Inequality*. London: Longman.

Epstein, C.F., Seron, C., Oglensky, B. and Sauté, R. (1999) *The Part-time Paradox: Time Norms, Professional Life, Family and Gender*. London: Routledge.

Esping-Andersen, G. (1996) After the golden age? Welfare state dilemmas in a global economy, in G. Esping-Andersen (ed.) *Welfare States in Transition: National Adaptations in Global Economies*. London: Sage.

Etzioni, A. (1994) *The Spirit of Community: The Reinvention of American Society*. New York: Touchstone Books.

Etzioni, A. (1997) *The New Golden Rule: Community and Morality in a Democratic Society*. London: Profile Books.

Etzioni, A. (1998) The responsive communitarian platform: Rights and responsibilities, in A. Etzioni (ed.) *The Essential Communitarian Reader*. Lanham, MD: Rowman & Littlefield.

Etzioni-Halevy, E. (1993) *The Elite Connection: Problems and Potential of Western Democracy*. Cambridge: Polity Press.

Everingham, C. (1994) *Motherhood and Modernity: An Investigation into the Rational Dimension of Mothering*. Buckingham: Open University Press.

Fantasia, R. (1988) *Cultures of Solidarity: Consciousness, Action and Contemporary American Workers*. Berkeley, CA: University of California Press.

Fardon, R. (1999) *Mary Douglas: An Intellectual Biography*. London: Routledge.

Ferge, Z. (1993) Winners and losers after the collapse of state socialism, in R. Page and J. Baldock (eds) *Social Policy Review 5*. Canterbury: Social Policy Association.

Fieldhouse, E. and Hollywood, E. (1999) Life after mining: Hidden unemployment and changing patterns of activity amongst miners in England and Wales, 1981–1991, *Work, Employment and Society*, 13(3): 483–502.

Finch, J. (1989) *Family Obligations and Social Change*. Cambridge: Polity Press.

Finch, J. (1997) Individuality and adaptability in English kinship, in M. Gullestadt and M. Segalen (eds) *Family and Kinship in Europe*. London: Pinter.

Finch, J. and Mason, J. (1993) *Negotiating Family Responsibilities*. London: Routledge.

Finch, J. and Summerfield, P. (1991) Social reconstruction and the emergence of companionate marriage, 1945–59, in D. Clark (ed.) *Marriage, Domestic Life and Social Change*. London: Routledge.

Firth, R., Hubert, J. and Forge, A. (1969) *Families and their Relatives: Kinship in a Middle-class Sector of London: An Anthropological Study*. London: Routledge & Kegan Paul.

Fowkes, B. (1995) *The Rise and Fall of Communism in Eastern Europe*, 2nd edn. Basingstoke: Macmillan.

Francis, H. and Smith, D. (1998) *The Fed: A History of the South Wales Miners in the Twentieth Century*. Cardiff: University of Wales Press.

Frankenberg, R. (1976) In the production of their lives, men(?) . . . sex and gender in British community studies, in D. Leonard Barker and S. Allen (eds) *Sexual Divisions and Society: Process and Change*. London: Tavistock.

Frazer, E. (1999) Unpicking political communitarianism: A critique of 'the communitarian family', in G. Jagger and C. Wright (eds) *Changing Family Values*. London: Routledge.

Frazer, E. and Lacey, N. (1993) *The Politics of Community: A Feminist Critique of the Liberal-Communitarian Debate*. Hemel Hempstead: Harvester Wheatsheaf.

Freie, J. (1998) *Counterfeit Community: The Exploitation of Our Longings for Connectedness*. Lanham, MD: Rowman & Littlefield.

French, S. (1994) The disability movement, in S. French (ed.) *On Equal Terms: Working with Disabled People*. Oxford: Butterworth-Heinemann.

Frisby, D. and Sayer, D. (1986) *Society*. London: Tavistock.

Frydman, R., Murphy, K. and Rapaczynski, A. (1998) *Capitalism with a Comrade's Face: Studies in the Postcommunist Transition*. Budapest: CEU Press.

Fukuyama, F. (1995) *Trust: The Social Virtues and the Creation of Prosperity*. New York: Free Press.

Furlong, A. and Cartmel, F. (1997) *Young People and Social Change: Individualization and Risk in Late Modernity*. Buckingham: Open University Press.

Gane, M. (1992) Durkheim: Woman as outsider, in M. Gane (ed.) *The Radical Sociology of Durkheim and Mauss*. London: Routledge.

Gerth, H. and Mills, C.W. (eds) (1970) *From Max Weber: Essays in Sociology*. London: Routledge & Kegan Paul.

Gibson, C. (1994) *Dissolving Wedlock*. London: Routledge.

Gibson-Graham, J.K. (1996) *The End of Capitalism (as we knew it): A Feminist Critique of Political Economy*. Oxford: Blackwell.

Giddens, A. (1971) *Capitalism and Modern Social Theory: An Analysis of the Writings of Marx, Durkheim and Max Weber*. Cambridge: Cambridge University Press.

Giddens, A. (1972) Introduction, in A. Giddens (ed.) *Emile Durkheim: Selected Writings*. Cambridge: Cambridge University Press.

Giddens, A. (1991) *Modernity and Self-Identity: Self and Society in the Late Modern Age*. Cambridge: Polity Press.

Giddens, A. (1992) *The Transformation of Intimacy: Sexuality, Love and Eroticism in Modern Societies*. Cambridge: Polity Press.

Giddens, A. (1994a) *Beyond Left and Right: The Future of Radical Politics*. Cambridge: Polity Press.

Giddens, A. (1994b) Risk, trust, reflexivity, in U. Beck, A. Giddens and S. Lash (eds) *Reflexive Modernization: Politics, Tradition and Aesthetics in the Modern Social Order*. Cambridge: Polity Press.

Gilbert, D. (1992) *Class, Community, and Collective Action: Social Change in Two British Coalfields, 1850–1926*. Oxford: Clarendon Press.

Gillis, J. (1997) *A World of Their Own Making: Myth, Ritual and the Quest for Family Values*. Cambridge, MA: Harvard University Press.

Gilroy, P. (2000) *Between Camps: Race, Identity and Nationalism at the End of the Colour Line*. London: Penguin.

Gordon, L. (1994) *Pitied but not Entitled: Single Mothers and the History of Welfare*. Cambridge, MA: Harvard University Press.

Gorell Barnes, G., Thompson, P., Daniel, G. and Burchardt, N. (1998) *Growing Up in Stepfamilies*. Oxford: Clarendon Press.

Gouldner, A. (1962) Introduction, in E. Durkheim, *Socialism*. New York: Collier Books.

Gouldner, A. (1980) *The Two Marxisms: Contradictions and Anomalies in the Development of Theory*. London: Macmillan.

Graham, H. (1987) Being poor: Perceptions and coping strategies of lone mothers, in J. Brannen and G. Wilson (eds) *Give and Take in Families: Studies in Resource Distribution*. London: Allen & Unwin.

Gray, J. (1997) *Endgames: Questions in Late Modern Political Thought*. Cambridge: Polity Press.

Hall, S. (1992) The question of cultural identity, in S. Hall, D. Held and T. McGrew (eds) *Modernity and Its Futures*. Cambridge: Polity Press.

Harris, C.C. (1980) The changing relation between family and societal form in western society, in M. Anderson (ed.) *Sociology of the Family*, 2nd edn. Harmondsworth: Penguin.

Harris, C.C. (1990a) *Kinship*. Buckingham: Open University Press.

Harris, C.C. (1990b) Reflections on family, economy and community, in C.C. Harris (ed.) *Family, Economy and Community*. Cardiff: University of Wales Press.

Harris, C.C. and Brown, P. (1987a) The determinants of labour market experience, in C.C. Harris and the Redundancy and Unemployment Research Group, *Redundancy and Recession in South Wales*. Oxford: Blackwell.

Harris, C.C. and Brown, P. (1987b) Redundancy and social transition, in C.C. Harris and the Redundancy and Unemployment Research Group, *Redundancy and Recession in South Wales*. Oxford: Blackwell.

Harvey, D. (1989) *The Urban Experience*. Oxford: Blackwell.

Harvey, D. (1993) Class relations, social justice and the politics of difference, in M. Keith and S. Pile (eds) *Place and the Politics of Identity*. London: Routledge.

Hauser, E., Heyns, B. and Mansbridge, J. (1993) Feminism in the interstices of politics and culture: Poland in transition, in N. Funk and M. Mueller (eds) *Gender Politics and Post-Communism: Reflections from Eastern Europe and the Former Soviet Union*. London: Routledge.

Hechter, M. (1975) *Internal Colonialism: The Celtic Fringe in British National Development, 1536–1966*. London: Routledge & Kegan Paul.

Hechter, M. (1987) *Principles of Group Solidarity*. Berkeley. CA: University of California Press.

Hechter, M. (2000) *Containing Nationalism*. Oxford: Oxford University Press.

Hechter, M. and Levi, M. (1994) Ethno-regional movements in the West, in J. Hutchinson and A. Smith (eds) *Nationalism*. Oxford: Oxford University Press.

Hobbes, T. (1949) *De Cive or the Citizen*. New York: Appleton-Century-Crofts.

Hobbes, T. (1968) *Leviathan*. Harmondsworth: Penguin.

Hochschild, A. (1990) *The Second Shift: Working Parents and the Revolution at Home*. London: Piatkus.

Hochschild, A. (1996) The emotional geography of work and family life, in L. Morris and E. Stina Lyon (eds) *Gender Relations in Public and Private: New Research Perspectives*. Basingstoke: Macmillan.

Hochschild, A. (1997) *The Time Bind: When Work Becomes Home and Home Becomes Work*. New York: Henry Holt.

Hodder, E. (1989) *Stepfamilies Talking*. London: Macdonald.

Hoggart, R. (1958) *The Uses of Literacy: Aspects of Working Class Life with Special Reference to Publications and Entertainments*. Harmondsworth: Penguin.

Hoggart, R. (1995) *The Way We Live Now*. London: Pimlico.

Hoggett, P. (ed.) (1997) *Contested Communities: Experiences, Struggles, Policies*. Bristol: Policy Press.

Holmes, L. (1997) *Post-Communism: An Introduction*. Cambridge: Polity Press.

Homans, G. (1951) *The Human Group*. London: Routledge & Kegan Paul.

Hoogvelt, A. (1997) *Globalization and the Postcolonial World: The New Political Economy of Development*. Basingstoke: Macmillan.

Hornsby, A. (1998) Surfing the net for community: A Durkheimian analysis of electronic gatherings, in P. Kivisto (ed.) *Illuminating Social Life: Classical and Contemporary Theory Revisited*. Thousand Oaks, CA: Pine Forge Press.

Hudson, M. (1995) *Coming Back Brockens: A Year in a Mining Village*. London: Vintage.

Hughes, H. (1974) *Consciousness and Society: The Reorientation of European Social Thought 1890–1930*. Frogmore: Paladin.

Humphrey, M. and Humphrey, H. (1988) *Families with a Difference: Varieties of Surrogate Parenthood*. London: Routledge.

Hutson, S. and Jenkins, R. (1989) *Taking the Strain: Families, Unemployment and the Transition to Adulthood*. Milton Keynes: Open University Press.

Ignatieff, M. (1990) *The Needs of Strangers*. London: Hogarth Press.

Ignatieff, M. (1996) There's no place like home: The politics of belonging, in S. Dunant and R. Porter (eds) *The Age of Anxiety*. London: Virago.

Jackson, B. (1968) *Working Class Community: Some General Notions Raised by a Series of Studies in Northern England*. London: Routledge & Kegan Paul.

Jamieson, L. (1998) *Intimacy: Personal Relationships in Modern Societies*. Cambridge: Polity Press.

Jerrome, D. (1992) *Good Company: An Anthropological Study of Old People in Groups*. Edinburgh: Edinburgh University Press.

Johnsen, E. (1998) Structures and processes of solidarity: An initial formalization, in P. Doreian and T. Fararo (eds) *The Problem of Solidarity: Theories and Models*. Amsterdam: Gordon & Breach.

Jones, G. (1995) *Leaving Home*. Buckingham: Open University Press.

Jordan, B. (1996) *A Theory of Poverty and Social Exclusion*. Cambridge: Polity Press.

Jordan, B. (1998) *The New Politics of Welfare*. London: Sage.

Jordan, B., Redley, M. and James, S. (1994) *Putting the Family First: Identities, Decisions, Citizenship*. London: UCL Press.

Keane, J. (1998) *Civil Society: Old Images, New Visions*. Cambridge: Polity Press.

Kideckel, D. (1993) *The Solitude of Collectivism: Romanian Villagers to the Revolution and Beyond*. Ithaca, NY: Cornell University Press.

Kiernan, K. (1992) The impact of family disruption in childhood on transitions made in young adult life, *Population Studies*, 46(2): 213–34.

Kiernan, K. and Mueller, G. (1999) Who Divorces?, in S. McRae (ed.) *Changing Britain: Families and Households in the 1990s*. Oxford: Oxford University Press.

Kilminster, A. (1992) Socialist models of development, in T. Allen and A. Thomas (eds) *Poverty and Development in the 1990s*. Oxford: Oxford University Press.

Kivisto, P. (1998) *Key Ideas in Sociology*. Thousand Oaks, CA: Pine Forge Press.

Konrad, G. (1992) Anti-politics, in J. Allen, P. Braham and P. Lewis (eds) *Political and Economic Forms of Modernity*. Cambridge: Polity Press.

Kovács, J. (1998) Uncertain ghosts: Populists and urbans in postcommunist Hungary, in P. Berger (ed.) *The Limits of Social Cohesion: Conflict and Mediation in Pluralist Societies*. Boulder, CO: Westview Press.

Kowalik, T. (1994) The great transformation and privatisation: Three years of Polish experience, in C. Bryant and E. Mokrzycki (eds) *The New Great Transformation? Change and Continuity in East-Central Europe*. London: Routledge.

Laba, R. (1991) *The Roots of Solidarity: A Political Sociology of Poland's Working-Class Democratization*. Princeton, NJ: Princeton University Press.

LaCapra, D. (1985) *Emile Durkheim: Sociologist and Philosopher*. Chicago, IL: University of Chicago Press.

Lane, D. (1996) *The Rise and Fall of State Socialism: Industrial Society and the Socialist State*. Cambridge: Polity Press.

Laslett, P. (1996) *A Fresh Map of Life*, 2nd edn. Basingstoke: Macmillan.

Lee, D. and Newby, H. (1983) *The Problem of Sociology*. London: Hutchinson.

Lees, L. (1998) *The Solidarities of Strangers: The English Poor Laws and the People, 1700–1948*. Cambridge: Cambridge University Press.

Le Gall, D. and Martin, C. (1997) Fashioning a new family tie: Step-parents and step-grandparents, in M. Gullestadt and M. Segalen (eds) *Family and Kinship in Europe*. London: Pinter.

Lehmann, J. (1993) *Deconstructing Durkheim: A Post-post-structuralist Critique*. London: Routledge.

Lehmann, J. (1994) *Durkheim and Women*. Lincoln, NB: University of Nebraska Press.

Lemert, C. (1997) *Social Things: An Introduction to the Social Life*. Lanham, MD: Rowman & Littlefield.

Leonard, A. (1991) Women in struggle: A case study in a Kent mining community, in N. Redclift and M. Thea Sinclair (eds) *Working Women: International Perspectives on Labour and Gender Ideology*. London: Routledge.

Levitas, R. (1998) *The Inclusive Society? Social Exclusion and New Labour*. Basingstoke: Macmillan.

Lewenstein, B. and Melchior, M. (1992) Escape to the community, in J. Wedel (ed.) *The Unplanned Society: Poland During and After Communism*. New York: Columbia University Press.

Lewis, G. (1998) Review, in G. Lewis (ed.) *Forming Nation, Framing Welfare*. London: Routledge.

Lewis, P. (1983) Legitimacy and the Polish communist state, in D. Held, J. Anderson, B. Gieben, *et al.* (eds) *States and Societies*. Oxford: Martin Robertson.

Lewis, P. (1993) Democracy and its future in Eastern Europe, in D. Held (ed.) *Prospects for Democracy: North, South, East, West*. Cambridge: Polity Press.

Lewis, P. (1997) Democratization in Eastern Europe, in D. Potter, D. Goldblatt, M. Kiloh and P. Lewis (eds) *Democratization*. Cambridge: Polity Press.

Lichterman, P. (1996) *The Search for Political Community: American Activists Reinventing Community*. Cambridge: Cambridge University Press.

Lister, R. (1997) *Citizenship: Feminist Perspectives*. Basingstoke: Macmillan.

Llewelyn-Davies, M. (1978) Two contexts of solidarity among pastoral Maasai women, in P. Caplan and J. Bujra (eds) *Women United, Women Divided: Cross-Cultural Perspectives on Female Solidarity*. London: Tavistock.

Lockwood, D. (1975) Sources of variation in working-class images of society, in M. Bulmer (ed.) *Working-class Images of Society*. London: Routledge & Kegan Paul.

Lockwood, D. (1992) *Solidarity and Schism: 'The Problem of Disorder' in Durkheimian and Marxist Sociology*. Oxford: Clarendon Press.

Lockwood, D. (1995) Marking out the middle class(es), in T. Butler and M. Savage (eds) *Social Change and the Middle Classes*. London: UCL Press.

Lukes, S. (1975) *Emile Durkheim: His Life and Work: A Historical and Critical Study*. Harmondsworth: Penguin.

Lukes, S. (1985) Conclusion, in M. Carrithers, S. Collins and S. Lukes (eds) *The Category of the Person*. Cambridge: Cambridge University Press.

Lynch, K. (1989) Solidary labour: Its nature and marginalisation, *Sociological Review*, 37(1): 1–14.

Maffesoli, M. (1996) *The Time of the Tribes: The Decline of Individualism in Mass Society*. London: Sage.

Mann, M. (1986) *The Sources of Social Power, Vol. I: A History of Power from the Beginning to A.D. 1760*. Cambridge: Cambridge University Press.

Mansfield, P. and Collard, J. (1988) *The Beginning of the Rest of Your Life? A Portrait of Newly-wed Marriage*. Basingstoke: Macmillan.

Marshall, G. (1997) *Repositioning Class: Social Inequality in Industrial Societies*. London: Sage.

Marshall, G., Rose, D., Newby, H. and Vogler, C. (1988) *Social Class in Modern Britain*. London: Unwin Hyman.

Martin, B. (1981) *A Sociology of Contemporary Cultural Change*. Oxford: Blackwell.

Marx, K. (1959) *Capital, Vol. 3*. London: Lawrence & Wishart.

Marx, K. and Engels, F. (1969a) *Selected Works, Vol. 1*. Moscow: Progress Publishers.

Marx, K. and Engels, F. (1969b) *Selected Works, Vol. 2*. Moscow: Progress Publishers.

Mason, D. (1985) *Public Opinion and Political Change in Poland 1980–1982*. Cambridge: Cambridge University Press.

Massey, D. (1994) *Space, Place and Gender*. Cambridge: Polity Press.

McDonald, L. (1994) *The Women Founders of the Social Sciences*. Ottawa: Carleton University Press.

McDowell, L. (1999) *Gender, Identity and Place: Understanding Feminist Geographies*. Cambridge: Polity Press.

Mele, C. (1999) Cyberspace and disadvantaged communities: The Internet as a tool for collective action, in M. Smith and P. Kollock (eds) *Communities in Cyberspace*. London: Routledge.

Melucci, A. (1989) *Nomads of the Present: Social Movements and Individual Needs in Contemporary Society*. London: Radius.

Melucci, A. (1996a) *The Playing Self: Person and Meaning in the Planetary Society*. Cambridge: Cambridge University Press.

Melucci, A. (1996b) *Challenging Codes: Collective Action in the Information Age*. Cambridge: Cambridge University Press.

Meštrović, S. (1997) *Postemotional Society*. London: Sage.

Mills, C.W. (1963) *The Marxists*. Harmondsworth: Penguin.

Misztal, Barbara (1996) *Trust in Modern Societies: The Search for the Bases of Social Order*. Cambridge: Polity Press.

Misztal, Barbara (2000) *Informality: Social Theory and Contemporary Practice*. London: Routledge.

Misztal, Bronislaw and Jenkins, J. (1995) Starting from scratch is not always the same: The politics of protest and the postcommunist transitions in Poland and Hungary, in J. Jenkins and B. Klandermans (eds) *The Politics of Social Protest: Comparative Perspectives on States and Social Movements*. London: UCL Press.

Monks, J. (1999) 'It works both ways': Belonging and social participation among women with disabilities, in N. Yuval-Davis and P. Werbner (eds) *Women, Citizenship and Difference*. London: Zed Books.

Moore, B. (1978) *Injustice: The Social Bases of Obedience and Revolt*. Basingstoke: Macmillan.

Moore, R. (1974) *Pit-men, Preachers and Politics: The Effects of Methodism in a Durham Mining Community*. Cambridge: Cambridge University Press.

Moore, R. (1975) Religion as a source of variation in working-class images of society, in M. Bulmer (ed.) *Working-class Images of Society*. London: Routledge & Kegan Paul.

Morgan, G. (1999) Work and organizations, in S. Taylor (ed.) *Sociology: Issues and Debates*. Basingstoke: Macmillan.

Morrow, V. (1998) *Understanding Families: Children's Perspectives*. London: National Children's Bureau.

Mulgan, G. (1997) *Connexity: How to Live in a Connected World*. London: Chatto & Windus.

Murphy, R. (1988) *Social Closure: The Theory of Monopolization and Exclusion*. Oxford: Clarendon Press.

Nicholson, T. (1997) Masculine status and working-class culture in the Cleveland ironstone mining communities, 1850–1881, in K. Laybourn (ed.) *Social Conditions, Status and Community 1860–c.1920*. Stroud: Sutton Publishing.

Nisbet, R. (1970) *The Sociological Tradition*. London: Heinemann.

Oakley, A. (1992) *Social Support and Motherhood*. Oxford: Blackwell.

Oakley, A. and Rigby, A. (1998) Are men good for the welfare of women and children?, in J. Popay, J. Hearn and J. Edwards (eds) *Men, Gender Divisions and Welfare*. London: Routledge.

O'Byrne, D. (1997) Working-class culture: Local community and global conditions, in J. Eade (ed.) *Living the Global City: Globalization as Local Process*. London: Routledge.

Offe, C. (1996a) *Varieties of Transition: The East European and East German Experience*. Cambridge: Polity Press.

Offe, C. (1996b) *Modernity and the State: East, West*. Cambridge: Polity Press.

Ost, D. (1991) *Solidarity and the Politics of Antipolitics: Opposition and Reform in Poland since 1968*. Philadelphia, PA: Temple University Press.

Pahl, R.E. (1970) *Patterns of Urban Life*. London: Longman.

Pahl, R.E. (1984) *Divisions of Labour*. Oxford: Blackwell.

Pahl, R. (1998) Friendship: The social glue of contemporary society?, in J. Franklin (ed.) *The Politics of Risk Society*. Cambridge: Polity Press.

Pahl, R. (2000) *On Friendship*. Cambridge: Polity Press.

Pakulski, J. and Waters, M. (1996) *The Death of Class*. London: Sage.

Parker, T. (1986) *Red Hill: A Mining Community*. London: Heinemann.

Parkin, F. (1979) *Marxism and Class Theory: A Bourgeois Critique*. London: Tavistock.

Parkin, F. (1982) *Max Weber*. London: Tavistock.

Parkin, F. (1992) *Durkheim*. Oxford: Oxford University Press.

Parsons, T. (1968) *The Structure of Social Action*, Vol. 1. New York: Free Press.

Pasley, K. and Ihinger-Tallman, M. (1988) Remarriage and stepfamilies, in C. Chilman, E. Nunnally and F. Cox (eds) *Variant Family Forms*. Newbury Park, CA: Sage.

Pearce, F. (1989) *The Radical Durkheim*. London: Unwin Hyman.

Peel, J. (1971) *Herbert Spencer: The Evolution of a Sociologist*. London: Heinemann.

Pelczynski, Z. (1988) The rebirth of civil society, in J. Keane (ed.) *Civil Society and the State: New European Perspectives*. London: Verso.

Phillips, A. (1993) *Democracy and Difference*. Cambridge: Polity Press.

Phillips, A. (1999) *Which Equalities Matter?* Cambridge: Polity Press.

Pickering, W. (1984) *Durkheim's Sociology of Religion: Themes and Theories*. London: Routledge & Kegan Paul.

Poggi, G. (1972) *Images of Society: Essays on the Sociological Theories of Tocqueville, Marx and Durkheim*. Stanford, CA: Stanford University Press.

Pope, W. (1998) Emile Durkheim, in R. Stones (ed.) *Key Sociological Thinkers*. Basingstoke: Macmillan.

Pringle, R. (1989) *Secretaries Talk: Sexuality, Power and Work*. London: Verso.

Pryce-Jones, D. (1996) *The War that Never Was: The Fall of the Soviet Empire 1985–1991*. London: Orion Books.

Putnam, R. (1993) *Making Democracy Work: Civic Traditions in Modern Italy*. Princeton, NJ: Princeton University Press.

Putnam, R. (2000) *Bowling Alone: The Collapse and Revival of American Community*. New York: Simon & Schuster.

Ray, L. (1993) *Rethinking Critical Theory: Emancipation in the Age of Global Social Movements*. London: Sage.

Ray, L. (1996) *Social Theory and the Crisis of State Socialism*. Cheltenham: Edward Elgar.

Ray, L. (1999) *Theorizing Classical Sociology*. Buckingham: Open University Press.

Rayside, D. (1991) *A Small Town in Modern Times: Alexandria, Ontario*. Montreal: McGill-Queens University Press.

Reading, A. (1992) *Polish Women, Solidarity and Feminism*. Basingstoke: Macmillan.

Rees, T. (1999) *Women and Work: Twenty-five Years of Gender Equality in Wales*. Cardiff: University of Wales Press.

Ribbens, J. (1994) *Mothers and their Children: A Feminist Sociology of Childrearing*. London: Sage.

Richards, L. (1990) *Nobody's Home: Dreams and Realities in a New Suburb*. Melbourne: Oxford University Press.

Ritzer, G. (1992) *Classical Sociological Theory*. New York: McGraw-Hill.

Roberts, E. (1985) *A Woman's Place: An Oral History of Working-Class Women 1890– 1940*. Oxford: Blackwell.

Roberts, E. (1995) *Women and Families: An Oral History, 1940–1970*. Oxford: Blackwell.

Roberts, K., Cook, F., Clark, S. and Semeonoff, E. (1977) *The Fragmentary Class Structure*. London: Heinemann.

Robertson, R. (1995) Glocalization: Time–space and homogeneity–heterogeneity, in M. Featherstone, S. Lash and R. Robertson (eds) *Global Modernities*. London: Sage.

Robinson, M. (1991) *Family Transformation through Divorce and Remarriage: A Systemic Approach*. London: Routledge.

Robinson, M. and Smith, D. (1993) *Step by Step: Focus on Stepfamilies*. Hemel Hempstead: Harvester Wheatsheaf.

Rose, N. (1995) Towards a critical sociology of freedom, in P. Joyce (ed.) *Class*. Oxford: Oxford University Press.

Rose, N. (1999) *Powers of Freedom: Reframing Political Thought*. Cambridge: Cambridge University Press.

Rosser, C. and Harris, C. (1965) *The Family and Social Change: A Study of Family and Kinship in a South Wales Town*. London: Routledge & Kegan Paul (abridged edition).

Rowlingson, K. and McKay, S. (1998) *The Growth of Lone Parenthood: Diversity and Dynamics*. London: Policy Studies Institute.

Runciman, W.G. (1989) *A Treatise on Social Theory, Vol. Two: Substantive Social Theory*. Cambridge: Cambridge University Press.

Sakwa, R. (1999) *Postcommunism*. Buckingham: Open University Press.

Salaman, G. (1974) *Community and Occupation: An Exploration of Work/Leisure Relationships*. Cambridge: Cambridge University Press.

Salaman, G. (1986) *Working*. London: Tavistock.

Samuel, R. (1977) Mineral workers, in R. Samuel (ed.) *Miners, Quarrymen and Saltworkers*. London: Routledge & Kegan Paul.

Savage, M., Barlow, J., Dickens, P. and Fielding, T. (1992) *Property, Bureaucracy and Culture: Middle-Class Formation in Contemporary Britain*. London: Routledge.

Scott, Alan (2000) Risk society or angst society? Two views of risk, consciousness and community, in B. Adam, U. Beck and J. Van Loon (eds) *The Risk Society and Beyond: Critical Issues for Social Theory*. London: Sage.

Scott, Alison (1994) *Divisions and Solidarities: Gender, Class and Employment in Latin America*. London: Routledge.

Seabrook, J. (1978) *What Went Wrong? Working People and the Ideals of the Labour Movement*. London: Victor Gollancz.

Sennett, R. (1971) *The Uses of Disorder: Personal Identity and City Life*. London: Allen Lane.

Sennett, R. (1977a) Destructive *gemeinschaft*, in N. Birnbaum (ed.) *Beyond the Crisis*. New York: Oxford University Press.

Sennett, R. (1977b) *The Fall of Public Man*. Cambridge: Cambridge University Press.

Sennett, R. (1998) *The Corrosion of Character: The Personal Consequences of Work in the New Capitalism*. New York: Norton.

Sharpe, S. (1994) *Fathers and Daughters*. London: Routledge.

Sibley, D. (1995) *Geographies of Exclusion: Society and Difference in the West*. London: Routledge.

Sibley, D. (1998) Social exclusion and the Roma in transition, in J. Pickles and A. Smith (eds) *Theorising Transition: The Political Economy of Post-Communist Transformations*. London: Routledge.

Silva, E. and Smart, C. (1999) The 'new' practices and politics of family life, in E. Silva and C. Smart (eds) *The New Family?* London: Sage.

Simmel, G. (1978) *The Philosophy of Money*. London: Routledge & Kegan Paul.

Simpson, B. (1998) *Changing Families: An Ethnographic Approach to Divorce and Separation*. Oxford: Berg.

Simpson, B. (1999) Nuclear fallout: Divorce, kinship and the insecurities of contemporary family life, in J. Vail, J. Wheelock and M. Hill (eds) *Insecure Times: Living with Insecurity in Contemporary Society*. London: Routledge.

Smart, C. and Neale, B. (1999) *Family Fragments?* Cambridge: Polity Press.

Smith, D. (1982) *Conflict and Compromise*. London: Routledge & Kegan Paul.

Smith, M. (2001) *Transnational Urbanism: Locating Globalization*. Oxford: Blackwell.

Spencer, H. (1868) *Social Statics*. London: Williams & Norgate.

Spencer, H. (1969) *The Man Versus the State*. Harmondsworth: Penguin.

Spencer, H. (1971) *Structure, Function and Evolution*. London: Michael Joseph.

Stacey, J. (1996) *In the Name of the Family: Rethinking Family Values in the Postmodern Age*. Boston, MA: Beacon Press.

Stacey, J. (1998) *Brave New Families: Stories of Domestic Upheaval in Late Twentieth-Century America*. Berkeley, CA: University of California Press.

Stacey, J. (1999) Virtual social science and the politics of family values in the United States, in G. Jagger and C. Wright (eds) *Changing Family Values*. London: Routledge.

Stead, J. (1987) *Never the Same Again*. London: The Women's Press.

Sułek, A. (1992) Farewell to the party, in J. Wedel (ed.) *The Unplanned Society: Poland during and after Communism*. New York: Columbia University Press.

Sullivan, O. (1997) Time waits for no (wo)man: An investigation of the gendered experience of domestic time, *Sociology*, 31(2): 221–39.

Sydie, R. (1987) *Natural Women, Cultured Men: A Feminist Perspective on Sociological Theory*. Milton Keynes: Open University Press.

Szelenyi, I. (1988) *Socialist Entrepreneurs: Embourgeoisement in Rural Hungary*. Cambridge: Polity Press.

Sztompka, P. (1999) *Trust: A Sociological Theory*. Cambridge: Cambridge University Press.

Taylor, M. (1995) Community work and the state: The changing context of UK practice, in G. Craig and M. Mayo (eds) *Community Empowerment: A Reader in Participation and Development*. London: Zed Press.

Taylor, R. (1979) Migration and the residual community, *Sociological Review*, 27(3): 475–89.

Thane, P. (1982) *The Foundations of the Welfare State*. London: Longman.

Therborn, G. (1995) *European Modernity and Beyond: The Trajectory of European Societies 1945–2000*. London: Sage.

Thompson, K. (1976) *Auguste Comte: The Foundation of Sociology*. London: Nelson.

Thompson, K. (1982) *Emile Durkheim*. London: Tavistock.

Tilly, C. (1998) *Durable Inequality*. Berkeley, CA: University of California Press.

Tilly, C. and Tilly, C. (1998) *Work Under Capitalism*. Boulder, CO: Westview Press.

Tönnies, F. (1955) *Community and Association*. London: Routledge & Kegan Paul.

Tönnies, F. (1971) *On Sociology: Pure, Applied and Empirical*. Chicago, IL: University of Chicago Press.

Torrance, J. (1977) *Estrangement, Alienation and Exploitation: A Sociological Approach to Historical Materialism*. Basingstoke: Macmillan.

Touraine, A. (2000) *Can We Live Together? Equality and Difference*. Cambridge: Polity Press.

Touraine, A., Dubet, F., Wieviorka, M. and Strzelecki, J. (1983) *Solidarity: Poland 1980–81*. Cambridge: Cambridge University Press.

Vail, J. (1999) Insecure times: Conceptualising insecurity and security, in J. Vail, J. Wheelock and M. Hill (eds) *Insecure Times: Living with Insecurity in Contemporary Society*. London: Routledge.

Waddington, D., Jones, K. and Critcher, C. (1989) *Flashpoints: Studies in Public Disorder*. London: Routledge.

Waddington, D., Wykes, M. and Critcher, C. (1991) *Split at the Seams? Community, Continuity and Change after the 1984–5 Coal Dispute*. Buckingham: Open University Press.

Waddington, D., Parry, D. and Critcher, C. (1998) Keeping the red flag flying? A comparative study of two worker takeovers in the British deep coalmining industry, 1992–1996, *Work, Employment and Society*, 12(2): 317–49.

Wallman, S. (1984) *Eight London Households*. London: Tavistock.

Warde, A. (1997) *Consumption, Food and Taste: Culinary Antinomies and Commodity Culture*. London: Sage.

Warwick, D. and Littlejohn, G. (1992) *Coal, Capital and Culture: A Sociological Analysis of Mining Communities in West Yorkshire*. London: Routledge.

Watier, P. (1998) Georg Simmel, in R. Stones (ed.) *Key Sociological Thinkers*. Basingstoke: Macmillan.

Watts Miller, W. (1996) *Durkheim, Morals and Modernity*. London: UCL Press.

Weber, M. (1978) *Economy and Society*. Berkeley, CA: University of California Press.

Wedel, J. (1992) Introduction, in J. Wedel (ed.) *The Unplanned Society: Poland during and after Communism*. New York: Columbia University Press.

Weeks, J. (2000) *Making Sexual History*. Cambridge: Polity Press.

Weeks, J., Heaphy, B. and Donovan, C. (1999a) Families of choice: Autonomy and mutuality in non-heterosexual relationships, in S. McRae (ed.) *Changing Britain: Families and Households in the 1990s*. Oxford: Oxford University Press.

Weeks, J., Heaphy, B. and Donovan, C. (1999b) Partnership rites: Commitment and ritual in non-heterosexual relationships, in J. Seymour and P. Bagguley (eds) *Relating Intimacies: Power and Resistance*. Basingstoke: Macmillan.

Wellman, B. and Berkowitz, S. (1988) Communities, in B. Wellman and S. Berkowitz (eds) *Social Structures: A Network Approach*. Cambridge: Cambridge University Press.

Wellman, B. and Gulia, M. (1999) Virtual communities as communities: Net surfers don't ride alone, in M. Smith and P. Kollock (eds) *Communities in Cyberspace*. London: Routledge.

Wellman, B., Carrington, P. and Hall, A. (1988) Networks as personal communities, in B. Wellman and S. Berkowitz (eds) *Social Structures: A Network Approach*. Cambridge: Cambridge University Press.

Wellman, D. (1995) *The Union Makes Us Strong: Radical Unionism on the San Francisco Waterfront*. Cambridge: Cambridge University Press.

Wesolowski, W. (1995) The nature of social ties and the future of postcommunist society: Poland after solidarity, in J. Hall (ed.) *Civil Society: Theory, History, Comparison*. Cambridge: Polity Press.

Widegren, Ö. (1997) Social solidarity and social exchange, *Sociology*, 31(4): 755–71.

Wight, D. (1993) *Workers not Wasters: Masculine Respectability, Consumption and Employment in Central Scotland*. Edinburgh: Edinburgh University Press.

Wignaraja, P. (ed.) (1993) *New Social Movements in the South: Empowering the People*. London: Zed Books.

Williams, C. (1981) *Open Cut: The Working Class in an Australian Mining Town*. Sydney, NSW: George Allen & Unwin.

Williams, R. (1975) *The Country and the City*. Frogmore: Paladin.

Williams, R. (1976) *Keywords: A Vocabulary of Culture and Society*. Glasgow: Fontana.

Williamson, B. (1982) *Class, Culture and Community: A Biographical Study of Social Change in Mining*. London: Routledge & Kegan Paul.

Williamson, B. (1990) *The Temper of the Times: British Society since World War II*. Oxford: Blackwell.

Willmott, P. (1986) *Social Networks, Informal Care and Public Policy*. London: Policy Studies Institute.

Wolfe, A. (1989) *Whose Keeper? Social Science and Moral Obligation*. Berkeley, CA: University of California Press.

Wolfe, A. (1992) Democracy versus sociology: Boundaries and their political consequences, in M. Lamont and M. Fournier (eds) *Cultivating Differences: Symbolic Boundaries and the Making of Inequality*. Chicago, IL: University of Chicago Press.

Wolff, K. (ed.) (1964) *The Sociology of Georg Simmel*. New York: Free Press.

Wood, R. (1995) *The Sociology of the Meal*. Edinburgh: Edinburgh University Press.

Worsley, P. (1997) *Knowledges: What Different Peoples Make of the World*. London: Profile Books.

Wrong, D. (1994) *The Problem of Order: What Unites and Divides Society*. Cambridge, MA: Harvard University Press.

Young, I. (1995) The ideal of community and the politics of difference, in P. Weiss and M. Friedman (eds) *Feminism and Community*. Philadelphia, PA: Temple University Press.

Young, M. (1988) *The Metronomic Society: Natural Rhythms and Human Timetables*. London: Thames & Hudson.

Young, M. and Willmott, P. (1957) *Family and Kinship in East London*. London: Routledge & Kegan Paul.

Zbierski-Salameh, S. (1999) Polish peasants in the 'Valley of Transition': Responses to postsocialist reforms, in M. Burawoy and K. Verdery (eds) *Uncertain Transition: Ethnographies of Change in the Postsocialist World*. Lanham, MD: Rowman & Littlefield.

Zirakzadeh, C. (1997) *Social Movements in Politics: A Comparative Study*. London: Longman.

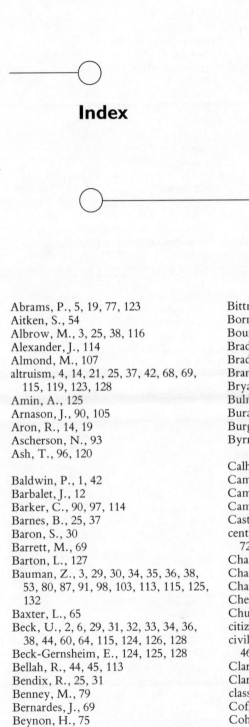

Index

CITIZENSHIP IN A GLOBAL AGE
SOCIETY, CULTURE, POLITICS

Gerard Delanty

- What is citizenship?
- Is global citizenship possible?
- Can cosmopolitanism provide an alternative to globalization?

Citizenship in a Global Age provides a comprehensive and concise overview of the main debates on citizenship and the implications of globalization. It argues that citizenship is no longer defined by nationality and the nation state, but has become de-territorialized and fragmented into the separate discourses of rights, participation, responsibility and identity. Gerard Delanty claims that cosmopolitanism is increasingly becoming a significant force in the global world due to new expressions of cultural identity, civic ties, human rights, technological innovations, ecological sustainability and political mobilization. Citizenship is no longer exclusively about the struggle for social equality but had become a major site of battles over cultural identity and demands for the recognition of group difference. Delanty argues that globalization both threatens and supports cosmopolitan citizenship. Critical of the prospects for a global civil society, he defends the alternative idea of a more limited cosmopolitan public sphere as a basis for new kinds of citizenship that have emerged in a global age.

Contents
Introduction – Part 1: Models of citizenship – The liberal theory of citizenship: rights and duties – Communitarian theories of citizenship: participation and identity – The radical theories of politics: citizenship and democracy – Part 2: The cosmopolitan challenge – Cosmopolitan citizenship: beyond the nation state – Human rights and citizenship: the emergence of the embodied self – Globalization and the deterritorialization of space: between order and chaos – The transformation of the nation state: nationalism, the city, migration and muliticulturalism – European integration and post-national citizenship: four kinds of post-nationalization – Part 3: Rethinking citizenship – The reconfiguration of citizenship: post-national governance in the multi-levelled polity – Conclusion: the idea of civic cosmopolitanism – Bibliography – Index.

192pp   0 335 20489 9   (Paperback)   0 335 20490 2   (Hardback)

SURVEILLANCE SOCIETY
MONITORING EVERYDAY LIFE

David Lyon

- In what ways does contemporary surveillance reinforce social divisions?
- How are police and consumer surveillance becoming more similar as they are automated?
- Why is surveillance both expanding globally and focusing more on the human body?

Surveillance Society takes a post-privacy approach to surveillance with a fresh look at the relations between technology and society. Personal data is collected from us all the time, whether we know it or not, through identity numbers, camera images, or increasingly by other means such as fingerprint and retinal scans. This book examines the constant computer-based scrutiny of ordinary daily life for citizens and consumers as they participate in contemporary societies. It argues that to understand what is happening we have to go beyond Orwellian alarms and cries for more privacy to see how such surveillance also reinforces divisions by sorting people into social categories. The issues spill over narrow policy and legal boundaries to generate responses at several levels including local consumer groups, internet activism, and international social movements. In this fascinating study, sociologies of new technology and social theories of surveillance are illustrated with examples from North America, Europe, and Pacific Asia. David Lyon provides an invaluable text for undergraduate and postgraduate sociology courses, for example in science, technology and society. It will also appeal much more widely to those with an interest in politics, social control, human geography, public administration, consumption, and workplace studies.

Contents
Introduction – Part one: Surveillance societies – Disappearing bodies – Invisible frameworks – Leaky containers – Part two: The spread of surveillance – Surveillant sorting in the city – Body parts and probes – Global data flows – Part three: Surveillance scenarios – New directions in theory – The politics of surveillance – The future of surveillance – Notes – Bibliography – Index.

208pp   0 335 20546 1   (Paperback)   0 335 20547 X   (Hardback)

CHILDHOOD AND SOCIETY
GROWING UP IN AN AGE OF UNCERTAINTY

Nick Lee

- What happens to childhood when the nature of adulthood becomes uncertain?
- What impact is globalization having on adult-child relationships?
- How are we to study 'growing up' today?

Traditionally, children and adults have been treated as different kinds of person, with adults seen as complete, stable and self-controlling, and children seen as incomplete, changeable and in need of control. This ground-breaking book argues that in the early twenty-first century, 'growing up' can no longer be understood as a movement towards personal completion and stability. Careers, intimate relationships, even identities, are increasingly provisional, bringing into question the division between the mature and the immature and thereby differences between adults and children.

Childhood and Society charts the emergence of the conceptual and institutional divisions between adult 'human beings' and child 'human becomings' over the course of the modern era. It then examines the contemporary economic and ideological trends that are eroding the foundations of these divisions. The consequences of this age of uncertainty are examined through an assessment of sociological theories of childhood and through a survey of children's varied positions in a globalizing and highly mediated social world. In all, this accessible text provides a clear, up-to-date and original insight into the sociological study of childhood for undergraduates and researchers alike. It also develops a new set of conceptual tools for studying 'growing up'.

Contents
Introduction – Part one: Human beings and human becomings – What do you want to be when you grow up? – Defining the dependent child – Beings in their own right?: The recognition and mis-recognition of children – Part two: Ambiguities of childhood – Children out of place: ambiguity and social order – Children in their place: home, school and media – New places for children: voice, rights and decision-making – Part three: Human becomings and social research – Childhood and extension: the multiplication of becoming – Towards an immature sociology – Conclusion: Growing up and slowing down – References – Index.

176pp   0 335 20608 5   (Paperback)   0 335 20609 3   (Hardback)